CHING, Eugene. 201 Chinese verbs: compounds and phrases for everyday usage, by Eugene Ching and Nora Ching. Barron's Educational
Series, 1977. 264p 77-8811. 8.95 pa ISBN 0-8120-0674-7. C.I.P.
Eugene Ching, an experienced teacher and scholar of the Chinese language, is well known in the field for several useful articles published on
various aspects of Chinese. The format of this book necessarily differs
from that of the other languages represented in the "201" series. Since
Chinese verbs are uninflected, the authors have chosen to list some of
the most useful compounds, phrases, and idiomatic expressions under
each monosyllabic verb entry. The entries are selected from two frequency lists, one reflecting usage in the People's Republic of China, the
other in Taiwan. Entries are arranged in alphabetical order according to
the pinyin system of romanization (there is no character index, the
assumption being that the user already knows the pronunciation of the
verb, and wishes to examine instances of its usage). A handy reference
work for the student, the book is not without its technical faults. The
breaking of the one-verb-per-page sequence, beginning on page 23 and
widening thereafter, is not reflected in the entry numbers of the Chinese
character texts at the back of the book, which maintain the ideal sequence. There are a number of errors in marking tones of syllables, and

Continued

CHING

an occasional error in representing the pronunciation of a character.
The introduction, which treats the Chinese verb, its role and function in
the sentence, contains some insights that will be of interest to students
of linguistics at the undergraduate level.

201 CHINESE VERBS

COMPOUNDS AND PHRASES
FOR EVERYDAY USAGE

Eugene and Nora Ching

The Ohio State University

BARRON'S EDUCATIONAL SERIES
Woodbury, New York

© Copyright 1977 by Barron's Educational Series, Inc.

All inquiries should be address to:
Barron's Educational Series, Inc.
113 Crossways Park Drive
Woodbury, New York 11797

Library of Congress Catalog Card No. 778811

International Standard Book No. 0-8120-0674-7

Library of Congress Cataloging in Publication Data

Ching, Eugene, 1921-
  201 Chinese verbs.

  English and Chinese.
  Includes bibliographical references.
  1. Chinese language — Verb.   2. Chinese Language — Terms
and phrases.   I. Ching, Nora C., 1937-   joint author.   II. Title.
PL1235.C5   495.1'82'421   77-8811
ISBN 0-8120-0674-7

PRINTED IN THE UNITED STATES OF AMERICA

Dedicated to our father,
Professor Tieh-han Chao,
a devoted teacher and scholar

CONTENTS

PREFACE

Since Chinese is an uninflected language, the format of this book is completely different from the others in the 201 series. Instead of the neat conjugation tables, which the verbs of other languages have, for each of the 201 monosyllabic verbs selected, the most useful compounds, phrases, and idioms containing the verb are listed. Although most of them remain verbs in these contexts, some of them may not. To show the differences, grammatical labels are used. It is hoped that students who became familiar with the characteristics of these classifications will be able to use the entries as an active part of their knowledge of Chinese. Considering the items listed under the 201 monosyllabic verbs, we could have called this book *2001 Chinese Verbs*.

In the preparation of this book, the first problem is a matter of selection. The 201 monosyllabic verbs are selected from two frequency lists: *A Study of the High Frequency Words Used in Chinese Elementary School Reading Materials* (Taipei, Chung Hua Book Co., 1967) and *Wenhua Xuexi Chang Yong Zibiao* (Shanghai, Huadong Renmin Chubanshe, 1951). In principle, only free forms should have been selected. However, a few bound forms are included because of the useful constructions in which they are components. Some free forms are omitted not because they are rarely used but because of the paucity of the constructions in which they are components. Entries under each verb have been selected also for their frequency and usefulness. For verbs with fewer entries, some items not so frequently used may be included as well as more examples. For verbs with abundant expressions, the problem becomes a painful process of elimination. Nevertheless, we have tried to exclude those lexical terms which are easily found in a dictionary and those combinations which are synthesizable or endocentric. In other words, special emphasis is given to items of which the real meaning or grammatical function can not be readily figured out just by examining the components. Although items with the monosyllabic verb as the initial component are the overwhelming majority of the entries, items in which it occupies other positions may also be listed after the former, both alphabetically.

The second problem we face is the labeling of the entries. For many of them labeling is not difficult. For some, we have to leave them unanalyzed and unclassified. For verbal constructions, we have to limit our labels to V (for verb) and SV (for status verbs, including quality verbs). Beyond those, we urge our readers to consult *A Grammar of Spoken Chinese* if our introduction in this book cannot help. Adj (for adjective) is used to indicate an item which is primarily used as a nominal modifier, unlike a status verb which may also be used as a predicate. The labels are usually in this order: analysis of construction / classification of form class. Classification of form class may be omitted whenever it is obvious. For example, when a V-O (verb-object) is in its usual role as a verbal, only V-O is given. However, when a V-O functions as a noun or transitive verb, N or TV will follow: V-O/N or V-O/TV. In order to take care of the ionization problem of a verb-object construction, VO is for solid verb-object, V-O for limited separability, and V O for phrases. Although the labels are given last for each entry, they are for the entries themselves rather than for the examples.

Wherever possible, English translations follow this order: literal translation precedes an approximate equivalent separated by a slant (/). A comma or semicolon instead of a slant would mean that the item may be used both literally and figuratively. For example, *zǒu mǎ kàn huā* means literally "to view the flowers on horseback" while it is used for "going over things quickly." *Chī dòufu* means both "to eat bean curd" and "to flirt."

These two items are listed as follows:

zǒu mǎ kàn huā 走馬看花　to view the flowers on horseback / to go over things quickly.

chī dòufu 吃豆腐　to eat bean curd, to flirt

One other problem lies in the treatment of verbs with different pronunciations and / or different ideographic written forms. Some have been treated as different verbs listed on separate pages, such as *dǎo* 倒 and *dào* 倒, *zuò* 作 and *zuò* 做. Many have been put together with the differences marked, such as *dāng* 當 and *dàng* 當, *diào* 調 and *tiáo* 調, and *qingjia* under *qīn* 親. *Yóu* 遊 and *yóu* 遊 are treated as one word. Those who are interested in this kind of problem in the Chinese language may read Liu Ping-nan, *P'o Yin Tzu Chi Chieh* (Taipei: Yi Chih Bookstore, 1973) and Tung Kuei-hsien, *T'ung Tzu Yi Yin Tzu Tien* (Taipei: P'ing P'ing Ch'upanshe, 1964). The romanization system used in the book is the one known as *pinyin*, officially adopted by the People's Republic of China in 1957. Other systems which are commonly used in this country are presented in the appended contrastive table. Chinese characters for the entries are those of the regular forms. A table to show the difference between the regular and simplified forms is also appended in the back of the book.

To prepare a book of this nature, we have consulted many dictionaries and vocabulary lists. The ones we depend upon heavily are Lin Yutang's *Chinese-English Dictionary of Modern Usage*, Wang Yi's *Kuo Yu Tz'u Tien*, Matthews' *Chinese-English Dictionary*, He Jung's *Kuoyu Jihpao Tz'u Tien*. Appendix II, "From Regular to Simplified Characters" is taken from *Jianhuazi Zongbiao Jianzi*, published by Wenzi Gaige Chubanshe, Peking, 1964 with the asterisks and footnote reference numbers removed. It is hardly necessary to say that we owe Professor Y. R. Chao more than anybody else for drawing freely from his monumental work *A Grammar of Spoken Chinese*. If anything has been left unexplained, answers will be found from his book. Our gratitude is due to some of our students who, after using some of our trial pages, enthusiastically endorsed this project. James R. Moore and Josephine Matthews participated in the final stages of the project. In this connection we wish to thank the federally supported work-study program for making it possible for them to work for us. Our thanks are also due to Mr. Charles Lin, who did the calligraphical work, and to Mrs. Gloria Corrigan for putting our manuscript in a form which is ready for the camera. To Professor Fang-yu Wang who read the manuscript and offered valuable suggestions we wish to express our sincere thanks also. It goes without saying, all the mistakes remain our own.

INTRODUCTION

This introduction discusses the major differences between the Chinese verb and the English verb, gives a brief description of the Chinese verb, particularly in relation with aspect makers, adverbs of degree, reduplication, and compounds, and provides examples in which Chinese verbs are used. Since there are not any neat conjugation tables to begin with, this introduction may offer a kind of framework in which the question how Chinese verbs function may in a very modest way be answered.

The Difference Between the Chinese Verb and the English Verb

As Chinese is not an inflective language, it is not possible to construct a Chinese conjugation. We must adopt a different approach for *201 Chinese Verbs*. Let us begin by discussing some unique qualities of Chinese verbs.

First, Chinese verbs do not indicate tense. Whether they are used in the past, present, or future, the form of the verb remains the same. For example, the verb *chī* "to eat" is always *chī* in each of the following sentences:

1. *cóngqián wǒ chī Zhōngguo fàn.*   "Formerly I ate Chinese food."

2. *Xiànzài wǒ chī Zhōngguo fàn.*   "Now I eat Chinese food."

3. *Jiānglái wǒ chī Zhōngguo fàn.*   "In the future I shall eat Chinese food."

Note that in each of the above examples, the tense of the Chinese sentence is expressed by such time words as *cóngqián, xiànzài,* etc. while the tense of the English sentence has to be indicated by the verb itself.

Second, Chinese verbs do not indicate person or number. Whether the subject is in first, second, or third person, singular or plural, the form of the verb is always the same. For example:

1. *Wǒ chī Zhōngguo fàn.*   "I eat Chinese food."

2. *Nǐ chī Zhōngguo fàn.*   "You eat Chinese food."

3. *Tā chī Zhōngguo fàn.*   "He (or she) eats Chinese food."

In the above sentences, if any of the subjects had been in plural number, the verb would still have been *chī*.

Third, Chinese verbs, particularly the dissyllabic ones, may be used as nouns without changing their morphological forms. For example, *dàibiǎo* may be "to represent" or "a representative"; *xuǎnjǔ*, "to elect" or "an election." Of course, English has verbs like "walk," "work," "vote," etc., which may all be used as nouns; but this kind of class overlap is more common in Chinese.

Fourth, Chinese verbs include adjectives. *Gāo* "tall," for example, may be used attributively in *gāo lóu* "a tall building," or predicatively without the verb "to be" as in *Tā gāo* "He is tall."

Fifth, English prepositional expressions are verbal expressions in Chinese. "In New York" would be *zài Niǔyuē; "*work for me," *gěi wo zuòshì; eat with chopsticks," *yòng kuàizi chī.*

Sixth, unlike English, Chinese verbs have no voice distinction. The forms for both active and passive voices are the same. Only the context can give some clue to the direction of the action. For example, in *Wǒ xiǎng chī fàn* "I would like to eat," and in *Fàn hái méi chī ne* "The food has not been eaten yet," without any change, *chī* is in the active voice in the former sentence while it is in the passive in the latter. *Yú hái méi chī ne* may mean the active voice "The fish has not eaten yet." or the passive voice "The fish has not been eaten yet." Only the context makes the intended meaning clear.

Naturally, this increased reliance on context for clarity has, in turn, led to preferred syntactical patterns. The topic-comment pattern is very common in Chinese. In English a topic is usually introduced by a preposition, while in Chinese a topic can take the position of the subject, even though it may not be the beginning point of the action. Using the same examples given to illustrate the lack of voice distinction of verbs in Chinese, we can say that in *Fàn hái méi chī ne* and *Yú hái méi chī ne,* both *fàn* and *yú* may be considered the topic of the sentence; *hái méi chī ne* is the comment that can be another sentence with the subject omitted.

Fàn (wǒ) hái méi chi ne.	"So far as the food is concerned, (I) have not eaten it yet."
Yú (wǒ) hái méi chī ne.	"So far as the fish is concerned, (I) have not eaten it yet."

From the translations we can see that in English, we have to introduce these topics with "so far as . . . is concerned," "concerning . . . ," "talking about . . . ," etc.

While verbal sentences are preferred in English, adjectival sentences are often preferred in Chinese. For example:

"He eats a lot."	*Tā chīde hěn duō.*	(Literally, what he eats is very much.)
"He walks very fast."	*Tā zǒude hén kuài.*	(Literally, his walking is very fast.)

With this understanding, a student of Chinese as a foreign language should avoid the following mistake:

Although *Wǒ bùshuō Zhōngguo huà hěn hǎo* means "It is very good that I don't speak Chinese," an English speaker may mistakenly use it for "I don't speak Chinese very well," which has to be the adjectival sentence *Wǒde Zhōngguo huà shuōde hùhǎo* (literally, "So far as my Chinese is concerned, the speaking is not good."). This point has been reinforced by Professor Y. R. Chao in *A Grammar of Spoken Chinese*, in which he says that Chinese adjectives are used predominantly in the predicative positions.[1] The example he gives is *Wǒmen rén duō, cháwǎn shǎo, chá gòule wǎn búgòu*. Literally, it means "So far as we are concerned, people are many, teacups are few, tea is enough but cups are not enough." Idiomatic English would be "There are many of us but few teacups; we have enough tea, but not enough cups."[2]

Aside from purely grammatical considerations, other differences, like unequal ranges of meaning with lexical items and different cultural settings for usage often appear when we compare Chinese and English. *Wánr* for example, means "play." However, one cannot but feel uncomfortable when one translates *Nǐ yòu kòngr qǐng dào wǒ jiā lái wánr* into "When you have time, please come to my house to play." Conversely, "He plays an important role in this matter" can hardly be translated into *Tā duì jèi jiàn shì wánr zhòngyàode rènwù*. "Visit" would probably be a better translation for *wánr*, even though the Chinese version for "visit" is usually *bàifǎng*. *Zhàn zhòngyàode wèizhi* (literally, "occupy an important location") probably should be used for "play an important role." Cultural differences usually dictate different responses to similar stimuli under similar situations. An American accepts a compliment with "Thanks," while a Chinese, at least in appearance, tries hard to deny it by saying *Náli Náli*, literally, "Where, where?"[3]

What then is a Chinese verb?

A Chinese verb has been defined as "A syntactic word which can be modified by the adverb *bu* (except for the verb *yǒu* "to have," which takes *méi*) and can be followed by the phrase suffix *le*."[4] These are the two common characteristics shared by all verbs in Chinese. Without going into the finer divisions of the Chinese verb, the following major types may be recognized:[5]

(1)   Action verbs: intransitive verbs like *lái* "to come," *qù* "to go," *zuò* "to sit," etc; transitive verbs like *kàn (xì)* "to see (a play)," *chī (fàn)* "to eat (food)," *shā (rén)* "to kill (people)," etc.

(2)   Quality verbs: intransitive verbs or adjectives like *dà* "big," *hǎo* "good," *xíng* "all right," etc.; transitive verbs like *ài (cái)* "to love (wealth)," *xìn (jiào)* "religious," *yǒu (qián)* "to have (money), rich," etc.

(3)   Status verbs: *bìng* "to be sick," *zuì* "to be drunk," *è* "to be hungry."

(4)   Classificatory verbs: *xìng (Lǐ)* "to have the family name of (Lǐ)," *zuò (guān)* "to serve as (an official)," *dāng (bīng)* "to serve as (a soldier)," etc.

(5) Auxiliary verbs: *huì (fēi)* "can (fly)," *xiǎng (shuì)* "would like to (sleep)," *kěn (zuò)* "willing to (do it)," etc.

(6) *Shì* and *yǒu: shì (rén)* "is a person," *yǒu (shū)* "to have (a book)," etc.

Verbs may be discussed in terms of their behavior with (1) aspect markers *-le, -guo, -zhe*, etc., (2) adverbs of degree *hěn, gèng*, etc., (3) reduplication, (4) compounds.

Aspect Markers

-Le as a word suffix should be distinguished from *.le* as a phrase suffix. Although all verbs may be followed by *.le*, only transitive verbs of Types (1) and (2) may be followed by *-le* without any restrictions. Intransitive verbs take the suffix *-le* only before cognate objects or quantified objects, as in *bìngle sāntiān* "sick for three days."[6] The two *le*'s are used primarily for complete action and new situations, often the two sides of the same thing: a new situation takes place after something has been completed.[7] It is wrong to assume that completed action is the same as past tense in English. Let's examine the following sentences:

(1) *Wǒ zuòle.*   "I did it."

(2) *Wǒ zuòle cái néng zǒu.*   "I cannot leave until I have done it."

(3) *Wo zuòle cái zǒu de.*   "I didn't leave until I had done it."

(4) *Zuòle zài shuō, hǎo ma?*   "Talk about it after it's done, O.K.?"

In the above sentences, *zuòle* has been used in each case without any formal change. It is interesting to note that the negative versions of the sentences reveal the nature of the verb even more clearly. Compare those four sentences with their negative versions.

(1) *Wǒ méizuò.*   "I didn't do it."

(2) *Wǒ búzuò jiù bùnéng zǒu.*   "I can't leave if I don't do it."

(3) *Wǒ méizuò jiù zǒu le.*   "I left before I had done it."

(4) *Méizuò bíe shuō, hǎo ma?*   "Don't talk about it if it's not done, O.K.?"

The negative version of sentence (2) clearly shows that the completed action is not the same as the English past tense. While the affirmative uses *-le* in the verb *zuòle*, the negtive uses *bu-*, usually considered the present negative, instead of *mei-*, usually considered the past negative. The affirmative (4) is definitely referring to the future perfect tense, while the negative refers to the present status of the work. Sometimes, the completed action is the same as the past tense, as in sentence (1). Very often, the completed action *-le* is used in a dependent clause that begins with "after" in English, while the literal Chinese equivalent, *yǐhòu*, is optional:

Nǐ chīle fàn. (yǐhòu) zǒu.   "You leave after eating."

Meanwhile the negative form of completed action is often used in a dependent clause that begins with "before" in English, and the literal Chinese equivalent, *yĭqián,* is also optional.

Tā méichīfàn (yĭqián) jiù zǒu le.   "He left before eating."

Tā méichīfàn (yĭqián) wǒ jiù zǒu le.   "I left before he ate."

For the use of *mei-* in the *yĭqián* clause, there is a positive alternate form: *Tā chīfàn yĭqián wǒ jiù zǒu le.* "I left before he ate." The reason why an *yĭqián* clause in Chinese may take either the affirmative or the negative form lies in the difference between the two versions of the *yĭqián* clause. With the negative form, *yĭqián* is optional as well as redundant, while in the positive form *yĭqián* is obligatory.

.Le for a new situation is usually connected with adjectives (intransitive quality verbs), intransitive status verbs, and auxiliary verbal phrases. For example:

(1) *Tā hǎo le.*   "He is well now."

(2) *Tā bìng le.*   "He is sick now."

(3) *Tā huì zǒu le.*   "He knows how to walk now."

Without *.le,* these sentences mean   (1) He is well,   (2) He is sick, and   (3) He knows how to walk, without considering how he was before. With *.le,* they imply   (1) He has not been well,   (2) He has been well, and   (3) He did not know how to walk before.

-Guo as a verbal suffix means "to have the experience of doing something at least once up to a certain point of time." For example, *Tā chīguo Zhōngguo fàn.* "He has had the experience of eating Chinese food." When *-guo* and *-le* are used together, the *-guo* is actually redundant. *Tā chīguole fàn le.* is not really much different from *Tā chīle fàn le.* "He has eaten." Again, we may use the negative forms to prove it. In *Tā méichīguo Zhōngguo fàn.* "He has not had the experience of eating Chinese food." both *mei-* and *-guo* are used; while in *Tā méichīfàn.* "He didn't eat." *-guo* cannot be used. With *-guo* it would mean "He has not had the experience of eating rice."

-Guo may be used with adjectives or status verbs to mean that one has or has not had the experience of being such and such. For example, *Tā cónglái méibìngguo.* "He has never been sick."

-Guo as a suffix is unstressed, while *guò* as a verb or a verb-complement ending is generally stressed. In *Ta méiguòguo hǎorìzi.* "He has never had a good day." the first *guò* is a verb, while the second is a suffix. In *Nǐ dǎdeguò ta ma?* "Can you beat him (in a fight)?" *guò* is a verb-complement (VC) compound ending.

Zhe is usually translated as the '-ing' of English. However, one may get into trouble if one always tries to use *-zhe* in Chinese the way one uses *-ing* in English. When one wants to say that an action is in the midst of taking place, *-zhe* is suffixed to the verb. For example, *Wǒ chīzhe fàn ne.* "I am eating." A *-zhe* phrase may be used as a setting for another action: In *Wǒ chīzhe fàn kàn bào.* "I read the paper while eating." *chīzhe fàn* "eating" is the setting for *kàn bào* "read paper." In *Kànzhe tian yào hēi le.* "Soon it will be dark." *kànzhe* "looking" is used here as an adverb, as if to mean "As one is looking at the sky, it is getting dark." The English gerund should not be translated into the Chinese verb + *-zhe*. "His acting is good" should not be translated as *Tāde yǎnzhe hǎo*. Instead, it should be *Tā yǎnde hǎo*.

Adverbs of Degree

We will use *hěn* "very" for illustration. It is usually used as a tester for adjectives. Although most adjectives can be modified by *hěn*, items which can be so modified are not always adjectives. Let's examine the following sentences:

(1) *Tā hěn hǎo.*   "He is very good."   (*Hǎo* is an adjective.)

(2) *Tā hěn huì shuōhuà.*   "He knows how to talk very well."

(*Huì shuōhuà* is a verbal phrase with an auxiliary verb.)

(3) *Tā hěn chīle jǐwǎn fàn.*   "He ate quite a few bowls of rice."

(*Chīle jǐwǎn fàn* is a verbal phrase without an auxiliary verb, but with a quantified object.)[8]

(4) *Tā hěn zhīdao téng ni.*   "He knows how to care about you very much."

(*Zhīdao téng ni* is a verbal phrase without either an auxiliary verb or a quantified object. Verbs that involve mental activity or physical action may have something to do with this.)

This proves one thing: in the above sentences, the constructions after *hěn* have been used as adjectives. Even (3), without *hěn*, means "He ate quite a few bowls of rice." However, with *hěn*, the sentence shifts its emphasis from how much he actually ate to the fact that he is a big eater.

Similarly, a Chinese sentence without an aspect marker is usually a description or a statement of truth or principle. Only when the center of attention is shifted to the verb itself do we need the aspect markers to show whether the action has or has not been completed, whether the action is in the midst of taking place, or whether one has or has not had the experience of doing something. In one Chinese reader, in connection with a professor's conducting a class, a student is quoted, *"Gāo Xiānsheng zěnmo bùjiǎng shū ne?"*[9] "How come Mr. Gao did not give lectures?" Since it was said after the class (as a matter of fact the first one), a past tense is definitely required. In Chinese, however, the sentence describes how Mr. Kao conducts his class, rather than whether or not he gave any lecture in the first class; *bu*, instead of *mei* is used. In *"Tāmen kànjiàn yǒu hěn duō xuésheng zài ner niànshū."*[10] "They saw there were many students reading there." the absence of the aspect marker *-le* shows the sentence stresses what they saw not whether they actually saw it or not. If we change the sentence around a little bit, it will be easier to see the difference: *Yǒu hěn duō xuésheng zài ner niànshū, tāmen kànjiànle ma?* "There were manys students reading there, did they see?" As the center of attention in this sentence has been shifted from what they saw to whether or not they saw, the aspect marker *-le* must be used.

Reduplication

Reduplication is an important morphological process in Chinese.[11] Verbs are generally reduplicated in the following forms:

Vv   chī. chi

Vlev   chī. lechi

Vyiv   chī. yichi

Vle. yiv chīle. yichi

If there is an object, it follows the reduplicated verb. Two-syllable verbs are reduplicated in an ABAB fashion with the reduplicated portion unstressed as the one-syllable verb. For the two syllable verbs, however, there is no AByiAB form. Sometimes it is possible to reduplicate a two-syllable verb as if it were two one-syllable verbs. For example, the two-syllable verb *qīngsuàn* "to liquidate" may be reduplicated normally *qīngsuànqingsuan*, or for special effect, *qīngyiqing suànyisuan*. But there is no *qīngsuànyiqingsuan*.*

Adjectives re reduplicated somewhat differently: the reduplicated part is changed to a high level tone if the original is not, and is suffixed with a retroflex *-er*. Examples in all four tones are given below:

1st Tone:	*gāo*	"tall"	*gāogāor (de)*
2nd Tone:	*hóng*	"red"	*hónghōngr (de)*
3rd Tone:	*hǎo*	"good"	*hǎohāor (de)*
4th Tone:	*màn*	"slow"	*mànmānr (de)*

Two-syllable adjectives are generally reduplicated in AABB fashion.

Rènào	"exciting"	*rèrenaonāorde*
Qingchu	"clear"	*qīngqingchūchurde*

Most AABB reduplication of two-syllable adjectives occurs, however, with coordinative compounds. Other kinds of compounds are either not reduplicable or reduplicated differently. *Haokàn* "good-looking," a subordinative compound, cannot be reduplicated. *Xuěbái* "white as snow" is, however, reduplicated in the manner of a two-syllable verb.

A verb may be reduplicated in AABB fashion to be used as an adjective, while an adjective which is usually reduplicated in AABB fashion may be reduplicated in ABAB fashion to be used as a verb. *Shāngliang* "to discuss" may be reduplicated *shāngliangshangliang* (ABAB), "to discuss a little," or *shāngshangliangliāngde* (AABB), "to be indecisive." *Rènào* "to be exciting" as an adjective is usually reduplicated *rèrenaonāorde;* but may be reduplicated *rènaorenao* "to have some excitement" to become a verb. A very interesting example is found in the compound noun *yìsi* "idea." It is reduplicated *yìyisisīde* (AABB) "hesitant" and *yìsiyisi* (ABAB) "to show friendship, to give something as a token of friendship."

The functions of reduplication for verbs are (1) trial, (2) casualness, (3) duration of time, and (4) quantity of object; and primarily for adjectives, (5) vividness. The following examples illustrate these points.

(1) Trial: *Nǐ zěnmo bújìde le? Zài xiángxiang kàn.* "How can it be that you don't remember it? *Try to think* and see whether or not you can remember."

(2) Casualness: *Tā búguò shuōshuo bale, nǐ hébì rènzhēn ne?* "He was *just talking,* why should you take it so seriously?"

(3) Duration of time: *Nǐ búhui shuō zhèju huà, liànxilianxi jiu huì le.* "If you don't know how to say this, *practice aslittle* and you will."

(4) Quantity of the object: *Shuō liangju hǎo huà, dàodaoqiàn, bújiu wánle ma?* "Say a few nice words, *apologize a little,* and won't it be all right?" It is worth noting that in this sentence, *shuō liangju hǎo huà* may be replaced with *shuōshuo hǎo huà,* and *dàodaoqiàn* may be replaced by *dào (yi) ge qiàn* without changing the meaning.

(5) Vividness: *Tāmen gāogaoxīngxingrde jìnlai le.* "They came in *in high spirits* (very happily)."

There is a variant reduplicated form for adjectives, A*li*AB, which carries a pejorative connotation. *Húdu,* "muddle-headed," is obviously a word with pejorative meaning. However, *húhududū* may be used to describe a person that the speaker is fond of, while *húlihudū* definitely conveys the speaker's displeasure.[12]

Compounds

Chinese morphemes are primarily monosyllabic except for a few like *pútao* "grapes," *wúgong* "centipede," etc.[13] Since there are only four hundred syllables (without considering the tones) in modern Mandarin Chinese, compounding becomes one of the most important devices for word construction. Generally speaking, there are five basic kinds of compounds; that is, coordinate compounds (CC), subordinative compounds (SC), verb-object compounds (VO), verb-complement compounds (VC), and subject-predicate compounds (SP). Some examples are listed in the following:

CC: *xǐhuān*   "joy and happy / to like"

       mǎnzú   "full and sufficient / to satisfy"

       zhāohu   "beckon and call / to greet, to take care of"

       qíguài   "strange and odd / strange"

SC:	*qiángdiào*	"strong accent / to emphasize"
	bùxíng	"footstep-go / go on foot"
	rèxīn	"hot heart / enthusiastic; to devote oneself to"
	xiǎokàn	"small look upon / to despise"
VO:	*bǎoxiǎn*	"to insure; to be reliable"
	dézuì	"get offense / to offend"
	chūbǎn	"issue an edition / to publish"
VC:	*kànjiàn*	"look see / to see"
	chībǎo	"to eat full"
	dǎdǎo	"to knock down"
	shuìzháo	"to fall asleep"
SP:	*tóuteng*	"headache"
	dìzhèn	"the earth quakes"
	dǎnxiǎo	"spleen-small / timid"
	mìngkǔ	"luck-hard"

Without going into the details of the characteristic behaviors of these compounds, which by itself would need more space than this introduction, a brief statement on the general behavior of the Chinese verb seems necessary.[14]

As a rule, Chinese verbs may take an auxiliary verb to indicate potentiality or an aspect marker such as *le* to indicate actuality. In their original forms, they are used to state habits, principles, and state of being. For example, *néng chī* means "can eat, able to eat"; *chīle*, "ate (the eating has been done)"; *chī*, "eat (one usually eats such and such, one would eat, as a rule one eats, etc.)." Verb-complement compounds have, in addition, two infixes for the potential forms; *-de-* for positive potentiality, *-bu-* for negative potentiality. For example, *chīdebǎo* "can eat to satisfaction," and *chībubǎo* "cannot eat to satisfaction." The following sentences which use all of these forms may be helpful:

Tā chī Zhōngguo fàn.	"He eats Chinese food (When Chinese food is served, he will eat)."
Tā néng chī Zhōngguo fàn.	"He can (is able to) eat Chinese food."
Tā chīle fàn le.	"He has eaten."

Tā chīzhe fàn ne.	"He is in the midst of eating."
Tā chīguo Zhōngguo fàn.	"He has had the experience of eating Chinese food."
Tā néng chīzhe fàn shuōhuà.	"He can talk while eating."
Tā děi chībǎo.	"He must eat his fill."
Tā chī Zhōngguo fàn chībubǎo.	"He can't eat to his satisfaction when he eats Chinese food."
Tā chī Zhōngguo fàn chīdebǎo.	"He can eat to his satisfaction when he eats Chinese food."
Tā chībǎole.	"He ate his fill."
Tā méichībǎo.	"He didn't eat his fill."
Tā chībǎole cái zǒu de.	"He left after he had eaten his fill."
Nǐ chībǎole zài zǒu.	"Don't leave until you have eaten your fill."

Chinese verbs may be used together without changing them into gerunds, participles, or infinitives. However, they may appear in different relationships.

(1) Coordinate relationship: *Tā chīyān hējiǔ dōu lái.* 'He smokes and drinks." Monosyllabic verbs, particularly bound ones, are used together in more or less fixed orders; for example, *chī-hē-piáo-dǔ* "eat, drink, visit prostitutes, and gamble"; *shēng-lǎo-bìng-sǐ* "to be born, to get old, to be sick, and to die"; *chuī-pāi-piàn* "boast, flatter, and cheat."

(2) Subordinative relationship: *Yòng kuàizi chīfàn* "to eat with chopsticks"; *Chile fàn dào xuéxiào qù* "to go school after eating."

(3) Sequential relationship: *Yi kànjiàn ta jiù shēngqì* "get mad immediately upon seeing him"; *Shuō gei wo tīng* "say it so that I can hear"; *Jiào ta qǐng yigi rén lái gei wo zuò fàn* "tell him to get somebody to cook for me."

(4) Verb-object relationship: *Wǒ tīng shuō tā zǒu le* "I heard it said that he left."

---

*Generally speaking, monosyllabic verbs are reduplicated more freely and frequently than dissyllabic verbs. *Yi* may be easily infixed in the reduplicated forms of monosyllabic verbs, but not so with dissyllabic verbs. See Lu Shuxiang, *"Xiandai Hanyu Dan Shuang Yinjie Wenti Chutan," Zhongguo Yuwen,* January, 1963, p. 19. Those who are interested in this problem may read also Wang Huan, *"Dongci chongdie," Zhongguo Yuwen,* January, 1963; Li Ren-jian, *"Guanyu Dongci Chongdie," Zhongguo Yuwen,* August, 1964; and Fan Fang-lian, *"Shilun Suowei 'Dongci Chong-die'," Zhongguo Yuwen,* August, 1964.

Footnotes

1. Y. R. Chao, *A Grammar of Spoken Chinese,* Berkeley, California, University of California Press, 1968, p. 679.

2. *Ibid.*

3. Eugene Ching, "Cultural Implications in the Teaching of Chinese," *Papers of the CIC Far Eastern Language Institute, University of Michigan, 1963,* edited by Joseph K. Yamagiwa, Ann Arbor, Michigan, 1964.

4. Y. R. Chao, *Mandarin Primer,* Cambridge, Mass., Harvard University Press, 1947, p. 47.

5. In the body of the book, verbs are not even classified in this manner. As has been mentioned in the Preface, only (V) and (SV) are used as labels to denote their functions. Examples are given wherever possible to show the usage.

6. Chao, *Mandarin Primer,* p. 48.

7. *Ibid,* pp. 193-195.

8. Rao Jiting, "Hen Plus Verbal Constructions," *Zhongguo Yuwen* (Chinese Language), No. 107, 1961.

9. Richard Chang, *Read Chinese Book Two,* New Haven, Far Eastern Publications, 1966, p. 68.

10. *Ibid,* p. 59.

11. Eugene Ching, "Reduplication in Chinese," *Papers of the CIC Far Eastern Language Institute, Indiana University, 1964,* Ann Arbor, Michigan, 1965.

12. Chao, *Grammar,* pp. 205-210.

13. Eugene Ching, "Dissyllabicity of Modern Mandarin," *Chinese Culture Quarterly,* Dec. 1969, pp. 88-104 and George A. Kennedy, "The Monosyllabic Myth," *Selected Works of George A Kennedy,* edited by Tien-yi Li, New Haven, Far Eastern Publications, 1964, pp. 104-118.

14. For the most authoritative treatment on the subject, see Chao, *Grammar,* Chapters 6 and 8.

PRONUNCIATION

A typical Chinese syllable consists of a consonantal initial and a final with a vowel nucleus. The final may be further analyzed into a medial, a main vowel (or the vowel nucleus), and an ending. The main vowel being the obligatory element, a Chinese syllable may be any of the following: a vowel (such as *a*); an initial and a vowel (such as *la*); an initial, a medial, and a vowel (such as *lia*); and an initial, a medial, a vowel, and an ending (such as *lian* with consonantal ending and *liao* with vowel ending). Suffix *er* is added to a syllable simply by affixing *r* to its end without consideringg the phonological change involved (such as *wanr*). Tone marks are put over the main vowel as follows: first tone ā, second tone á, third tone ǎ, fourth tone à, neutral or unstressed tone a (no tone mark).

1. Initials

b   as in English buy, but without voicing like English p in spy, *bài* "to worship"

c   like the ts in English its with the initial i left off, but with a stronger puff of breath, *cài* "vegetable"

ch   a cross between the initial sounds of true and choose as though we said chrue instead of true, *chu* "exit"

d   as in English die, but without voicing like English t in sty, *dài* "to put on"

f   as in English father, *fa* "law"

g   as in English guy, but without voicing like k in English sky, *gài* "to cover"

h   like the English h in how but with friction at the back of the mouth, *hǎo* "good"

j   Like Chinese q but without puff of breath, *jì* "remember"

k   as in English kite, but with a stronger puff of breath, *kāi* "to open"

l   as in English law, *lǎo* "old"

m   as in English mother, *mā* "mother"

n   as in English now, *nào* "to annoy"

p   as in English pie, but with a stronger puff of breath, *pài* "to appoint" q   much as ch in English cheat, but with the tip of the tongue held down behind the lower front teeth, *qì* "air"

r   as in English run, but without rounding of the lips, *rén* "person"

s   as in English sign, *sài* "to compete"

t   as in English tie, but with a stronger puff of breath, *tài* "too"

w   as in English way, *wèi* "to feed"

x   much as sh in English she, but with the tip of the tongue held down behind the lower front teeth, and without any rounding of the lips, *xī* "west"

y   as in English yeah, *yá* "tooth"

z   like the ds in English adds with the initial a left off, *zài* "again"

zh   like Chinese ch but without puff of breath, *zhū* "pig"

2. Medials (medials are main vowels when no other vowel follows them.)

i   like the English i in machine except as main vowel after z, c, s, zh, ch, sh, r, *liá* "two"

u   like the English u in suave, *luàn* "mess"

u   like the French u in nuance, with umulaut after l, n, only, *nǚ* "female," *qù* "to go"

3. Main Vowels

a   (1) like the English a in father, *mǎ* "horse,"   (2) between i or y and n, like the English a in hand, *liǎn* "face," *yān* "smoke";   (3) between u and n, like the English a in bat, *yuàn* "courtyard";   (4) between u or w and ng, like (1) or the English o in long, *huáng* "yellow"

ai   like the English ai in aisle, *ài* "love"

ao   like the English au in umlaut, *lǎo* "old"

e   (1) about like the English u in but or huh, *hē* "to drink"; (2) after i and *ü*, like the English e in met, *yě* "also," *yuè* "moon"

ei   like the English ei in reign, *lèi* "tired"

i   (1) final in the syllable except (3) and (4), like the English ee in see, *xǐ* "to wash,"   (2) not final in the syllable, like the English i in pin, *pín* "poor"; (3) after z, c, and s, like the English oo in look without rounding the lips, *zì* "character," *cì* "jab," *sì* "four;"   (4) after zh, ch, sh, r, like the middle-western American English ir in shirt, or ur in hurt, *chī* "to eat," *zhī* "to know," *shì* "yes," *rì* "sun"

o   like the English u in urn, *wǒ* "I"

ou   like the English ow in know, *hòu* "behind"

u   (1) final and not after j, q, x, y, like the English oo in moon, *wù* "fog"; (2) after j, q, x, y, like the French u in nuance or the Chinese ü, *yu* "rain"

ü   like the French u in nuance, or the English oo in moon and the ee in see pronounced simultaneously: while, pronouncing ee, round your lips without other changes, *lǘ* "donkey"

4. **Endings:** Vowel endings are pronounced as described above. The following consonants occur as endings:

n   like the English n in tan, *tán* "to talk"

ng   like the English ng in sing or singer, but not like the ng in finger, *xíng* "O.K."

r   (1) like the English r in bar, fur, *wánr* (pronounced wár) "to play";   (2) after ng, the vowel is strongly nasalized, r as (1), *héngr* "horizontal stroke"

Everybody knows that nobody can learn the pronunciation of a foreign language by reading the description of its sounds only. It is of utmost importance that one should get the assistance of a native speaker. Ask him to read the Chinese words in which a particular sound is found. After one has more or less mastered the sound system, he should go on to learn to read the expressions, phrases, and sentences, still with a native speaker as the model. Unless he is a trained linguist, the native speaker should not be asked to explain how a sound is pronounced and why a certain expression or group of words is spoken in such a way. Just imitate him, repeat after him again and again until you have learned it. Although recording is no substitute for a native speaker, it could be used when a native speaker is not available.

ABBREVIATIONS USED IN THE TEXT

Adj	Adjective
Budd.	Buddhist
CC	Coordinate Construction
Conj	Conjunction
Col. pron.	Colloquial pronunciation
esp.	especially
fig.	figuratively
LC	Literary Chinese
lit.	literally
math.	mathematics
N	Noun
PRC	People's Republic of China
SC	Subordinative Construction
SP	Subject-predicate Constructions
SV	Status Verb
Transli.	Transliteration
TV	Transitive Verb
TW	Time Word
V	Verb
VC	Verb-complement Construction
VO	Verb-object Construction (solid)
V-O	Verb-object Construction (with limited separability)
V O	Verb-object Construction (free components)

愛

àicái 愛財	to love money, to be covetous [VO/SV]	

àigù 愛顧 (of superior) to bestow favor, to take interest in (one below): *Duō xiè nínde àigù.* I am very grateful for your kind interest in me. [CC/V, N]

àiguó 愛國 to love one's country, to be patriotic: *àiguóxīn*, patriotism [V-O/SV]

àihào 愛好 to be fond of (dress, gambling, etc.) [CC/V]

àihǎo(r) 愛好兒 to desire to be good; to be particular about being good [VO/SV]

àihù 愛護 to cherish, support, and protect (country, children, reputation, etc.): *Yàoshi yíge rén àihù tāde míngyù, tā jué búhuì zuòchū zhèzhǒng jiànbude rén de shì de.* If one cares about his reputation, he definitely cannot do this kind of shameful thing. [CC/V]

àilián 愛憐 to love, to show tenderness towards (an orphan, a young widow, etc.) [CC/V]

ài měi 愛美 to love beauty, to be esthetic: *àiměide guānniàn*, esthetic sense [V O]

àimiànzi 愛面子 to care about "face" [VO/SV]

àimù 愛慕 to love, to adore (lover, a great author, etc.) [CC/V]

àiqíng 愛情 love, especially romantic love between man and woman [SC/N]

ài qù búqù 愛去不去 Go if you want, stay if you don't.

àiren 愛人 lover, sweetheart, spouse (PRC) [SC/N]; to love others: *ài rén rú jǐ*, to love one's neighbors as one's self [V O]

àishang 愛上 to fall in love with: *Nǐ zěnmo huì àishang tā?* How could it be possible for you to fall in love with her? [VC]

ài wū jí wū 愛屋及烏 to love the house to love the crow on the roof/ "love me, love my dog"

àixī 愛惜 to love and cherish [CC/V]

àixiǎo 愛小 to be greedy for small gains or profits [VO/SV]

ài (zhàn) xiǎo piányi 愛佔小便宜 to love trifling advantages, to be keen on petty profits

ān
to install, to pacify   安

ānchā 安插		to place (friend, etc.) in organization, to find a job for (a person): *Qǐng nǐ gěi tā ānchā yíge zhíwèi.* Please arrange a position for him. [CC/V]

ān diànhuà 安電話 to install a telephone

āndìng 安定 to settle down: *Děng tā āndìng-yixia zài shuō ba.* Wait until he has settled down a bit and then talk about it. [CC/V]; to be peaceful and secure: *Zhùzai zhèr hěn āndìng.* It is very peaceful to live here. [SV]

ānfèn 安分 to be law-abiding: *ānfèn shǒu jǐ* [VO/SV]

ānhǎo 安好 to install well [VC]; to be well, in good health [CC/SV]

ānjiā 安家 to settle down a family: *ānjiā fèi*, allowance for setting up a family [V-O]

ānjìng 安靜 peaceful and quiet (place, person) [CC/SV]

ān jū lè yè 安居樂業 to make a good living and be contented, each in his station

ānlèwō 安樂窩 a happy retreat

ānpái 安排 to arrange (things), to provide (meals, jobs, etc.) [CC/V]

ānquán 安全 to be safe [CC/SV]; safety, security

ānran 安然 to be calm [SV]; calmly: *Tā ānran dùguò nánguān.* He calmly went through the difficulties. [Adv]

ānshén 安神 to calm down nerves, to relax one's mind [V-O]

ānxián 安閒 to be leisurely: *Tā rìzi guòde hěn ānxián.* He leads an easy life.

ān zhěn wú yōu 安枕無憂 to be free of worries

ānzhì 安置 to place a person (=*ānchā*), to install (=*ānzhuāng*)

ānzhuāng 安裝 to install: *Diànhuà yǐjing ānzhuānghǎole.* The telephone has been installed.

bùān hǎo xīn 不安好心 to be malicious, with bad intentions: *Tā zhèiyang duì nǐ xiǎnrán shì bùān hǎo xīn.* That he treats you this way shows clearly his bad intentions.

xīnli bùān 心裏不安 to feel uneasy

2

bàn'àn 辦案 (of judge, official) to take charge of a case [V-O]

bànbudào 辦不到 impossible to do it: *Zhège bànbudào.* It is impossible to do this.

bànchāi 辦差 to take charge of assignments [V-O]

bàn hòushi 辦後事 to make preparations for a funeral

bàn huò 辦貨 to purchase supplies [V O]

bàn jiǔxí 辦酒席 to prepare a banquet

bànlǐ 辦理 to take charge of (affairs): *Zhèjian shì yóu wǒ bànlǐ.* Let me take charge of this matter.[CC/V]

bàn sāngshi 辦喪事 to make preparations for a funeral

bàn shēngri 辦生 to make preparations for a birthday celebration

bàn shì 辦事 to handle administrative affairs, to do things: *Tā hěn huì bàn shì.* He knows how to handle things. [V O]

bàn shòu 辦壽 to make preparations for a birthday celebration (for elders) [V O]

bàn zuì 辦罪 to punish a criminal [V O]

bāngbàn 幫辦 an assistant (diplomatic service) [CC/N]

chábàn 查辦 to investigate charges [CC/V]

chuàngbàn 創辦 to establish (schools, hospitals, etc.), to found: *Zhège xuéxiào shì shénmo shíhou chuàngbàn de?* When was this school founded? [CC/V]

dūbàn 督辦 commissioner [CC/N]

kāibàn 開辦 =*chuàngbàn* [CC/V]

mǎibàn 買辦 compradore [CC/N]

méibànfa 沒辦法 There is no way out: *Méibànfa zuò.* Cannot be done.

méifazi bàn 沒法子辦 no way to do it

zhàobàn 照辦 to do accordingly (official documents), will do as you wish: *Zhǐyào nǐ shuōchulai, wǒ yídìng zhàobàn.* If you will only tell me, I will do as you say. [CC/V]

3

bāo
to wrap up, to include, to surround   包

bāobàn 包辦	to take full responsibility for an assignment: *Zhè shì yóu wǒ bāobàn.* I will be solely responsible for this matter.
bāobì 包庇	to shelter someone for wrongdoing [CC/V]
bāochāo 包抄	to outflank and attack (enemy) [CC/V]
bāofēng 包封	to seal (package) [CC/V]
bāofu 包袱	wrapping cloth (for travel); burden of past habits of thinking [SC/N]
bāofu dǐr 包袱底兒	the bottom of the wrapping cloth/secrets, the most precious possessions, best act in performance: *dǒulou bāofu dǐr.* Show one's best act (usually reserved for the last).
bāoguǎn 包管	to guarantee, to assure: *Bāoguǎn méicuò.* I guarantee it is all right. *bāoguǎn láihuír,* to guarantee satisfaction or exchange of merchandise purchased [CC/V]
bāogōng 包工	contract for labor [V-O/N]: *bāogōng zhì,* piece-work basis; *bāogōng huó,* piece-work jobs
bāoguǒ 包裹	parcel [CC/N]; to wrap [V]
bāohán 包含	to include, to contain: *Zhèjù huà bāohánde yìsi hěn duō.* This sentence means more than is apparent. [CC/V]
bāojīn 包金	leasing fee: *Yíge yuè de bāojīn shì duōshǎo?* How much is the leasing fee for a month? gold-plated
bāokuò 包括	to include [CC/V]
bāoluó wànxiàng 包羅萬象	to cover and contain everything: *Nèiben xiǎoshuōr zhēn shì bāoluó wànxiàng, shénmo dōu yǒu.* That novel covers everything.
bāoqilai 包起來	to wrap up [VC]
bāoróng 包容	to forgive, to pardon [CC/V]
bāowéi 包圍	to surround [CC/V]
bāoxiāng 包廂	box at theater [SC/N]
bāoyuánr 包圓兒	to buy the whole lot [V-O]
bāozhā 包扎	to tie up (bundle) to bandage [CC/V]

4

bǎoān jīguān 保安機關 security organization

bǎobiāo 保鏢 bodyguard [VO/N]

bǎobuzhù 保不住 cannot guarantee [VC]

bǎochí 保持 to maintain (road condition, temperature, liaison, etc.) [CC/V]

bǎocún 保存 to preserve [CC/V]

bǎodān 保單 certificate of guarantee; insurance policy [SC/N]

bǎoguǎn 保管 to be in charge of (jewelry, property, etc.): *bǎoguǎnrén*, custodian [CC/V]

bǎohù 保護 to protect [CC/V]; protection: *bǎohù guó*, protectorate; *bǎohù sè*, protective coloration

bǎojiàn 保薦 to recommend (someone for employment) [CC/V]

bǎoliú 保留 to reserve (rights, etc.) [CC/V]; reservation

bǎomǔ 保姆 nurse-maid (also written 保母)[SC/N]

bǎoquán 保全 to protect (reputation, life, property, etc.) [VC]

bǎorén 保人 guarantor [SC/N]

bǎoshǒu 保守 to be conservative [CC/SV]

bǎoxiǎn 保險 to insure [V-O]; insurance; dependable [SV]: *Nèige bǎoxiǎn gōngsī bùbǎoxiǎn.* That insurance company is not dependable.

bǎozhàng 保障 to protect (civil rights, life, property, etc.) [CC/V]; protection: *Rénquánde bǎozhàng*, protection of human rights

bǎozhèng 保證 guarantee [CC/V,N]: *bǎozhèngrén*, guarantor; *bǎozhèng shū*, certificate of guarantee

bǎozhòng 保重 to take good care of (oneself): *Qǐng hǎohāor bǎozhòng shēntǐ.* Please take very good care of your health. [CC/V]

bǎozhǔnr 保准兒 I guarantee: *bǎozhǔnr méishì.* I guarantee nothing will happen to you. [VC]

nánbǎo 難保 it is hard to say that: *Nánbǎo tā búhuì shēngqì.* It's hard to say that he will not be mad. [SC/ADV]

報

bàoàn 報案 to register complaints at court, to submit official report on case [V-O]

bàochóu 報仇 to revenge for grudge [V-O]

bàodá 報答 to pay back debt of gratitude [CC/V]

bàodào 報到 to report arrival, to report for duty [V-O]

bàodào 報導 to report (news, intelligence, etc.) [CC/V]; report: *xīnwén bàodào*, news report

bàoēn 報恩 to recompense for kindness: *bào fùmǔ yǎngyù zhī ēn*, to make oneself worthy of parents' care and upbringing [V-O]

bàofèi 報廢 to invalidate, to be declared worthless: *Zhèbù chēzi bàofèi le*. This car has been junked. [VO]

bàogào 報告 report [CC/V,N]

bàogōng 報功 to report achievement (victory, etc.), to claim credit [V-O]

bàoguān 報關 to pay custom duties [V-O]

bàoguó 報國 to serve the country worthily: *lì zhì bào guó*, to make a resolution to serve the country [V-O]

bàokǎo 報考 to register for examination [V-O]

bào kǔqióngr 報苦窮兒 to pretend poverty

bàomíng 報名 to register (for school, entrance examination, etc.) [V-O]

bàomìng 報命 to respond to an order or command: *wú yǐ bào mìng*, without anything to respond to an order [VO]

bào shuì 報稅 to pay tax [V O]

bàosōng 報喪 to announce death [V-O]

bàoxǐ 報喜 to announce joyful events (wedding, birth, etc.): *bàoxǐ búbàoyōu*, to report joyful vents but not saddening news [V-O]

bàoxìn 報信 to report news [V-O]

bàoxiè 報謝 to pay back debt of gratitude, to show gratitude [CC/V] *bèidòng* 被動   passive (opposite of *zhǔdòng*, active)

bèifùxiàn 被覆線   insultated wire

bèigào 被告   to be accused; the defendent (opposite to *yuángào*, the plaintiff)

bèihài 被害   to be murdered, to be harmed

bèijiǔ 被酒   drunk

bèilèi 被累   to be implicated

bèinàn 被難   to be killed in an uprising (martyr): *Zhècì qǐyì bèinànde lièshi hěn duō.* In this uprising many were killed.

bèipiàn 被騙   to be cheated

bèiqī 被欺   to be humiliated

bèiqiǎng 被搶   to be robbed

bèiqǐng 被請   to be invited: *Zěnmo nǐ méi bèiqǐng?* How come you've not been invited?

bèiqū 被屈   to be wronged

bèi rén tīngjian 被人聽見   to be heard, overheard by others: *Nǐ shuō zhè huà búpà bèi rén tīngjian?* Aren't you afraid that somebody may overhear what you have said?

bèishā 被殺   to be killed

bèi ta názǒule 被他拿走了 was taken away by him

bèi xuǎn 被選   to be elected

bèixuǎnquán 被選權   the right to be elected

bèizhuō 被抓   to be arrested: *Zéi bèizhuōzhule.* The thief has been caught.

bèi
to prepare, to provide, to furnish 備

bèiàn 備案	to register for the record [V-O]
bèibàn 備辦	to prepare (luggage, banquet, etc.) [CC/V]
bèibǔ 備補	qualified candidate waiting for appointment
bèichá 備查	to keep for future reference or investigation
bèichē 備車	to provide with cars, to get the car ready [V-O]
bèi ér búyòng 備而丂用	to prepare for future needs
bèikǎo 備考	to keep for future investigation; an appendix for reference
bèiqǔ 備取	alternates for admission (college, office, etc.)
bèiwànglù 備忘錄	memorandum
bèi wèi chōng shù 備位充數	just to fill a post (self-depreciatory)
bèiwén 備文	to prepare a document [V-O]
bèixì 備細	the details
bèiyòng 備用	to provide for use
bèizhàn 備戰	to prepare for war [V-O]
bèizhu 備註	a note for future investigation
chóubèi 籌備	to plan and provide (funds, proposals, etc.) [CC/V]
fángbèi 防備	to provide against: *Wǒmen děi shíshí fángbèi dírende xíjí.* We must be prepared to deal with enemy attack all the time.[CC/V]
jièbèi 戒備	to be on the alert: *Zài díren dìqū, wǒmen bìxū shíshí jièbèi.* In enemy territory, we must be on the alert at all times. [CC/V]
jūnbèi 軍備	armament, military preparedness [SC/N]
yǒu bèi wú huàn 有備無患	with all the preparations, there is nothing to worry about.
yùbèi 預備	to prepare [SC/V]
zhànbèi 戰備	military preparedness [SC/N]
zhǔnbèi 準備	to prepare, to be prepared

---

bǐbushàng 比不上   to be inferior to: *Wǒ bǐbushàng ta.* I am not as good as he. [VC]

bǐfāng 比方   for instance; a supposition, an illustration by example: *bǐfāng shuō*, for example; *jǔ ge bǐfāng*, to give an example

bǐhuà 比畫   to make hand gestures, to demonstrate with gestures [CC/V]

bǐjiān zuòzhàn 比肩作戰   to fight shoulder to shoulder

bǐjiǎo 比較   to compare; comparatively, relatively: *bǐjiǎo hǎo*, relatively better; comparative: *bǐjiǎo yǔyán xué*, comparative linguistics [CC/V, Adv]

bǐ kwài 比快   to compete in speed [V O]

bǐlì 比例   comparison, example: *Ná...zuò bǐlì*, to take...as an example; proportion, ratio: *bǐlìchǐ*, scale (of map)

bǐrè 比熱   (physics) specific heat [SC/N]

bǐrú 比如   for example

bǐsài 比賽   to have a contest: *bǐsài jiǎnggùshi*, to have a contest in story telling [CC/V]; contest: *jiǎngyǎn bǐsài* speech contest

bǐ shàng bùzú, bǐ xià yǒu yú 比上不足 比下有餘   worse off than some, better off than many (formula for contentment)

bǐ shǒu huà jiǎo 比手畫脚   to make lively gestures while talking

bǐyù 比喻   a parable, a metaphor, an allegory [CC/N]

bǐzhào 比照   to follow the model: *bǐzhàozhe zhèzhāng huàr huà*, to paint by using this picture as a model [CC/V]

bǐzhòng 比重   specific weight or gravity [SC/N]

bǐzuò 比作   to compare someone as: *Nǐ bǎ ta bǐzuò shénmo?* What do you compare him to be? [CC/V]

rén bǐ rén, qìsǐ rén 人比人氣死人   One may be upset to death if he compares himself with those who are more successful.

tā bǐ wo gāo 他比我高   He is taller than I.

yòng shǒu bǐfang 用手比方   to describe with hands

biānding 編訂   to edit (book) with the idea of restoring the correct version, to establish (correct list of names, numbers, etc.) [CC/V]

biāndui 編隊   to organize troop units, to form groups [V-O]

biānhào(r) 編號兒 to assign a number (to a list of persons or things) [V-O]

biānhù 編戶   to register residents (for police record) [V-O]

biānjí 編輯   to edit (paper, magazine, etc.) [CC/V]; editor

biānjié 編結   to tie, to weave [CC/V]

biānjù 編劇   to write plays [V-O]; script writer

biānlèi 編類   to classify [V-O]; classification

biānliè 編列   to arrange in order [CC/V]

biān míngcè 編名冊   to make a roster

biānnián(shǐ) 編年史   form of history arranged by years and months, chronicles

biānpai 編派   to criticize, to make up stories about persons: *Bié lǎoshi biānpai rén, hǎo ma?* Don't criticize people all the time, O.K.? [CC/V]

biānpái 編排   to arrange in order, to write and to direct [CC/V]; writing and directing of a play

biānqiǎn 編遣   to disband (troops, personnel) in breaking up a unit or for reassignment [CC/V]

biānshěn 編審   to examine and approve, to pass judgement on books, publications [CC/V]; person who examines and approves

biānshū 編書   to compile a book [V O]

biānyì 編譯   to edit and to translate [CC/V]; editor and translator

biānzào 編造   to fabricate: *biānzào yáoyán*, to fabricate rumors [CC/V]

biānzhī 編織   to knit [CC/V]

biānzhì 編制   to organize [CC/V]; organization, chain of command

biānzhù 編著   to compile [CC/V]; compilation, compiler

biān zidiǎn 編字典, to compile a dictionary

biàndòng 變動 to change [CC/V]: drastic change: *Biàndòng hěn dà*. The change is great.

biànfǎ 變法 to reform [V-O]; political reform; ways to change

biàngé 變革 change for the new (in system, policy) [CC/N]

biàngēng 變更 change of course, of action [CC/N]

biàngù 變故 any untold change or turn of events [SC/N]

biànhǎo 變好 to grow better: *Zhè háizi biànhǎole*. This child becomes better. [VC]

biànhuà 變化 to change in form or character [CC/V]; change: *qiān biàn wàn huà*, unending changes

biànhuáng 變黃 to become yellow [VC]

biànjié 變節 to switch loyalty; to remarry [V-O]

biànliǎn 變臉 to change countenance (when mad) [V-O]

biànmài 變賣 to sell (estate, store, etc.) [CC/V]

biànqiān 變遷 change in trend, conditions [CC/V]

biànsè 變色 to change color; to change countenance [V-O]

biàntài 變態 change of attitude, abnormal: *biàntài xīnlǐ*, abnormal psychology [SC]

biàntiān 變天 (weather) to turn overcast: *Biàntiān le. Bié wàngle dài sǎn.* The weather has changed. Don't forget to bring your umbrella. [V-O]

biàntōng 變通 to use another method to: *biàntōng bànlǐ*, to do it by circumventing the rules [VC]

biànxiàng 變相 change in appearance: *biànxiàng màiyín*, prostitution in a different form [VO]

biàn xìfǎ 變戲法 to perform magic, to play tricks

biànxīn 變心 to change heart/to change mind (about love, etc.): *Tā yǐjing biànle xīn. Nǐ jiù bié zài sǐ xīnyǎnr le.* She has already changed her mind. You shouldn't be so obstinate (about her). [V-O] *cānbài* 參拜   to pay respect to (high officials), to worship (gods) [CC/V]

cāncuò 參錯   to shuffle about [CC/V]

cāndìng 參訂   to revise text [CC/V]

cānguān 參觀   to visit as a tourist, to observe [CC/V]

cānjiā 參加   to take part in, to join [CC/V]

cānjiàn 參見   to see (superior) [CC/V]

cānjiào 參校   to collate, to compare [CC/V]

cānkàn 參看   to compare [CC/V]

cānkǎo 參考   to use as a reference: *Xiě wénzhāng nǐ děi cānkǎo hěn duō shū.* Writing a paper, you must use many books as references. [CC/V]; reference materials: *gěi nǐ zuò ge cānkǎo*, give you as a reference

cānlíng 參靈   ceremony of respect to the coffin before procession [V-O]

cānmóu 參謀   staff officer [CC/N]

cāntòu 參透   to penetrate, to understand (mysteries, profundities) [CC/V]

cānwù 參悟   to understand (mystery from meditation) [CC/V]

cānxiǎng 參想   to reflect, to consider [CC/V]

cānyàn 參驗   to verify (truth by personal experience): to personally inspect [CC/V]

cānyè 參謁   to pay respect to (high official, god) [CC/V]

cānyì 參議   to partake in deliberations of policy [CC/V]; a senator

cānyù 參與   to take part in (discussion, plan): *Cóng zuótian qǐ, wǒ cānyùle tāmende tǎolùn.* Starting yesterday, I've taken part in their discussion. [CC/V]

cānzàn 參贊   to act as advisor on project [CC/V]; a counsellor

cānzhàn 參戰   to participate in the war [V-O]

cānzhèng 參政   to participate in government [V-O]

chábān 查班   to inspect class [V-O]

chábàn 查辦   to investigate and prosecute (case, person) [CC/V]

cháchāo 查抄   to take inventory/to confiscate (property) [CC/V]

chádiǎn 查點   to check item by item [CC/V]

chá duì wú é 查對無訛   After checking, no error was found. (formula for okaying accounts)

cháfēng 查封   to confiscate and seal up (property, goods) [CC/V]

cháhè 查核   to examine (accounts) [CC/V]

chá hùkǒu 查戶口   to check residents, to take census

chájìn 查禁   to search and ban (smuggled goods, etc.) [CC/V]

chájīng 查經   to study the Bible: *chájīngbān*, Bible study class [V-O]

chájiù 查究   to investigate and follow up (a case) [CC/V]

chákàn 查勘   to investigate on the spot [CC/V]

chámíng 查明   to find out: *chámíng zhēnxiàng*, to find out the true facts [VC]

cháqīng 查清   to clear up by an investigation [VC]

cháshào 查哨   to serve as a sentry [V-O]

cháshōu 查收   (letter writing) please receive: *Suí xìn jì gei nǐ xiàngpiàn sānzhāng. Qǐng cháshōu.* I am enclosing in the letter three photographs. Please receive. [CC/V]

cháyuè 查閱   to read (report, correspondence) [CC/V]

cházhàng 查賬   to audit accounts [V-O]

cházhào 查照   (in official documents) to submit for your attention: *Qǐng cházhào bànlǐ.* Please consider and act accordingly. [CC/V]

chá zìdiǎn 查字典   to look up in a dictionary: *Nǐ yàoshi yǒu búrènshide zì, jiù chá zìdiǎn.* If there are words you don't know, look them up in a dictionary.

chá
to observe, to inspect

察

chá'àn 察案	to investigate a case
chábàn 察辦	to investigate and take measures [CC/V]
cháchū 察出	to find out [VC]
cháduó 察奪	(official document) please use your discerning judgment [CC/V]
cháfǎng 察訪	to go about to find out (conditions, rumors) [CC/V]
cháhé 察核	(official document) please use your discerning judgment [CC/V]
chájué 察覺	to scent, to read [CC/V]
chákàn 察看	to look into, to inspect [CC/V]
chákàn 察勘	to examine (place of robbery, landmarks, etc.) on the spot [CC/V]
cháming 察明	to ascertain clearly: *cháming zérèn*, to ascertain clearly who is responsible [VC]
cháshōu 察收	to examine and receive [CC/V]
cháwèn 察問	to inquire into [CC/V]
chá yán guān sè 察言觀色	to pay attention to what is said and to how it is said
cházhào 察照	to take notice and do accordingly [CC/V]
dūchá 督察	to supervise, to watch over [CC/V]
guānchá 觀察	to observe [CC/V]
jiānchá 監察	to supervise, to watch over [CC/V]
jǐngchá 警察	police [CC/N]
jiūchá 糾察	to investigate (a case) [CC/V]
shīchá 失察	to commit mistake of omission [VO]
shìchá 視察	to inspect [CC/V]; inspector
xìchá 細察	to observe carefully: *xìchá lái yì*, to judge the motive of his coming [SC/V]

產

chǎndì	產地	origin of products [SC/N]
chǎn'é	產額	rate of volume of production [SC/N]
chǎnfáng	產房	maternity ward [SC/N]
chǎnfù	產婦	lying-in woman (woman in maternity) [SC/N]
chǎnhòurè	產後熱	puerperal fever
chǎnkē	產科	obstetrics, maternity department [SC/N]
chǎnliàng	產量	capacity or volume of production [SC/N]
chǎnpǐn	產品	products [SC/N]
chǎnpó	產婆	midwife [SC/N]
chǎnshēng	產生	to produce (fish, grapes, etc.); to create (misunderstanding, trouble, etc.) [CC/V]
chǎnwù	產物	products of land [SC/N]
chǎnyè	產業	property, industry [CC/N]
cáichǎn	財產	property [CC/N]
dòngchǎn	動產	movable effects: *búdòngchǎn*, realty [SC/N]
fángchǎn	房產	realty [CC/N]
Gòngchǎndǎng	共產黨	Communist Party
jiāchǎn	家產	family property [SC/N]
nánchǎn	難產	difficult labor (maternity) [SC/N]
pòchǎn	破產	to go into bankruptcy [V-O]
shuǐchǎn	水產	marine products (fish, etc.) [SC/N]
sīchǎn	私產	private property [SC/N]
tǔchǎn	土產	local products [SC/N]
xiǎochǎn	小產	to give premature birth [SC/V]
yíchǎn	遺產	inherited property [SC/N]
zhèr chǎn mǐ	這兒產米	This place produces rice.

15

chàng
to sing, to shout out aloud

唱

chàngběn(r) 唱本兒 song text [SC/N]

chàngchàngrde 唱唱兒的 street singer

chàng gāodiàor 唱高調兒 to brag without actual deeds: *Tā jiù huì chàng gāodiàor. Bié zhǐwàng tā zuòchu shénmo lai.* He just talks. Don't expect him to do anything.

chàng gēr 唱歌兒 to sing a song [V O]

chànghǎo 唱好 to sing well [VC]; to give cheers as audience [V-O]

chànghé 唱和 to write (poem) in reply

chàng hēitóu 唱黑頭 to sing the role of a painted face (Chinese opera)

chàngjī 唱機 a singing machine/record player (also, *liúshēngjī*) [SC/N]

chàngjiào 唱叫 to yell and scream [CC/V]

chànglǐ 唱禮 (Buddhist) prayer at end of mass with "five forgivenesses" and "five wishes" [SC/N]

chàngmíng 唱名 to make roll call [V-O]

chàngpiàn(r) 唱片兒 singing disc/records [SC/N]

chàng piào 唱票 to call votes [V O]

chàngr 唱兒 a song, ditty: *chàng ge chàngr*, to sing a ditty

chàng shī 唱詩 to chant, to sing hymns [V O]

chàngxì 唱戲 to hold, have, or sing an opera: *Jīntian wǎnshang chéngli chàngxì.* Tonight, there is an opera in the city.

dúchàng 獨唱 to perform a solo [SC/V]

fū chàng fù suí 夫唱婦隨 husband sings and wife follows/to have a harmonious married life

héchàng 合唱 to sing in chorus [SC/V]

mài chàng 賣唱 to sell singing/to sing as minstrel at restaurants, streets [V O]

qīngchàng 清唱 to sing without accompaniment or stage makeup [SC/V]

chēngbà	稱霸	to assume hegemony, to declare oneself as superpower [V-O]
chēngbiàn	稱便	to consider it good and convenient: *Rénrén chēngbiàn.* Everybody considers it good and convenient. [VO]
chēngdài	稱貸	to borrow money [VO]
chēngdào	稱道	to praise, to declare: *chēngdào bùjué*, to praise unceasingly [CC/V]
chēng gū dào guǎ	稱孤道寡	to call oneself king
chēnghào	稱號	title [SV/N]
chēnghè	稱賀	to congratulate [VO]
chēnghu	稱呼	to address [CC/V]; way by which one is addressed
chēngměi	稱美	to call good, to praise [VO]
chēngqìng	稱慶	to offer congratulations [VO]
chèngshēn	稱身	to fit well: *Zhèjian yīshang hěn chèngshēn.* This dress fits well. [VO]
chēngsòng	稱頌	to praise, to adore [CC/V]
chēngwèi	稱謂	way of addressing a person [CC/N]
chēngxiè	稱謝	to give thanks [VO]
chēngxióng	稱雄	to declare oneself as leader, to be considered as leader [V-O]
chēng xiōng dào dì	稱兄道弟	to address each other in great familiarity
chēngxǔ	稱許	to praise, to show approval (especially by a superior) [CC/V]
chēngzàn	稱讚	to praise [CC/V]
chèngzhí	稱職	to be competent [VO/SV]
chènqián	稱錢	to be rich [VO/SV]
chènxīn	稱心	to have as one wishes [VO/SV]
chènyì	稱意	to be satisfactory, to be satisfied [VO]

chéngbài 成敗	success and failure/result: *bújì chéngbài*, don't care about what the result will be [CC/N]	
chéngběn 成本	capital: *Chéngběn tài gāo de shēngyi bùhǎo zuò.* Business requiring high capital is not easy to do. [SC/N]	
chénggōng 成功	to be successful [VO/SV]	
chénghūn 成婚	to get married [V-O]	
chéngjī 成績	achievement, results [SC/N]	
chéngjiā 成家	to establish family/to get married [V-O]	
chéngjiàn 成見	set views/prejudice [SC/N]	
chéngjiāo 成交	to complete the business deal [V-O]	
chéngjiù 成就	accomplishment, achievement [CC/N]	
chéngle shénmo le 成了甚麼了	What has it (one) become to?	
chénglì 成立	to establish [CC/V]	
chéngmíng 成名	to become famous [V-O]	
chéngnián 成年	to become adult, to have grown up [SC/V]; the whole year [TW]	
chéngqīn 成親	to become relatives/to get married [V-O]	
chéngquán 成全	to help complete: *Wǒ zhèyang zuò háibúshì xiǎng chéngquán tā nà yípiàn xiàoxīn.* I do this to help him fulfill his filial obligation. [CC/V]	
chéngshú 成熟	to be mature [CC/SV]	
chéngtiān 成天	the whole day [TW]	
chéngwéi 成為	to become [CC/V]	
chéngwù 成物	ready-made things [SC/N]	
chéngxiào 成效	effect, result [SC/N]	
chéngxīn 成心	intentionally: *Tā chéngxīn qì ta māma.* He intentionally angers his mother. [VO]	
chéngyǔ 成語	established sayings/proverbs [SC/N]	
chéngzhǎng 成長	to grow [CC/V]	

乘

chéngbiàn 乘便 to do something at one's convenience: *Qǐng chéngbiàn bǎ ta dài huí qu.* Please take him home at your convenience (since you are going that way). [V-O]

chéngchú 乘除 multiplication and division [CC/N]

chéngfǎ 乘法 (method of) multiplication [SV/N]

chéngfāng 乘方 (mathematics) square, cube, power of nth degree

chéng fēng pò làng 乘風破浪 to ride the wind and waves/to have a smooth and swift trip

chéngjī 乘機 to take the chance and...: *chéngjī tuōtáo*, to take the chance and escape; to ride a plane [V-O]

chéngjiān 乘間 to take the chance (of a good opportunity to speak, attack, etc.) [VO]

chéng jīhuì 乘機會 to take advantage of the opportunity

chéngkè 乘客 passenger [SC/N]

chéngkòng(r) 乘空兒 to take advantage of a free moment or unguarded situation: *Nǐ xiànzài méishì, hái bù chéng kòngr bǎ nèifeng xìn xiěwán?* Since you are not busy now, why don't you finish that letter? [V-O]

chéngliáng 乘涼 to enjoy cool air [V-O]

chéng mǎ 乘馬 to ride a horse [V O]

chéng rén bú bèi 乘人不備 to take advantage of other's unpreparedness

chéngshí 乘時 to take advantage of an opportune time [VO]

chéngshì 乘勢 to avail oneself of the opportunity, to strike while the iron is hot [VO]

chéngshù 乘數 a multiple [SC/N]

chéngxìng 乘興 to do something on impulse to enjoy: *chéngxìng duō huà jǐzhāng ba.* You'd better paint a few more while you are enjoying it. [VO]

chéngxū 乘虛 to do something when the opponent is weak [VO]

sān chéng sān dé jiǔ 三乘三得九 Three multiplied by three is nine.

---

chī cù 吃醋 to eat vinegar, to be jealous

chī dà guō fàn 吃大鍋飯 to eat rice cooked in a big pot (institutional food)

chī dòufu 吃豆腐 to eat bean curd, to flirt (with opposite sex), to make fun of (person of the same sex)

chī ěrguāng 吃耳光 to be slapped on the face

chī fànguǎnr 吃飯館兒 to eat at a restaurant

chījǐn 吃緊 to be tense: *Shíjú hěn chījǐn.* The situation is very tense. [VO/SV]

chījìn 吃勁 to be hard, to try: *Zhèjian shì hěn chījìn.* This is hard. *Nǐ děi chījìn lā.* You have to pull hard.

chījīng 吃驚 to be frightened: *dà chī yìjīng*, to be greatly frightened [V-O]

chīkǔ 吃苦 to suffer hardship [V-O]

chīkuī 吃虧 to suffer loss; to be disadvantageous [V-O]

chīlì 吃力 to be difficult, requiring strength [VO/SV]

chī nǚzhāodài 吃女招待 to eat at a restaurant because of its pretty waitresses

chī rǎn bù chī yìng 吃軟不吃硬 to bully the weak but yield to the strong

chī rǎn fàn 吃軟飯 to eat soft rice, to live on one's wife (or woman)

chīshuǐ 吃水 to be absorbent: *Zhèzhong zhǐ bútài chīshuǐ.* This kind of paper is not too absorbent. [VO/SV]

chīsù 吃素 to abstain from eating meat [V-O]

chī xián fàn 吃閒飯 to eat leisure food/to be a loafer or sponger

chīxiāng 吃香 to be popular: *Tā xiànzài hěn chīxiāng.* He is now very popular. [VO/SV]

chī yādàn 吃鴨蛋 to eat a duck egg, to fail to win any points

chīzhòng 吃重 hard to do: *Zhèjian shì hěn chīzhòng.* This is hard to do. [VO/SV]

持

chí bǐ	持筆	to hold a pen/to write [V-O]
chífǎ	持法	to maintain the law: *chífǎ sēnyán*, to administer sharp justice [VO]
chífú	持服	to resign and stay home during parent's mourning of three years [V-O]
chígēng	持更	to keep night watch by sounding drum at invervals [V-O]
chíjiā	持家	to run a household, to maintain family fortune and status [VO]
chíjiǔ	持久	to hold out long, to last: *chíjiǔ zhàn*, protracted warfare [VC]
chílùn	持論	to hold views: *chílùn gōngzhèng*, to hold impartial views [VO]
chípíng	持平	to hold just views: *chípíng zhī lùn*, a balanced view [VO]
chíshēn	持身	to conduct oneself [VO]
chíxíng	持行	(Budd.) conduct [VO]
chíxù	持續	to carry on, to last [CC]
chíyǎng	持養	to take good care (of health), to cultivate spiritual regimen [VO]
chízèng	持贈	to hold and give/to present a gift with both hands [CC/V]
chízhāi	持齋	to keep vegetarian fast (V-O)
chízhèng	持正	to support what is right [VO]
chízhòng	持重	to act with gravity (not frivolous): *lǎochéng chízhòng*, experienced and steady [VO/SV]
bǎchí	把持	to monopolize (power, position) [CC/V]
bǎochí	保持	to maintain (status, distance): *Gēn tā háishi bǎochí diǎnr jùlí hǎo xie.* It is better to keep a distance from him.
fúchí	扶持	to support (CC/V)
zhīchí	支持	to support, to sustain (person to stand up, tottering regime, etc.) [CC/V]
zhǔchí	主持	to be in charge [SC/V]

chūbǎn	出版	to publish: *chūbǎn yìběn shū*, to publish a book [V-O/TV]
chūchāi	出差	to be sent on a business trip [V-O]
chūchǎn	出產	to produce [CC/V]; products, natural products
chūchàr	出岔兒	to go wrong: *Yàoshi chū ge chàr shéi fùzé?* If anything goes wrong, who is going to take the responsibility? [V-O]
chū fēngtou	出風頭	to enjoy publicity
chūjiā	出家	to get out of home/to become a monk [V-O]
chūkǒu	出口	export, exit [SC]; to speak [V-O]
chūlù	出路	future, employment prospect: *Xué yīnyuè, chūlù bútài hǎo.* If one studies music, the employment prospects aren't too good. [SC/N]
chūménr	出門兒	to go out of the door, to be out of town [V-O]
chū mǐ	出米	to produce rice [V O]
chūmiàn	出面	to appear: *Zhè jianshì, yóu wǒ chūmiàn jiēqia.* Let me go to deal with this matter. [V-O]
chūmíng	出名	to become famous [V-O]
chūqì	出氣	to vent the spleen [V-O]
chūqián	出錢	to pay: *Mǎi qìchē, shéi chūqián?* Buy a car? Who is going to pay? [V-O]
chūqu	出去	to go out [VC], also used as complement to other verbs
chūrù	出入	difference, discrepancies [CC/N]
chūsè	出色	to be superior [VO/SV]
chūshēn	出身	background: *Tā shi zuò mǎimai chūshēn.* He has a business background. [VO/N]
chūshén	出神	to be completely absorbed by something, to be absent minded. [V-O]
chūshì	出事	to have an accident [V-O]

chūtóu 出頭   to become prominent in one's field: *Nǐ hǎohāor zuò, zǒng yǒu chūtóude yìtiān.* If you work hard, one day you will get ahead. [V-O]

chūxi 出息   ability, promise: *Zhè háizi zhēn méi chūxi.* This child has no ability (or future). [SC/N]

chūyáng 出洋   to go abroad [V-O]

chū yángxiàng 出洋相   to make fun of (oneself or sombody else)

chú
to remove, to exterminate, to dismiss   除

---

chú bào ān liáng 除暴安良 to drive out the rascals and protect good people

chúchóng 除蟲 to exterminate insects [V-O]

chúdiào 除掉 to remove [VC]

chúfǎ 除法 (math.) division [SC/N]

chúfēi 除非 unless, except: *Chúfēi nǐ qù bùxíng.* It won't do unless you go. [Conj]

chúgēn 除根 to uproot: *zǎn cǎo chú gēn*, to get rid of grass, it must be uprooted [V-O]

chúhài 除害 to suppress the evil: *Zhèngfǔ yīngdāng tì lǎobǎixìng chúhài.* Governments ought to suppress the evil on behalf of the people. [V-O]

chúhào 除號 (math.) sign of division "÷"

chúkāi 除開 to count off, to take away [VC]

chúle 除了 Besides: *Chúle nǐ (yǐwài) méiyou bié ren huì.* Besides you, there are no others who can. *Chúle nǐ (yǐwài) hái yǒu biérén qù.* In addition to you there are others who also go.

chúmíng 除名 to dismiss, to expel (to remove from list of names): *Tā chángcháng táoxué, suóyi bèi xuéxiào chúmíng le.* He was expelled from school because he was often truant. [V-O]

chúqù 除去 to remove [VC]

chúshù 除數 (math.) the divisor; *bèichúshù*, the dividend

chúwài 除外 not to be counted, to be excluded: *Xīngqīrì chúwài.* Sundays are excepted.

chúxī 除夕 New Year's Eve

fèichú 廢除 to abolish: *fèichú bùpíngděng tiáoyuē*, to abolish unequal treaties [CC/V]

kāichú 開除 see *chúmíng* [CC/V]

pòchú 破除 to abolish: *pòchú míxìn*, to abolish superstition [CC/V]

sān chú liù dé èr 三除六得二 Six divided by three is two.

zhēnchú 真除 to be appointed officially as

chǔbùlái	處不來	cannot get along: *Wǒ gēn tā chǔbùlái.* I can't get along with him.[VC]
chǔduàn	處斷	to decide [CC/V]
chǔfá	處罰	to punish [CC/v]
chǔfāng	處方	to prescribe [V-O]; prescription
chǔfèn	處分	to punish
chǔjìng	處境	circumstances [SC/N]
chǔjué	處決	to execute (criminal), to decide [CC/V]
chǔlǐ	處理	to dispose of, to arrange, to settle: *Zhèjian shì zhēn bùhǎo chǔlǐ.* This matter is really hard to deal with.(CC/V)
chǔshì	處士	a retired scholar [SC/N]
chǔshì	處世	to deal with the world: *Tā búhuì dài rén chǔshì, suóyi chángcháng dézuì rén.* He offends people often because he doesn't know how to deal with people. *chǔshì zhī dào,* a way of life [V-O]
chǔsǐ	處死	to sentence to death [VO]
chǔwōzi	處窩子	one shut away from society
chǔ xīn jī lù	處心積慮	to brood over a matter for a long time
chǔxíng	處刑	to punish: *chǔ jíxíng,* sentence to death [V-O]
chǔ yú sǐ dì	處於死地	to send somebody to his doom
chǔzhǎn	處斬	to execute (criminal) [CC/V]
chǔzhì	處治	to punish [CC/V]
chǔzhì	處置	=*chǔlǐ* [CC/V]
xiāngchǔ	相處	to get along with each other: *Tāmen liǎngge xiāngchǔde hěn hǎo.* The two of them get along fine.[SC/V]

chuán'àn 傳案 to summon to court [V-O]

chuánbō 傳播 to spread (news, ideas, disease, etc.) [CC/V]

chuánbù 傳佈 to spread, to publicize (CC/V)

chuándá 傳達 to communicate (thoughts, ideas); to transmit (order from above); *chuándá mìnglìng* [CC/V]

chuándān 傳單 a handbill, a publicity circular or flyer [SC/N]

chuándì 傳遞 to pass around (letter, message) [CC/V]

chuán'gei ta 傳給他 to pass on to him

chuánguān 傳觀 to circulate for people to see [CC/V]

chuánjiā 傳家 to bequeath to the family: *chuánjiā zhī bǎo*, art object kept as heirloom [VO]

chuánjiào 傳教 to preach: *chuánjiàoshì*, a missionary [V-O]

chuánpiào 傳票 a court summons, subpoena; (accounting) a voucher [SC/N]

chuánrǎn 傳染 to infect: *chuánrǎn bìng*, communicable disease [CC/V]

chuán rè 傳熱 to transmit heat [V O]

chuánshén 傳神 to be vivid, to give lively expression (of portraiture) [VO/SV]

chuánshěn 傳審 to summon for trial [CC/V]

chuánshòu 傳授 to teach [CC/V]

chuánsòng 傳送 to deliver (message, news) [CC/V]

chuánshuō 傳說 folktale [CC/N]

chuánwén 傳聞 It is reported that: *Chuánwén díren zhànlǐng Wáng Zhuāng.* It is reported that the enemy occupied Wang Chuang. [CC]

chuánxìn 傳信 to deliver letters, to communicate (tradition, belief); *chuán xìnr*, to deliver a message [V-O]

chuányáng 傳揚 to spread (teaching, etc.) [CC/V]

chuányuè 傳閱 to pass around for people to read [CC/V]

答

dá'àn	答案	answer, solution of mathematical problem [SC/N]
dábài	答拜	to pay a return call
dábiàn	答辯	to argue back [CC/V]
dábushanglai	答不上來	can't answer [VC]
dáchár	答碴	to make an answer to question, to strike up conversation [V-O]
dácí	答詞	a response (to an address of congratulation): *Xiànzài qǐng Wáng Bóshi zhì dácí.* Now we ask Dr. Wang to say a word (as a response). [SC/N]
dáduì	答對	to answer, to respond [CC/V]; to answer correctly [VC]
dáfu	答覆	to reply [CC/V]; a reply
dáhuà	答話	to answer [V-O]
dálǐ	答禮	to respond to a salutation [V-O]; a gift in return [SC/N]
dápin	答聘	to reply on acceptance of appointment [VO]; formal acknowledgement of betrothal gift
dáshù	答數	correct number in mathematical solutions [SC/N]
dáxiè	答謝	to return a courtesy call; a letter to thank someone
dāying	答應	to consent, to promise [CC/V]; *bùdāying*, to disapprove, to take offense at: *Nǐ luàn huā qián, Bàba bùdāying.* Dad will not approve your careless spending.
dáyǔ	答語	reply, words of reply [SC/N]
bàodá	報答	to repay person for kindness or favor [CC/V]
duì dá rú liú	對答如流	answer like flowing water/to answer quickly
huídá	回答	to answer [CC/V]; a reply
jiědá	解答	to explain [CC/V]; an explanation
suǒ dá fēi suǒ wèn	所答非所問	What was answered was not what was questioned/ answer evades the question
wèndá	問答	question and answer: *wèndá tí*, question and answer topics in an examination [CC/N]

dǎ
to strike, to fight, to do

打

---

dǎ bǎizi 打攏子 to have an attack of malaria [V-O]

dǎ biāngǔ 打邊鼓 to beat the side drum/to spread or circulate praise of actor, etc.

dǎchéng yípiàn 打成一片 to become one piece/to become a harmonious whole

dǎchū shǒur 打出手兒 (Chinese opera) to throw weapons back and forth on the stage

dǎ dànzi 打彈子 to play billiards [V O]

dǎ dìpù 打地鋪 to sleep on floor (due to lack of accommodation)

dǎ dìtānr 打地攤兒 to fall down flat on ground

dǎ dǐzi 打底子 to make a draft [V O]

dǎ diànhuà 打電話 to make a phone call

dǎgōng 打工 to have a temporary job (of students doing summer work) [V-O]

dǎ guānqiāng 打官腔 to put person off by talking formalities as excuse

dǎhāha 打哈哈 to laugh out loud, to make fun [V-O]

dǎjià 打架 to fight, to engage in a brawl [V-O]

dǎ jiāodao 打交道 to have dealings with

dǎ máoyī 打毛衣 to knit a sweater

dǎ qīng mà jiào 打輕罵俏 to flirt

dǎ qiūfēng 打秋風 to have a windfall/to obtain gifts of money (as by sending wedding invitations to people including mere acquaintances)

dǎshǒu 打手 professional rioters [SC/N]; to beat the hand [V O]

dǎtāi 打胎 to have an abortion [V-O]

dǎtīng 打聽 to find out [CC/V]

dǎ yájì 打牙祭 to have a good meal

dǎzá(r) 打雜兒 to do odd jobs as handyman [V-O]

dǎ zhāohu 打招呼 to say "hello"

dài'àn	帶案	to subpoena [VO]
dài biǎo	帶錶	to wear a watch [V O]
dài bīng	帶兵	to lead troops [V O]
dàidǎ	帶打	to rain fisticuffs; show of combat in Chinese opera [VO]
dàidào	帶道	to lead the way, to serve as guide [V-O]
dàidùzi	帶肚子	to be pregnant
dàifēnshu	帶分數	mixed fraction (mathematics)
dàigōu	帶鈎	best buckle [SC/N]
dài hǎo(r)	帶好兒	to carry greetings to: *Qǐng tì wǒ dài ge hǎor gěi nǐ fùmǔ.* Please remember me to your parents. [V O]
dài kǒuyīn	帶口音	to speak with an accent: *shuōhuà dài kǒuyīn*
dàilei	帶累	to involve someone in trouble or expense [CC/V]
dàilǐng	帶領	to lead, to be in charge of (troops) [CC/V]
dàilù	帶路	=*dàidào*
dài qián	帶錢	to carry money [V O]
dàishang mén	帶上門	to close the door [V O]
dài shēnzi	帶身子	to be pregnant [V O]
dàishǒu	帶手	wiping cloth carried by waiters [VO/N]
dàitóu(r)	帶頭兒	to lead [V-O]
dàixiào	帶孝	to wear mourning [V-O]
dài xiǎoháir	帶小孩兒	to bring up children: *Bié bǎ xiǎoháir dàihuàile.* Don't spoil the child.
dài xiāoxi	帶消息	to take message
dài xǐsè	帶喜色	to wear a pleased expression
lián dǎ dài mà	連打帶罵	to beat and scold at the same time
lián tī dài dǎ	連踢帶打	to mix kicks with hand blows

dāng (dàng)
to undertake, to fill an office, to treat as

當

dāngbīng	當兵	to be a soldier [V-O]
dāngchāi	當差	to run errand, to work for (someone) [V-O]; a servant
dāngdài	當代	the present age, that period [VO/TW]
dāng jī lì duàn	當機立斷	to decide on the spot or moment, to make quick decision
dāngjiā	當家	to be the head of, to oversee [V-O]
dāngjú	當局	the authorities [VO/N]
dāngmiàn	當面	face to face: *Nǐ dāngmiàn duì tā jiǎng.* You talk to him face to face.[VO/Adv]
dāngquán	當權	to be in power: *dāngquánpài,* faction in power [VO]
dāngran	當然	naturally [Adv]
dāng rén bú ràng	當仁不讓	in good causes, don't lag behind
dāngshí	當時	at that very moment, that time [VO/TW]
dāngshìrén	當事人	person in charge, parties to a quarrel or lawsuit
dāngtóu	當頭	right overhead: *dāng tóu bàng hè,* to give sharp advice for one to make up from error [VO/Adv]
dāngxīn	當心	to take care, to be careful [V-O]
dāngxuǎn	當選	to be elected [V-O]
dāng zhī wú kuì	當之無愧	to merit the credit, to be deserving
dāngzhòng	當眾	in the presence of all: *dāngzhòng xuānbù,* to announce publicly [VO/Adv]
cáiláng dāng dào	豺狼當道	wolf stands astride the road/bad person in power
mén dāng hù duì	門當戶對	(of betrothal) two families match in social status
shàngdàng	上當	to go to pawnshop/to be cheated [V-O]
dàng ěrbiān fēng	當耳邊風	to take advice as passing wind
dàngzhēn	當真	really: *Tā dàngzhēn búhuì.* He really cannot.[VO/Adv]
ná ta dàng péngyou	拿他當朋友	to treat him as a friend

倒

dǎobānr	倒班兒	to take turns [V-O]
dǎobāo	倒包	to substitute one thing for another [V-O]
dǎobì	倒閉	to go bankrupt: *Hǎo jǐjiā yínháng dǎobì le.* Quite a few banks went bankrupt. [CC/V]
dǎobuguòlai	倒不過來	=*dǎobùkāi* [VC]
dǎobukāi	倒不開	cannot meet the turnover in business [VC]
dǎodàn	倒蛋	to make trouble, to create mischief (also 搗蛋) [V-O]
dǎo fèng diān luán	倒鳳顛鸞	to have sexual intercourse
dǎogé	倒戈	to turn around weapon/to change sides (of warlords) [V-O]
dǎohuàn	倒換	to replace [CC/V]
dǎojià	倒價	selling-out price [SC/N]
dǎojiào	倒嚼	to chew the cud [SC/V]
dǎosǎng	倒嗓	to have a hoarse voice (of opera singers) [V-O]
dǎotā	倒塌	to tumble down [CC/V]
dǎoteng	倒騰	to turn upside down
dǎotì	倒替	to substitute, to replace [CC/V]
dǎotóu	倒頭	to lay down one's head to sleep, to die: *dǎotóu zhǐ*, paper money burned at death [V-O]
dǎoyùn	倒運	to have bad luck [V-O]; bad luck: *zǒu dǎoyùn*
dǎozhàng	倒帳	to go bankrupt becuase of deficit, to fail to collect debts
dǎozìr	倒字兒	to mispronounce (in Peking opera) [V-O]
biàndǎo	辯倒	to defeat by arguing [VC]
dǎdǎo	打倒	to knock down, down with ...!
tuīdǎo	推倒	to push down [VC]
zāidǎo	栽倒	to fall down [VC]

31

dàocǎi 倒彩   false applause: *hē dàocǎi*, to hiss a speaker or actor [SC/N]

dào chē 倒車   to back up a car [V O]

dào dǎ lór 倒打鑼兒   to beat the gong upside down/ everything is upside-down

dàoguà 倒掛   to hang upside down [SC/V]

dàoguolai 倒過來   to put in reverse

dàohǎor 倒好兒 false applause: *jiào ge dàohǎor*, to hiss at performance (=*dàocǎi*) [SC/N]

dàoliú 倒流   to flow back [SC/V]

dàoqì 倒氣   to gasp [V-O]

dàoqiàn 倒欠   to owe instead of gaining: *Tā yuánlái qiàn wǒ hěn duō qián. Hòulai wǒ dàoqiàn tā.* He owed me a lot of money originally. Later I owed him instead. [SC/V]

dàoshǔ 倒數   to count backward: *Tā shì dàoshǔ dìyī.* He is No. 1 counted backward. [SC/V]

dàotiē(r) 倒貼兒 to lose in bargain, to sell below cost; to pay her paramour instead of being paid [SC/V]

dàotuì 倒退   to fall back [SC/V]

dào xíng nì shī 倒行逆施 to govern or manage in opposition to right principles

dàoxuán 倒懸   to hang upside down, tyrannical treatment [SC/V]

dàoyǐng(r) 倒影兒 inverted image, reflection in water (SC/N)

dàozāicōng 倒栽蔥   to plant the onion upside down/to fall headfirst

dàozhì 倒置   to set up wrong: *yīn guǒ dàozhì*, cause and result are set up wrong/to put the carriage before the horse [SC/V]

dàozhuàn 倒轉   to turn in reverse [SC/V]

guàdàole 掛倒了 to hang something upside down [VC]

dàochāi 到差   to arrive at post, to appear for duty [V-O]

dàochù 到處   everywhere: *Dàochù shì shuǐ*. Water is everywhere. [VO/Adv]

dào cǐ wéi zhǐ 到此為止   to stop here

dàodá 到達   to reach: *Jīntian dòngshēn dehua, shénmo shíhou kéyi dàodá?* if you leave today, when can you arrive? [CC/V]

dàodǐ 到底   after all, to the bottom of the matter: *Zhè dàodǐ shì zěnmo huí shì?* What is the matter after all; to the end: *kàngzhàn dào dǐ*, to fight to the end

dàoguo 到過   to have been somewhere: *Wǒ dàoguo Niǔ Yuē.* I have been to New York.

dàojiār 到家兒   to be proficient: *Tāde huàr kě huàde dàojiār le.* His painting is really good [VO/SV] (cf. *dào jiā*, to reach home)

dào mòliǎor 到末了兒   to the end, finally, at last

dàoqī 到期   due time: *Báyuè yīhào dàoqī.* It is due August 1. *Nǐ jiè de shū dàoqīle ma?* Is the book you borrowed due today? [VO]

dào rújīn 到如今   until now

dàoshǒu 到手   to succeed in getting: *Nèixie qián shénmo shíhou cái néng dàoshǒu?* When can I get that money? [V-O]

dàotóulai 到頭來   in the end: *Dàotóulai quán diūle.* In the end everything was lost. [VO/adv]

bái tóu dào lǎo 白頭到老   to reach old age with white hair/to live together for an entire lifetime (husband and wife)

mǎ dào gōng chéng 馬到功成   horse gets there and job is done/to succeed without delay

niàn dào dìsānkè 念到第三課   study to Lesson 3

xiǎngdào 想到   to think of (something, someone): *Xiǎngdào zhèjian shì jiù tóuteng.* I get a headache whenever I think of this matter. [VC]

zhǎodào 找到   to be found: *Wǒde màozi zhǎodàole.* I have found my hat. [VC]

zhōudào 週到   to be considerate: *Tā zuòshì hěn zhōudào, cónglái bùdézuì rén.* Being considerate in his dealings, he never offends poeple. [CC/SV]

diǎn
to touch, to mark, to light 點

diǎnbīng	點兵	to muster soldiers [V-O]
diǎn cài	點菜	to select dishes from a menu [V O]
diǎnchuān	點穿	to point out the secret [VC]
diǎn huǒ	點火	to light a fire [V O]
diǎnjiāo	點交	to check and hand over [CC/V]
diǎnjiǎo(r)	點脚兒	to walk lamely [V-O]
diǎnmíng	點名	to make roll call [V-O]
diǎnmíng	點明	to point out (importance, meaning); to make a clear account [VC]
diǎnpò	點破	to expose (lie, falsehood) [VC]
diǎnshōu	點收	to check and receive [CC/V]
diǎn shū	點書	to punctuate a book [V O]
diǎn tóu	點頭	give a nod: diǎntóu péngyou, friends who don't know each other very well [V-O]
diǎn xì	點戲	to select play from repertoire offered [V O]
diǎnxīn	點心	a snack, pastry [VO/N]
diǎnxǐng	點醒	to remind gently [VC]
diǎnxuè	點穴	to hit at selected points (of Chinese kungfu, capable of causing internal bleeding) [VO]
diǎn yǎn	點眼	to apply eyedrop into the eye; to secure a point of anchorage in Chinese chess [V O]
diǎn yǎnyào	點眼藥	to apply eyedrop [V O]; diǎnyǎn yào, eyedrop [SC/N]
diǎnzhuì	點綴	to decorate; to add a lively detail on painting, writing, or furniture in a room [CC/V]
dǎdiǎn	打點	to put in order (baggage): dǎdiǎn xíngli
qīngting diǎn shuǐ	蜻蜓點水	dragonfly skims water surface/to use a light touch in writing, to travel around with short stopovers
zhǐdiǎn	指點	to point out, to show [CC/V]

定

dìngguī	定規	to set up rules [V-O]
dìnghūn	定婚	to be engaged to marry [V-O]
dìnghuò	定貨	to order goods [V-O]
dìngjì	定計	to decide, to set a plan [V-O]; a fixed plan [SC/N]
dìngjià	定價	to set the price [V-O]; fixed price, list price [SC/N]
dìngjū	定居	to settle down (in a town) [CC/V]
dìngjú	定局	a settled situation [SC/N]
dìnglǐ	定理	a maxim, theorem [SC/N]
dìnglǜ	定律	laws (moral, physical) [SC/N]
dìnglùn	定論	accepted opinion [SC/N]
dìngqī	定期	to set a time [V-O]
dìngqian	定錢	earnest money, deposit [SC/N]
dìngqíng	定情	to pledge love between lovers [V-O]
dìngshén	定神	to calm down [V-O]
dìng tiānxià	定天下	to bring peace and stability to country
dìngxīnwán(r)	定心丸兒	tranquillizer, hence, anything that soothes the nerves or help make up one's mind
dìngyì	定義	definition: *xià dìngyì*, to define [SC/N]
dìng zhǔyì	定主意	to make a decision
dìngzuì	定罪	to convict, to sentence [C-O]
dìngzuò	定做	to have it custom-made [CC/V
dìngzuòr	定座兒	to book seats, to make reservations [V-O]
shuōbudìng	說不定	cannot say for sure: *Shuōbudìng tā huì lái*. He may come. Who knows? [VC]
shuōdìng	說定	to settle after talking: *Wǒmen shuōdìngle míngtian yíkuàir zǒu*. We have decided to leave together tomorrow. [VC]
nádìng zhúyì	拿定主意	to make up one's mind

dòngbīng 動兵   to move the soldier/to start a war [V-O]

dòngbudong 動不動   very often, do something for no reason at all, for nothing: *Zhè háizi dòngbudong jiù kū.* This child cries for nothing.[Adv]

dòngcí 動詞   verb [SC/N]

dònggōng 動工   to commence work (on construction, building) [V-O]

dònghuǒ(r) 動火兒   to start fire/to feel angry [V-O]

dòng nǎojīn 動腦筋   to move the brain/do a lot of thinking

dòng niàntou 動念頭   to think of a plan, to plot

dòngqì 動氣   to get angry [V-O]

dòngrén 動人   to be moving, touching, attractive [VO/SV]

dòngshēn 動身   to set out, to depart [V-O]

dòngshǒu 動手   to raise hand to fight, to start (work), to begin: *Wǒde jiǎo dòngshǒu mále.* My feet have begun to feel numb.

dòng shǒu dòng jiǎo 動手動脚   to be fresh with girls

dòngtīng 動聽   (speech) to be moving, persuasive [SV/VO]

dòngtǔ 動土   to move dirt/to break ground [V-O]

dòngxīn 動心   to be moved (by attractive offer) [V-O]

dòngxiōng 動兇   to resort to violence (V-O)

dòngyòng 動用   to touch, to draw upon (funds): *dòngyòng gōngkuǎn*, to draw upon public funds (CC/V)

dòngyuán 動員   to move personnel/to mobilize: *dòngyuán mínzhòng*, to mobilize the people [VO/TV]

bié dòng 別動   Don't move!

bù wéi suǒ dòng 不為所動   not to be swayed (by speech) or attracted (by beauty)

nábúdòng 拿不動   cannot carry (too heavy) [VC]

wú dòng yú zhōng 無動於衷 to be completely indifferent

xindòng 心動 to be moved, to begin considering [SP/V]

yùndòng 運動 to do exercise [CC/V]; exercise, movement: *Wǔsì Yùndòng,* the May Fourth Movement

zhèige qián bùnéng dòng 這個錢不能動 This money cannot be touched.

dú
to read, to pronounce, to study

讀

dúběn	讀本	a reader, a school text [SC/N]; *Hànyǔ Dúběn*, <u>Chinese Reader</u>
dú dàxué	讀大學	to go to college or university
dúfǎ	讀法	way of pronouncing [SC/N]
dújīng	讀經	to read the Scripture, to read classics [V-O]
dúshū	讀書	to read a book: *dúshūrén*, a scholar, a literate person [V-O]
dú sǐshū	讀死書	to read dead books/to read without digesting
dú wàiwén	讀外文	to study foreign languages
dúwù	讀物	reading material [SC/N]
dú yèxiào	讀夜校	to go to night school
dúyīn	讀音	to pronounce [V-O]; pronunciation, literary pronunciation [SC/N]
dúzhě	讀者	a reader, one who reads: *Dúzhě Wénzhāi*, <u>Reader's Digest</u> [SC/N]
dú Zhōngwén xì	讀中文系	to study in the Chinese department, to major in Chinese
dúzǒule yīn	讀走了音	to pronounce incorrectly
jìdú	寄讀	to study as a boarding student
lǎngdú	朗讀	to read aloud [SC/V]
mòdú	默讀	to read silently [SC/V]
sān dú tōngguò	三讀通過	to have passed a proposal after three readings
zǒudú	走讀	to attend school while living at home

38

度

duò dé liàng lì 度德量力   to estimate one's virtue and measure one's strength/to assess one's ability before launching something

dùliàng 度量   capacity to tolerate: dùliang dà, can tolerate a lot

dù niánguān 度年關   to pass the New Year by paying all one's debts

duòzhī 度支   to estimate expenditures [VO]

duòliàng 度量   to consider, to measure [CC/V]

dùqū 度曲   to write words for popular song, to keep time in playing [VO]

dùrì 度日   to pass the day, to live [VO]

dù rì rú nián 度日如年   to spend a day like one year/the days are long (with waiting), to have a miserable life

chuǎiduò 揣度   =cǔnduò

chuǎi qíng duò lǐ 揣情度理   to make an intelligent appraisal

cǔnduò 忖度   to conjecture, imagine (another's attitude)

guòdù 過度   excessively, beyond measure; guòdù xiǎoxīn, excessively careful [VO/Adv].

nián huá xū dù 年華虛度   one's years spent for nothing/to waste one's live (especially for young women)

yǐ jǐ duò rén 以己度人   to place oneself in another's position

yǐ xiǎorén zhī xīn duò jūnzi zhī fù 以小人之心度君子之腹   to estimate a gentleman's mind with a hypocrite's way of thinking

zhì zhī duò wài 置之度外   to disregard entirely

---

fābiǎo 發表   to publish, to express: *fābiǎo yìjian*, to express ideas [CC/V]

fācái 發財   to get rich [V-O]

fāchóu 發愁   to be worried, sad [V-O]

fādāi 發呆   to be dazed [V-O]

fādòng 發動   to promote, initiate (movement, campaign, an engine): *fādòngjī*, dynamo, an electric motor [CC/V]

fāfēng 發瘋   to grow crazy: *Nǐ fāfēng le*. You are out of your mind. [V-O]

fāfú 發福   to grow fat (a compliment in Chinese) [V-O]

fāhěn 發狠   to work with angry determination [V-O]; diligently [Adv]

fāhéng 發橫   to become obstinate, violent (V-O)

fāhuāng 發慌   to panic (V-O)

fāhuǒ 發火   to become angry [V-O]

fākuáng 發狂   to become mad, to grow crazy (V-O)

fālèng 發楞   to be stunned [V-O]

fāmáo 發毛   to be afraid (to enter a diserted house), to be covered with goose pimples [V-O]

fāmíng 發明   to invent

fā píqi 發脾氣   to get mad

fāshāo 發燒   to have fever [V-O]

fāshēng 發生   to arise, to cause to happen: *fāshēng wùhui*, to cause misunderstanding [CC/V]

fāshì 發誓   to take an oath, to swear, also *fāzhòu* [V-O]

fāxiàn 發現   to discover [CC/V]

fāxiè 發洩   to blow off steam, anger [CC/V]

fāzǐ 發紫   to emit purple glow/to be extremely popular: *hóngde fāzǐ*, so popular (red), that one turns purple

反   to turn over, to counter, to oppose

fǎnbó	反駁	to reply to criticism
fǎncháng	反常	to be abnormal [VO/SV]
fǎnchuàn	反串	(of actor) to play a different role: *fǎnchuàn lǎoshēng*, to play the male character (female character being the customary role)
fǎndào	反倒	to the contrary [CC/Adv]
fǎndòng	反動	to be reactionary: *fǎndòngpài*, the reactionaries [SC/SV]
fǎnduì	反對	to oppose: *fǎnduìpài*, the political opposition [CC/V]
fǎnfù	反覆	again and again: *fǎnfù jiěshì*, to explain again and again; *fǎnfù wúcháng*, to change one's mind constantly (can't be trusted) [CC/Adv]
fǎngǎn	反感	reaction, bad reaction: *yǐnqǐ fǎngǎn*, to cause a bad reaction [SC/N]
fǎngémìng	反革命	counter-revolutionary
fǎngōng	反攻	to counterattack [SC/V]
fǎngòng	反共	to oppose Communism [V-O]; [SV] as in *Tā fēicháng fǎngòng*. He is very anti-Communist.
fǎnhuǐ	反悔	to repent
fǎnjí	反擊	to fight back, to counterattack [SC/V]
fǎnkàng	反抗	to resist [CC/V]; resistance
fǎn Kǒng	反孔	to oppose Confucius [V-O]
fǎnliǎn	反臉	to break the friendship: *fǎnliǎn búrèn rén*, to break the friendship without considering the past [V-O]
fǎnpàn	反叛	to rebel [CC/V]; rebellion
fǎnzhèng	反正	to defect the rebel troops and join the government (V-O); anyway: *Tā fǎnzhèng búhuì fǎnzhèng*. Anyway he will not defect.[Adv]
chuānfǎnle	穿反了	to wear it inside out (or in some other wrong way) [VC]
zàofǎn	造反	to rebel [V-O]

---

fēibái 飛白   a style of Chinese calligraphy with dry brush showing hollow lines (SC/N)

fēibēn 飛奔   to dash (away) [SC/V]

fēidàn 飛彈   flying bullet/a stray bullet, missile, rocket [SC/N]

fēidié 飛碟   flying saucer [SC/N]

fēi duǎn liú cháng 飛短流長   to spread rumors

fēi'é 飛蛾   moth [SC/N]

fēi huáng tēng dá 飛黃騰達   to get rapid promotions or series of successes in politics or business

fēijī 飛機   a flying machine/airplane [SC/N]

fēijiǎo 飛腳   a flying foot/a flying kick [SC/N]

fēi lái zhī huò 飛來之禍   unexpected trouble

fēimáotuǐ 飛毛腿   a fast walker [SC/N]

fēipǎo 飛跑   to run as if flying/to run very fast [SC/V]

fēipù 飛瀑   (flying) waterfalls [SC/N]

fēiqiáo 飛橋   a flying bridge/a very high bridge [SC/N]

fēishēng 飛昇   to fly up [CC/V]

fēitēng 飛騰   to go up (to the sky) [CC/V]

fēiwěn 飛吻   to fly a kiss [V-O]; a flying kiss

fēixíng 飛行   to fly, to go by plane: *fēixíngyuán*, airplane pilot [CC/V]

fēiyáng 飛揚   to float in the sky [CC/V]

fēiyáng báhù 飛揚跋扈   to become powerful and intransigent

fēiyǎnr 飛眼兒   to give a darting glance [V-O]

fēiyīng zǒu gǒu 飛鷹走狗   flying hawks and running hounds/underlings

fēizhǎng 飛漲   to go up like flying/(of price) sudden and rapid increase [SC/V]

gǎibiān	改編	to reorganize: *Gǎibiān jūnduì*, to regroup troops; to revise and rewrite [CC/V]
gǎibiàn	改變	to change: *Bǎ nèixie bùhǎode xíguàn gǎibiàn-guolai.* Change over those bad habits. [CC/V]
gǎigé	改革	to reform [CC/V]; reform
gǎiguān	改觀	to present a new look [V-O]
gǎiguò	改過	to repent: *gǎiguò zì xīn*, to repent and reform [V-O]
gǎiháng	改行	to change one's occupation [V-O]
gǎihuàn	改換	to exchange or substitute one for another, to make changes in (words, titles, etc.) [CC/V]
gǎijià	改嫁	to remarry [V-O]
gǎijìn	改進	to improve [CC/V]; improvement
gǎikǒu	改口	to give a different story or affidavit; also *gǎizuǐ* [V-O]
gǎiliáng	改良	to improve, to reform [SC/V]
gǎiqī	改期	to change date [V-O]
gǎirì	改日	to change a date/later: *gǎirì zài tán*, to talk about it later; also *gǎitiān* [VO/Adv]
gǎishàn	改善	to improve (treatment, method, etc.) [VC/V]
gǎi tóu huàn miàn	改頭換面	to change the head and face/ to make superficial changes
gǎixuǎn	改選	to hold a new election [V-O]
gǎiyàng	改樣	to refashion, remodel (room), to change manner (of person) [V-O]
gǎizào	改造	to remodel (building), to reform [CC/V]
gǎizhèng	改正	to correct errors: *gǎizhèng cuòwu* [CC/V]
gǎizhuāng	改裝	to change into another kind of dress, to disguise, to remodel (a building), to put in new containers [VO]
gǎizuòyè	改作業	to correct a student's homework

gào
to tell, to announce, to sue

告

gàobái	告白	public notice [CC/N]
gàobiàn(r)	告便兒	to bid goodbye, to go to the toilet [V-O]
gàobié	告別	to take leave, to say goodbye [V-O]
gàochéng	告成	to announce the completion of some important project: *Dà gōng gàochéng.* The great task has been completed.
gàocí	告辭	to bid goodbye, to take leave [V-O]
gàodài	告貸	to make a request for a loan, to borrow money [V-O]
gàofā	告發	to formally inform court of a crime, to lodge a complaint [CC/V]
gàojí	告急	to make an emergency request for help [VO]
gàojià	告假	to ask for leave of absence: *gào bìngjià,* to ask for sick leave [V-O]
gàojié	告捷	to announce victory [V-O]
gàojiè	告誡	to warn, to admonish [CC/V]
gàomì	告密	to give secret information against someone [V-O]
gàoshi	告示	a public announcement [CC/N]
gàosu	告訴	to tell; (law) to bring suit against someone [CC/V]
gào yíduànluo	告一段落	to consider one phase of a project completed
gàozhī	告知	to tell, to notify [CC/V]
gàozhuàng	告狀	to sue at court [V-O]
gàozuì	告罪	(courtesy) please excuse me for an unintentional offense: *Gàozuì! Gàozuì!* [V-O]
bùkě gào rén zhī shì	不可告人之事	an affair that is not mentionable
guǎnggào	廣告	advertisement [SC/N]
tōnggào	通告	public notice [CC/N]
wǒ gào ni	我告你	I will sue you.
zì gào fèn yǒng	自告奮勇	to volunteer one's service

革

géchú 革除	to expel, to dismiss [CC/V]
gé gù dǐng xīn 革故鼎新	to discard the old ways of life in favor of the new
gé miàn xǐ xīn 革面洗心	to start life anew
gémìng 革命	to revolt, to overthrow the established authorities [V-O]; revolution: *guómín gémìng*, people's revolution
gétuì 革退	to dismiss [CC/V]
géxīn 革心	to change one's mind [V-O]
géxīn 革新	to reform, to innovate
géyuán 革員	to have a reduction in force (=*cáiyuán*)
gézhí 革職	to dismiss, to be dismissed from office: *Tā xiānsheng bèi géle zhí.* Her husband was fired. [V-O]
biàngé 變革	to replace the old with the new [CC/V]
gǎigé 改革	to reform [CC/V]
kāigé 開革	to dismiss (=*géchú*) [CC/V]
xīnggé 興革	to introduce reforms [CC/V]

gěi (jǐ)
to give, to provide   給

gěifù	給付	to make payment [CC/V]
gěijià	給假	to grant leave of absence: *gěile sāntian jià*, granted three days' leave of absence [V-O]
gěiliǎn	給臉	to show courtesy to someone who does not really deserve it, to save someone's face: *gěiliǎn búyào liǎn*, to show courtesy to one, but he is not worthy of it [V-O]
gěi rén dǎ le	給人打了	was beaten by somebody (=*bèi rén dǎ le*)
gěi tā zuò fàn	給他做飯	to cook for him
jǐyǎng	給養	Provisions, allowance [CC/N]
jǐyǔ	給予	to present as a gift or favor [CC/V]
bǎ fànwǎnr gei zá le	把飯碗兒給砸了	to have the rice bowl smashed, to have lost one's job
gōngjǐ	供給	to supply with things [CC/V]
jiā jǐ hù zú	家給戶足	to be abundantly provided
jiāogěi	交給	to hand over to: *Qǐng nǐ bǎ zhèzhāng huàr jiāogei tā.* Please hand over this painting to him.[CC/V]
màigei ta	賣給他	to sell something to him. Sell it to him.
pèijǐ	配給	to ration [CC/V]
ràng rén gěi dǎ le	讓人給打了	=*gèi rén dà le*
sònggei ta	送給他	to give something to him as a gift
zì jǐ zì zú	自給自足	to be self-sufficient

跟

gēnbānr(de)	跟班兒的	servant of an official, entourage [VO/N]
gēnbāo(de)	跟包的	=*gēnbānr* [VO/N]
gēnmār	跟媽兒	personal maid of a prostitute [SC/N]
gēn nǐ xuéxí	跟你學習	to learn from you
gēn pái	跟牌	(of card game) to follow suit [V O]
gēnqian	跟前	place nearby: *jiǎngtái gēnqian*, near the platform; *Nǐ gēnqian yǒu méiyou xiǎoháir?* Do you have children with you? [SC/N]
gēnrén	跟人	an attendant, a follower [VO/N]; *gēn rén*, to follow someone [V O]
gēnshǒur	跟手兒	immediately, smoothly: *gēnshǒur qù zuò*, to do it at once [VO/Adv]
gēnsuí	跟隨	to follow someone [CC/V]; follower
gēn ta bànshì	跟他辦事	to work with him
gēn ta jiéhūn	跟他(她)結婚	to get married with him (or her)
gēn ta liáotiānr	跟他聊天	to chat with him
gēn ta yào qián	跟他要錢	to ask him for money
gēntou	跟頭	a fall: *zāi gēntou*, to have a fall; a somersault; *fān gēntou*, to do a somersault
gēnyǐr	跟尾兒	right away: *Tā gēnyǐr jiù chūlai le.* He will come out right away. [VO/Adv]
gēnzhe	跟着	in the wake of, right away: *gēnzhe jiù lái le*, came over right away; to follow: *Nǐ gēnzhe ta.* You follow him.
gēnzōng	跟踪	to follow in the track of, to shadow (someone) [V-O]
Tā gēn Lǎo Lǐ shì lǎo péngyou.	他跟老李是老朋友	He and Old Li are good friends.

gòngchǎn 共產   to share property: *gòngchǎndǎng*, Communist Party[V-O]

gòngcún gòngróng 共存共榮   co-existance and co-prosperity

gòngfàn 共犯   accomplice [SC/N]

gòngguǎn 共管   to manage together: *guójì gòngguǎn*, controlled internationally [SC/V]

gònghé dǎng 共和黨   Republican Party

gònghé zhèngtǐ 共和政體   republican form of government

gòngjì 共計   to sum up, altogether: *gòngjì duōshao qián?* How much altogether? [SC/Adv]

gòngmíng 共鳴   sympathy, sympathetic understanding [SC/N]

gòngmóu 共謀   to plan together [SC/V]

gòngshì 共事   to work together: *Nǐ gēn tā gòngguo shì ma?* Have you ever worked with him? [V-O]

gòngsù 共宿   to lodge in the same place [VO]

gòng xiāng shèng jǔ 共襄盛舉   to offer help to a great cause together

gòngyíng 共營   to manage jointly: *gōngsī gòngyíng*, managed by both public and private concerns [SC/V]

gòngyǒu 共有   to possess together: *Zhèxie dōngxi wéi wǒmen suǒ gòngyǒu.* These things are for our mutual possession.[SV/V]

gòngzǒng 共總   altogether (=*gòngjì*) [CC/Adv]

búgòng dài tiān 不共戴天   will not live under the same sky as the man who slew his father/inveterate hatred

zǒnggòng 總共   =*gòngzǒng* [CC/Adv]

---

guān'ài 關愛　　*guānxīn*, be concerned, and *àihù*, love/to express solicitude for the well-being of (someone) [CC/V]

guāndēng 關燈　　to close the lamp/to turn off the lights [V-O]

guāndiàn 關電　　to close the electricity/to turn off the electricity [V-O]

guān diànmén 關電門　　=*guāndiàn*

guānhuái 關懷　　*guānxīn*, to be concerned, and *huáiniàn*, to think of/to be concerned about, for, show interest in [CC/V]; solicitude

guānlián 關連　　relations, connections: *Zhèjian shì gēn nèijian shì méiyou shénmo guānlián.* This matter has no connection with that one. [CC/N]

guānmén 關門　　to close the door [V-O]; (Chinese medicine) the kidneys

guānqiè 關切　　to be concerned about (someone), to be intimately related, connected [CC/SV]

guānshang 關上　　to close (door, window, etc.) [VC]

guānshè 關涉　　*guānlián* and *qiānshè*, to involve/to have effects on something else: *guānshè biérén sīshì*, to have to do with the private business of others [CC/V]; relations, connections, effects

guāntuō 關託　　to request someone to intercede on one's behalf: *Guāntuō nín tì wǒ shuōshuo qíng.* Please put in a few good words for me. [CC/V]

guānxi 關係　　to be related to one another [CC/V]; relationship, consequences: *Tā gēn tā yǒu méi-you guānxi méi guānxi.* It is not important whether he and she have had any relationship. (CC/V]

guānxīn 關心　　to be concerned about (someone) or for (something): *Tā hěn guānxīn nǐ.* He is very concerned about you. *guānxīn guóshì*, to show interest in national affairs [VO/SV]

guānyu 關於　　regarding, concerning, about: *Guānyu zhèjian shì, wǒ yìdiǎnr dōu bùzhīdao.* I know nothing about this matter. [Preposition]

guānzhào 關照　　*guānxīn* and *zhàoying*, to take care of/to notify: *Yǒu shì, qǐng guānzhào yìshēng.* If anything comes up, please notify me. to take care of: *Qǐng nǐ duōduō guānzhào.* Please take good care of (him). [CC/V]

關

guānzhù 關注　*guānxīn* and *zhùyi*, to pay attention to/to pay close attention to, to be intensely concerned about, for [CC/V]

kāiguān 開關　to open and to close/to turn on and off; switch [CC/N]

shì bù guān jǐ 事不關己　The matter doesn't concern one personally.

觀

guāncè 觀測 to prognosticate through observation [CC/V]

guānchá 觀察 to look into, to observe [CC/V]; observation

guāndiǎn 觀點 point of view, standpoint: *Gèren yǒu gèrende guāndiǎn.* Each has his own viewpoint.[SC/N]

guānfēng 觀風 to look for an opportunity to do something, to stand watch for something expected to happen: *Nǐmen jìnqu, wǒ zài wàibianr guānfēng.* You go in and I'll keep watch outside for you.[VO]

guāngǎn 觀感 to observe and to react/observations and comments [CC/N]

guānguāng 觀光 to visit as a tourist, to take a tour: *guānguāngkè*, toruist; *guānguāng shìyè*, the tourist business [V-O]

guānkàn 觀看 to take a look at, to see [CC/V]

guānmó 觀摩 to study and fondle (works of art), to study by visiting other institutions [CC/V]

guānniàn 觀念 concept, idea, notion: *xīn guānniàn*, new concepts [CC/N]

guānshǎng 觀賞 *guānkàn*, to see, and *xīnshǎng*, to appreciate/to enjoy by sight (art, flower, view, etc.) [CC/V]

guānwàng 觀望 to take a wait-and-see attitude: *cǎi guānwàng tàidù; guānwàng bùqián*, to wait and see without taking any action [CC/V]

guānzhān 觀瞻 (of things) outward appearance: *yǒu ài guānzhān*, will adversely affect the outward appearance [CC/N]

guānzhòng 觀眾 the audience, spectators [SC/N]

bēiguān 悲觀 to be pessimistic [SC/SV]

cānguān 參觀 to visit (school, hospital, etc.) [CC/V]

kèguān 客觀 objective [SC/SV]; objectivity

lèguān 樂觀 to be optimistic [SC/SV]

míng ruò guān huǒ 明若觀火 as clear as viewing a fire/very clear

pángguān 旁觀 to look on: *xiù shǒu pángguān*, to look on with folded arms [SC/V]

zhǔguān 主觀 subjective [SC/SV]; subjective

guǎn
to manage, to be in charge of, to interfere

管

---

guǎnbǎo 管保 to guarantee, to be sure: *Wǒ guǎnbǎo tā bùlái.* I'm sure he will not come.[CC/V]

guǎn bǎo 管飽 to guarantee adequate food [V O]

guǎnbuliǎo 管不了 cannot manage: *Zhèijian shì wǒ kě guǎnbuliǎo.* It is really beyond my power to manage this affair.[VC]

guǎn chī guǎn zhù 管吃管住 to provide food and lodging

guǎn fàn 管飯 to provide food, to include board [V O]

guǎnjiā 管家 to be in charge of domestic affairs [V-O]; person in charge of domestic affairs, also *guǎnjiāde*, a butler

guǎnjiào 管教 to take care of and discipline (children): *guǎnjiào xiǎoháir*; to make or cause (someone) to do something: *Guǎnjiào tā gěi nǐ shuō hǎo huà.* I will see to it that he apologizes to you. [CC/V]

guǎnjiāpó 管家婆 a housewife, a woman who likes to interfere

guǎnlǐ 管理 to manage [CC/V]

guǎnménde 管門的 a doorkeeper

guǎnshì 管事 to be in charge of: *Zhèr shéi guǎnshì?* Who is in charge here? (V-O); person in charge, also *guǎnshìde*

guǎnshù 管束 *guǎnlǐ*, to manage, and *yuēshù*, to control/supervise (children, students, etc.) [CC/V]

guǎn tuì guǎn huàn 管退管換 to guarantee refund and exchange

guǎnxiá 管轄 to exercise control over [CC/V]

guǎn xiánshì 管閒事 to poke one's nose into another's business

guǎnzhàng 管賬 to do bookkeeping [V-O]; *guǎnzhàngde*, bookkeeper, person in charge of accounts

guǎnzhì 管制 *guǎnlǐ*, to manage, and *jiézhì*, to regulate/to administer, to control [CC/V]

bùguǎn 不管 don't care, no matter ...

dàiguǎn 代管 manage on behalf of (someone)

zhǔguǎn 主管 to be responsible for [SC/V]; head of an office

害

hài
to harm, to kill, to suffer from

hàibìng 害病　to be ill: *hàile liǎngtiān bìng*, to be ill for two days [V-O]

hài háizi 害孩子 =*hàixǐ*

hài guó yāng mín 害國秧民　to harm the country and the people

hàikǒu 害口　(of pregnant woman) to show appetite for certain foods [V-O]

hàipà 害怕　to fear, to be afraid of [VO]

hài qún zhī mǎ 害群之馬　horse that harms the group/person who gives the group a bad name

hài rén 害人　to harm people: *hái rén bùqiǎn*, to do someone a lot of harm [V O]

hài rén fǎn hài jǐ 害人反害己　a plot to harm others boomeranged

hàisào 害臊　to blush, to feel shy [VO]

hài shāyǎn 害沙眼　to contract trachoma

hàisǐ 害死　to murder, to harm severely: *Nǐ hàisǐ wǒ le.* You are killing me. [VC]

hàixǐ 害喜　to have morning sickness [V-O]

hàixiū 害羞　to feel shy, to feel ashamed [VO]

cánhài 殘害　to do severe injury [CC/V]

lìhài 利害　*lìyì*, advantage, and *hàichu*, disadvantage [CC/N]

lìhai 厲害　to be severe: *lìhaide hěn*, very severe; *bìngde hěn lìhai*, severely ill [CC/SV]

móu cái hài mìng 謀財害命　to kill for money

móuhài 謀害　to conspire [CC/V]

pòhài 迫害　*yāpò*, to oppress, and *móuhài*, to harm [CC/V]

shāhài 殺害　to kill [CC/V]

shānghài 傷害　to injure [CC/V]

xiànhài 陷害　to trap and harm/to betray [CC/V]

hé
to close, to join, to agree

合

hébìng	合併	to unite, to annex [CC/V]
héchàng	合唱	to sing together [SC/V]; a chorus
héchéng	合成	to complete by bringing together [VC]
hé duōshao měijīn	合多少美金	How much U.S. money does it correspond to?
héfǎ	合法	to be legal, in accordance with the law [VC/SV]
hégé	合格	to be up to standard, qualified [VO/SV]
hégòng	合共	altogether [CC/Adv]
héhu	合乎	to be in accordance with: héhu dàoli, to be in accordance with reason
héhuǒ(r)	合夥兒	to go into partnership [VO]
héjì	合計	to count together [SC/V]
hélǐ	合理	to be reasonable, right, in accordance with reason [VO/SV]
héqún	合群	to be gregarious, to go along with the group [VO/SV]
héshang	合上	to close (books, etc.) [VC]
héshí	合時	to be fashionable, to be timely [VO/SV]
héshi	合適	to be suitable [CC/SV]
hésuàn	合算	to be worthwhile, reasonable in price [SC/SV]
hétong	合同	contract: dìng hétong, to have a contract [CC/N]
héyì	合意	to be agreeable, in accordance with one's ideas [VO/SV]
Hézhòngguó	合衆國	the United States
hézhu	合住	to close (umbrella, etc.) [VC]
hézuò	合作	to cooperate [SC/V]; cooperation
mào hé shén lí	貌合神離	in appearance together in spirit apart/friends or allies in appearance only
tiān zuò zhī hé	天作之合	a Heaven-made match (marriage)

huābuqi 花不起 cannot afford to spend (so much): *huābuqi zhèmo duō qián* [VC]

huāfèi 花費 to spend money, to cost [CC/V]; the cost

huā héshang 花和尚 profligate monk

huāhuadada 花花搭搭 variegated

huāhuāgōngzǐ 花花公子 a playboy

huāhuālǜlǜ 花花綠綠 colorful

huāhuāshìjiè 花花世界 world of sensual pleasures

huā qián 花錢 to spend money [V O]

huāshao 花稍 to be pretty, to be romantic, to be fond of opposite sex [CC/SV]

huā tiān jiǔ dì 花天酒地 world of women and wine/to indulge oneself in worldly pleasures

huāxiàng 花項 items of expense: *Méi shénmo huāxiàng.* There is no occasion to spend.[SC/N]

huāxiāo 花消 expenses: *Dōngxi dōu zhǎngle. Huāxiāo tài dà.* Things are more expensive now. (Our) expenses have increased a lot.[CC/N]

huāyǎn 花眼 blurred eyes [SC/N]

huā yán qiǎo yǔ 花言巧語 to speak with flowery, deceiving words

tóu hūn yǎn huā 頭昏眼花 dizzy

yǎnhuā 眼花 eyes become blurred/cannot see clearly: *Kànde wǒ yǎnhuā.* I've read so much that my eyes have become blurred.[SP/V]

yǎn huā liáo luàn 眼花撩亂 dazzled (by the sight of things)

huà
to transform, to disguise, -ize

化

huàchú 化除 to abolish, to remove (prejudices): huàchú chéngjiàn [CC/V]

huà dí wéi yǒu 化敵為友 to convert enemy into friend

huà gāngé wéi yùbèi 化干戈為玉帛 "beat swords into plowshares"/to put an end to war and have peace

huàhé 化合 to combine in chemical process: huàhéwù, (chemical) compound [CC/V]

huàmíng 化名 to disguise one's name, to adopt a pseudonym [V-O]

huàshēn 化身 transmormation of Buddha in different manifestations, a personification (of love, piety, etc.) [SC/N]

huàshí 化石 fossil [SC/N]

huàxué 化學 chemistry [SC/N]

huàyàn 化驗 to do chemical analysis [CC/V]; chemical analysis

huàyù 化育 to grow and change naturally [CC/V]; such growth and change

huà zhěng wéi líng 化整為零 to break up whole into parts/to take care of things one by one

huàzhuāng 化妝 to apply makeup: huàzhuāngpǐn, cosmetics [V-O]

huàzhuāng 化裝 to dress in disguise [V-O]

biǎomiànhuà 表面化 to bring to the surface

chūn fēng huà yǔ 春風化雨 the kindly influence of a good teacher

èhuà 惡化 to worsen, to deteriorate

fēnghuà 風化 customs, public morals: fēnghuà qū, red-light district [CC/N]

jiàohuàzi 叫化子 a beggar, also jiàohuāzi or huāzi

ōuhuà 歐化 to Europeanize: Ōuhuà jùzi, Europeanized sentences

wénhuà 文化 civilization, culture [CC/N]

xiàndàihuà 現代化 to modernize

zàohuà 造化 creation, operation of nature, good luck: Zhèi dōu shì nǐde zàohuà. These are all your good luck. [CC/N]

畫

huà bǐng chōng jī 畫餅充饑 to draw a cake to satisfy hunger/a Barmecide feast

huàfēn 畫分 to divide in parts [CC/V]

huàfú 畫符 to write or draw spells or incantations [V-O]

huàgōng 畫供 to sign affidavit [V-O]

huà guǐ yì, huà gǒu nán 畫鬼易,畫狗難 It is easier to paint a ghost than a dog.

huà hǔ lèi quǎn 畫虎類犬 to paint the tiger but looks like a dog/ fail to achieve what one set out to do, to describe something unsuccessfully

huà huàr 畫畫兒 to draw a picture [V O]

huà huóle 畫活了 to paint something very vividly

huàjiā 畫家 a painter (SC/N]

huàjiàng 畫匠 (derogatory) commercial artist [SC/N]

huàjiè 畫界 to draw the boundary [V-O]

huà lóng diǎn jīng 畫龍點睛 to add the pupil while painting the eye of a dragon/to make the critical touch

huàmǎo 畫卯 to sign one's name to indicate punctual arrival in office [V-O]

huàméi 畫眉 to draw eyebrows [V-O]; the grey thrush

huà shé tiān zú 畫蛇添足 to paint a snake with feet/superfluous

huàshī 畫師 (courtesy) painter [SC/N]

huàtú 畫圖 to paint, to draw [V-O]; a painting, a drawing

huàxíng 畫行 to write a sign of assent, to give authorization [V-O]

huàyā 畫押 to make a sign (especially of an illiterate) in lieu of signature [V-O]

huàyàngzi 畫樣子 rough draft [SC/N]; to draw a model [V-O]

huàyī 畫一 to standardize; uniform

huān
to enjoy, to be joyful

歡

huānbiàn 歡忭	to be happy, overjoyed [CC/V]	
huānhū 歡呼	to shout cheerfully: *huānhū wànsuì*, to shout *banzai* [CC/V]	
huānhǔr 歡虎兒	happy tiger cub/a lively child; *Zhèige xiǎoháir huānhǔr side.* This child is as happy and gay as a tiger cub.	
huānjù 歡聚	to have a happy reunion, to meet happily together: *Dàjia huānjù yi táng.* Everybody is happy together. [SC/V]	
huānlè 歡樂	to be happy, delighted [CC/SV]	
huānlóng 歡龍	happy dragon (=*huānhǔr*)	
huānsòng 歡送	to give farewell party: *huānsònghuì*, farewell party [SC/V]	
huān tiān xǐ dì 歡天喜地	to be overjoyed	
huānxǐ 歡喜	to be happy, delighted; to like: *Wǒ huānxǐ ta.* I like her. (understatement for I love her) [CC/V]	
huānxiào 歡笑	to laugh heartily [CC/V]	
huānxīn 歡心	joy, love [SC/N]	
huānxīn 歡欣	to be exultant: *huānxīn gǔwǔ*, to dance for joy [CC/SV]	
huānxǐqiánr 歡喜錢兒	happy money/tips to servants on celebration	
huānxǐ yù kuáng 歡喜欲狂	crazy with happiness/overjoyed	
huānxù 歡敘	to meet for happy reunion [CC/V]	
huānyán 歡顏	happy countenance [SC/N]	
huānyàn 歡宴	to entertain guests with banquet: *huānyàn bīnkè* [CC/V]	
huānyíng 歡迎	to welcome: *shòu huānyíng*, to be well-liked, well received: *Tā nèiběn shū hěn shòu huānyíng.* That book of his is well received. [SC/V]	
huānyù 歡娛	to enjoy oneself [CC/V]	
huānyuè 歡悅	to be pleased [CC/SV]	
huānyuè 歡躍	to jump for joy [CC/V]	
xǐhuan 喜歡	to like [CC/V]	

huánbào	還報	to pay back [CC/V]; retribution
huánběn	還本	to recover capital invested: *gòu huánběn,* to come out even [V-O]
huándū	還都	(of government) to return to the capital after exile [V-O]
huánhún	還魂	the soul returns, dead person revives [V-O]
huánjià	還價	to haggle [V-O]
huánjìng	還敬	to return courtesy [VO]
huánkǒu	還口	to talk back [V-O]
huánlǐ	還禮	to return courtesy, to salute back, to give gift in return [V-O]
huánqián	還錢	to pay back money (owed to somebody)
huánqīng	還清	to repay in full [VC]
huán rénqíng	還人情	to make gift in return
huánshǒu	還手	to strike back [V-O]
huánsú	還俗	to return to secular life [V-O]
huánxí	還席	to give a return dinner, to vomit after being drunk (to throw out what was eaten) [V-O]
huánxiāng	還鄉	to return to one's native place [V-O]
huányáng	還陽	to return to life [V-O]
huányuàn	還願	to redeem a vow pledged before Buddha [V-O]
huányuán	還原	to be restored to the original shape or position [V-O]
huán zhài	還債	to pay debt [V O]
huán zhàng	還賬	to repay loan [V O]
huánzuǐ	還嘴	to answer back in abuse or self-defense [V-O]

huíbài	回拜	to return a visit [VO]
huíbào	回報	to bring back a report [V-O]
huídá	回答	to answer [CC/V]; a reply
huígù	回顧	to look back [SC/V]
huíguó	回國	to return to one's native country [V-O]
huíhuà	回話	to report (on errand), to answer charges [V-O]
huí jiā	回家	to return home [V O]
huíjiàn	回見	see you again (=*huítóur jiàn*)
huíjìng	回敬	to send present in return, to propose a toast in return: *huíjìng yìbēi*, to offer a drink in return [VO]
huíkòu	回扣	a kickback [SC/N]
huílǐ	回禮	to return a salute, to give a return gift [V-O]
huìmìng	回命	to return with message [V-O]
huíshēng	回聲	echo [SC/N]
huíshǒu	回手	to return a blow [V-O]
huí tóu shì àn	回頭是岸	to turn the head and there is the shore/ to repent and salvation is at hand
huítóu(r)	回頭兒	to turn the head; to repent, to reform [V-O]; later:*Huítóur jiàn*. See you later. [Adv]
huíwèi	回味	to savor enjoyment
huíxiǎng	回想	to recall, to reflect, to consider
huíxìn	回信	to answer a letter [V-O]; letter in reply
huíyì	回憶	to reminisce [SC/V]
huíyīn	回音	an answer, an echo [SC/N]
huízuǐ	回嘴	to talk back, to retort [V-O]
làng zǐ huí tóu	浪子回頭	the prodigal son's return

huì
to have the ability to, to understand, to meet

huìhé 會合	to assemble, to join forces [CC/V]	
huìhuà 會話	conversation	
huìjiàn 會見	to meet, to see (visitor) [CC/V]	
huìkǎo 會考	nationally unified examination [SC/V,N]	
huì kè 會客	to see guests or visitors [V O]	
huì lā huì chàng 會拉會唱	to know how to play a Chinese violin and to sing Chinese opera	
huìmiàn 會面	to meet face to face [V-O]	
huìqí 會齊	to assemble: *Wǒmen zài Wángjiā huìqí, ránhòu chūfā.* We will assemble at the Wang's and then set out.	
huìshāng 會商	to discuss together [CC/V]	
huìshī 會師	to join forces for battle, rendezvous [V-O]	
huìshì 會試	=*huìkǎo*	
huìshuǐ 會水	to be good at swimming [V-O]	
huìtóng 會同	jointly (manage): *huìtóng guǎnlǐ*	
huìwù 會悟	to realize (the truth) [CC/V]	
huìwù 會晤	to meet or see personally [CC/V]	
huì xiàyǔ 會下雨	It is going to rain.	
huìxīn 會心	silent appreciation: *huìxīnde wéixiào*, a smile of understanding	
huìyì 會意	to appreciate silently; one of the six principles of Chinese character formation [VO]	
huìzhàn 會戰	to meet for great battle	
huì zhàng 會賬	to pay the bill (as in a restaurant) [V O]	
huì zuò 會作	can do, knows how to do (something) [V O]	
xuéhuìle 學會了	to have learned it [VC]	
yì xué jiù huì 學就會	to learn quickly (of a fast learner)	

61

huó
to live, to be alive, to be flexible

活

huó dào lǎo, xué dào lǎo, xué bùliǎo
        Live to old age, learn to old age, can't learn everything

huódòng 活動
    to move around, to exercise; to run for (an office): *huódòng yī guān bàn zhí*, to run about to get an official post [CC/V]; to be active [SV]; activities

huógāi 活該
    it served you right, one deserves (to be punished, etc.): *Tā huógāi áidǎ. Shéi jiào tā nèimo huài ne.* He deserves to be spanked. Who asked him to be so bad.

huó jiàn guǐ 活見鬼
          Utter nonsence! Impossible!

huójù 活劇
    a drama in real life [SC/N]

huó kòuzi 活扣子
      a knot that can be easily untied

huólù 活路
    a way out, a chance to live [SC/N]

huómái 活埋
    to bury alive [SC/V]

huópo 活潑
    to be lively, energetic [CC/SV]

huór 活兒
    work: *gàn huór*, to do work

huó shòuzuì 活受罪
      to suffer terribly

huóshuǐ 活水
    fresh current [SC/N]

huó sǐrén 活死人 a walking corpse, a useless person

huótour 活頭兒
    something worth living for: *Lián xì dōu bùnéng kàn, hái yǒu shénmo huótour?* What does one want to live for if he can't even go to the opera?

huóyè 活頁
    loose leaf (album): *huóyè wénxuǎn*, selected readings in loose leaf [SC/N]

huóyòng 活用
    to make flexible use of [SC/V]

huóyuè 活躍
    to be very active, lively: *Tā zài zhèngzhi fāngmiàn hěn huóyuè.* He is very active in politics.[CC/SV]

huózhuō 活捉
    to capture alive [SC/V]

shēng lóng huó hǔ 生龍活虎
      live dragon and tiger/very much alive and vivid

yǎnghuo 養活 to raise (children), to support (parents); *yǎnghuó*, to bring life back to (orphan, animal, etc.) [VC]

集

jíchéng	集成	a grand compendium
jígǔ	集股	to form a stock company [V-O]
jíhé	集合	to assemble, to muster [CC/V]
jíhuì	集會	to hold a meeting [CC/V]
jíjǐn	集錦	collection of choice items of art or quotations [VO/N]
jíjù	集聚	to assemble in one place [CC/V]
jíquán	集權	to centralize [VO]; centralization: *Zhōngyāng jíquán*
jí shǎo chéng duō	集少成多	"many a little makes a mickle"
jí sī guǎng yì	集思廣益	to benefit by group discussion

jítǐ 集體 collective: *jítǐ chuàngzuò*, work done by many participants; *jítǐ lǐngdǎo*, collective leadership; *jítǐ lóngchǎng*; collective farm; *jítǐ ānquán*, collective security

jítuán 集團 a group of persons or nations: *gòngchǎn jítuán*, the Communist block of nations; *jítuán jiéhūn*, mass wedding

jí yè chéng qiú 集腋成裘 to make a garment by piecing together little pieces of fur/Many small contributions will make a great sum.

jíyì	集議	to hold a meeting to discuss [CC/V]
jíyóu	集郵	to collect postal stamps [V-O]: *jíyóujiā*, a philatelist
jízhōng	集中	to concentrate: *jízhōng zhùyì*, to concentrate one's mind [VO]; *jízhōngyíng*, concentration camp
jízī	集資	to collect capital for a business enterprise [V-O]

jì
to record, to remember

記

jìchóu 記仇	to bear a grudge [V-O]	
jìde 記得	to remember, can recall: *Wǒ jìde tā shì shéi.* I remember who he is.	
jìgōng 記功	to give credit for meritorious work [V-O]	
jìguà 記掛	to think of, to be concerned about [CC/V]	
jìguò 記過	to give a demerit [V-O]	
jìhaor 記號兒	a mark, a sign: *Zuòge jìhaor jiù búhuì wàngle.* Make a sign so that we will not forget. [SC/N]	
jìlù 記錄	to record [CC/V]; minutes of meetings	
jìmíng 記名	to register the name: *jìmíng tóupiào,* to sign one's name on ballot in voting [V-O]	
jìqǔ 記取	to recall, to remember: *jìqǔ jiàoxùn,* learn a lesson [CC/V]	
jìshì 記事	to record events [V-O]; written records, chronicles	
jìshìr 記事兒	to remember things (the first time a child shows its memory): *Nèishí wǒ cái jìshìr.* At that time I began to remember things. [V-O]	
jìxialai 記下來	to put down in writing [VC]	
jìxingr 記性兒	the memory power: *Wǒde jìxingr tài huài.* My memory is too bad. [SC/N]	
jìyì 記憶	to remember [CC/V]; memories: *jìyìlì,* memory power (=*jìxingr*)	
jìzai 記載	to put down in writing [CC/V]; written records	
jìzhàng 記賬	to make an entry in an account, to charge to an account [V-O]	
jìzhě 記者	a newspaper reporter [SC/N]	
jìzhu 記住	to bear in mind: *Jìzhu bié wàng le.* Keep this in mind and don't forget. [VC]	
bǐjì 筆記	to take notes [SC/V]; notes	
sǐjì 死記	to resort to rote memory [SC/V]	
sùjì 速記	to take shorthand [SC/V]	

jiābèi	加倍	to double [V-O]
jiāēn	加恩	to show favor [VO]
jiāfǎ	加法	addition (math.) [SC/N]
jiāgōng	加工	to do extra work [VO]; processing [N]: *shípǐn jiāgōng*, food processing
jiāhài	加害	to inflict injury on (someone) [VO]
jiāhao	加號	sign of addition (+)
jiājí	加級	to add a grade/to promote [V-O]
jiājiǎng	加奬	to award praise [VO]
jiājǐn	加緊	to intensify, to become tense
jiāméng	加盟	to join the league, alliance [V-O]
jiāmiǎn	加冕	to be coronated [V-O]; coronation
jiāqiáng	加強	to strengthen, to intensify [VO]
jiārù	加入	to join, to enter [VC]
jiāsù	加速	to accelerate, to increase speed [VO]
jiātiān	加添	to augment, to increase [CC/V]
jiā yán jiā cù	加鹽加醋	to add salt and vinegar/to add freely to the original version in retelling
jiāyī	加一	to add 10%: *xiǎofèi jiāyī*, to add 10% for tips [VO]
jiāyì	加意	to give special attention to: *jiāyì zhāohu*, to give special care [VO]
jiāyìn	加印	to apply the name chop or seal (on document) [V-O]; to make more printed copies [SC/V]
jiā yóu	加油	to add oil, to fill gasoline [V O]
jiā yóu(r)	加油兒	to encourage, to root (football team) [V-O]
jiāzhòng	加重	to add weight, to increase (penalty) [VO]
biàn běn jiā lì	變本加厲	to be more severe, cruel, violent

jiā
to add (to), to increase

加

gèngjiā 更加   all the more [Adv]

yì jiā yī shì èr 一加一是二   One plus one is two.

見
to see, to call on, to receive, to appear

jiàn bude rén 見不得人   to be unpresentable

jiàndì 見地   perception, viewpoint: *Zhèige rén hěn yǒu jiàndì.* This person is very clear-sighted.

jiàn fēng zhuǎn duò 見風轉舵 to turn the rudder with the wind/to be an opportunist

jiàn fèngr jiù zuān 見縫就鑽 to see a crack, enters/to behave like a social climber (a go-getter, a self-seeking person)

jiàngāodì 見高低 to see who beats whom, to see who is better

jiànguài 見怪 to take offense: *Qǐng bié jiànguài.* Please don't blame me. [VO]

jiàn guài bú guài 見怪不怪 to become inured to the unusual, weird, or uncanny

jiànguǐ 見鬼 to see the ghost/nonsense [VO]; also, *huó jiànguǐ*

jiànjiě 見解 *jiànshi*, viewpoint, and *liǎojiě*, understanding, judgment [CC/N]

jiàn jǐng shēng qíng 見景生情 to recall old memories at familiar sights

jiàn qián yǎn kāi 見錢眼開 (of blind person) to open his eyes to money if offered/to be influenced by money

jiànqīng 見輕 (illness) to get better: *Tāde bìng jiànqīng le.* He is getting better.

jiàn rén jiàn zhì 見仁見智 each according to his lights

jiàn rén jiù shuō 見人就說 to talk about it to whoever he sees

jiànshi 見識 insight, judgement [CC/N]

jiàn shìmian 見世面 to get to know the world

jiàn tiānrì 見天日 to see the sky and sun/injustice redressed

jiànwài 見外 to be considered as an outsider: *Qǐng nǐ búyào jiànwài.* Please don't treat me as an outsider.(used to urge one to accept gift or invitation)

jiànwén 見聞 what one sees and hears, general knowledge: *Tā jiànwén hěn guǎng.* His knowledge is very broad.[CC/N]

67

jiànxí	見習	to get practical experience by actual work [CC/V]
kànjiàn	看見	to see [VC]
mèngjiàn	夢見	to see in dream [VC]
pèngjiàn	碰見	to run into (somebody, something) [VC]
tīngjiàn	聽見	to hear [VC]
wénjiàn	聞見	to smell [VC]
yùjiàn	遇見	=pèngjiàn
zàijiàn	再見	Goodby [SC/V,N]

jiǎngdào 講道 to preach, to moralize [V-O]

jiǎnghé 講和 to hold peace talks, to negotiate peace, to settle differences amicably [V-O]

jiǎnghuà 講話 to talk informally [V-O]

jiǎngjià(r) 講價兒 to bargain over prices [V-O]

jiǎng jiāoqing 講交情 to care about friendship, to gain special favor through friendship: *Nǐ jiǎng jiāoqing bùjiǎng?* Do you care about our friendship?

jiǎngjiě 講解 to explain (as teacher to student) [CC/V]

jiǎngjiu 講究 to be particular about (clothing): *jiǎngjiu chuān*; matter to be taken into account [CC/SV]: *Tā zhèiyang zuò, yídìng yǒu shénmo jiǎngjiu.* There must be something in his doing so.

jiǎnglǐ 講理 to be reasonable; to settle disputes by appealing to reason [V-O]

jiǎng miànzi 講面子 to be particular about appearances, to save someone's face [V O]

jiǎngmíng 講明 to explain clearly [VC]

jiǎngqiú 講求 to study carefully, to delve into, to be fond of: *jiǎngqiú wàibiǎo*, to pay special attention to appearances [CC/V]

jiǎng (rén) qíng 講人情 to ask for special favor, to intercede for another [V-O]

jiǎngshòu 講授 to teach, to lecture, to offer (academic courses) [CC/V]

jiǎngtái 講台 a lecture platform, a lecturn [SC/N]

jiǎngtáng 講堂 a lecture hall, a classroom [SC/N]

jiǎngxí 講習 to hold discussion meetings, to conduct training classes [CC/V]

jiǎngxué 講學 to lecture on academic subjects [V-O]

jiǎngyǎn 講演 to lecture (to students), to give a public lecture [V-O]; a lecture

jiǎngyì 講義 lecture notes, usually given to students [VO/N]

69

jiāo baijuanr 交白卷兒 to hand in examination paper without answers

jiāochāi 交差 to render a report upon completion of an assignment [V-O]

jiāodài 交代 to transfer duties: *jiāodài chāishì*; to bid, to order: *Jiāodài ta búyào duōzuǐ*. Tell him not to talk too much. transfer: *bàn jiāodài*, to work on the transfer

jiāodao 交道 personal relations: *Hěn nán gēn tā dǎ jiāodao*. It's very hard to get along with him.

jiāohé 交合 to have sexual intercourse [CC/V]; sexual intercourse

jiāohuàn 交換 to change, to interchange, to exchange: *jiāohuàn jiàoshòu*, exchange professor [CC/V]

jiāojì 交際 social intercourse: *jiāojìhuār*, a social butterfly

jiāoliú 交流 to flow in opposite directions [SC/V]; alternating current; interchange: *wénhuà jiāoliú*, cultural interchange

jiāo (péng) yǒu 交朋友   to make friends [V-O]

jiāoqing 交情 *jiāowǎng*, social dealings, and *qíngyì*, friendship/friend-ship [CC/N]

jiāoshe 交涉 to negotiate, to discuss [CC/V]; negotiation, discussion

jiāotán 交談 to talk with

jiāotì 交替 to come one after another: *xīn jiù jiāotì*, the new come after the old have gone (in personnel shake-up)

jiāo tóu jiē ěr 交頭接耳   to whisper into each other's ears, to talk confidentially

jiāowǎng 交往 to associate with [CC/V]; social or business dealings

jiāo xuéfèi 交學費 to pay tuition

jiāoyì 交易 to do business, to engage in trade: *zhèngjuàn jiāoyìsuǒ*, stock market

jiāoyóu 交遊 to make friends [CC/V]; circle of friends

jiāoyùn 交運 to have a spell of good fortune [V-O]

jiāozhàn 交戰 to go to war: *jiāozhànguó*, belligerent [V-O]

chéngjiāo 成交 to close a business transaction [V-O]

jiào cài 叫菜   to call for takeout orders from restaurant [V-O]

jiàochī 叫吃   to call to indicate a checkmate (chess) [V-O]

jiào dàohǎor 叫倒好兒   to cry down a speaker or an actor [V-O]

jiàogēge 叫哥哥   a singing grasshopper [N]; to call one's older brother [V-O]

jiàohǎor 叫好兒   to shout "bravo" [V-O]

jiàohào 叫號   to yell out, to shout out [CC/V]

jiàohuan 叫喚   to shout [CC/V]

jiàohuàzi 叫化子   a beggar

jiàojiēde 叫街的   a beggar (roving the streets and crying for pity)

jiàojú 叫局   to send for a prostitute or singsong girl to wait on table (=*jiào tiáozi*) [V-O]

jiào kǔ lián tiān 叫苦連天   to constantly complain of hardship

jiàomài 叫賣   to cry goods for sale [CC/V]

jiàomén 叫門   to call for a door to be opened, to knock on the door [V-O]

jiàoqū 叫屈   to complain of unfair treatment [V-O]

jiào ta chūqu 叫他出去   to let him go out

jiào tiáozi 叫條子   to call a prostitute to entertain (=*jiàojú*)

jiàoxiāo 叫囂   to shout, to scream [CC/V]

jiào Zhāngsān 叫張三   to be called Chang San, to call Chang San

jiàozi 叫子   a whistle

jiàozìhao 叫字號   (of business firms) winning goodwill through superior quality of goods; (of person) earning popular respect for exemplary conduct

jiàozuo 叫做   to be called: *Zhèi jiu jiàozuo "zì tǎo kǔ chī."* This is called "self-inflicted hardship." *Wǒmen bǎ Kǒngzǐ jiàozuo zhì shèng xiān shī.* We call Confucius the greatest sage and teacher.

jiàozuòr 叫座兒   to be popular, to have good box office [VO/SV]

jié
to connect, to conclude, to bear fruit

結

jiébài	結拜	to become sworn brothers or sisters
jiébàn(r)	結伴	to form companionships [V-O]
jiéchóu	結仇	to become enemies: *gēn shéi jiéchóu?*
jiécún	結存	to leave a balance of: *jiécún yìqiān-kuài qián*, leaves a balance of 1,000 dollars; such balance
jié fǎ fū qī	結髮夫妻	partners by the first marriage
jiégòu	結構	construction, structure: *dòngbīn jiégòu*, verb-object construction (CC/N)
jiéguǒ	結果	to bear fruit [V-O]; to finish off, to kill (person) [VO] outcome, result [VO/N]; as a result [VO/Adv]
jiéhūn	結婚	to get married [V-O]
jiéjú	結局	the final outcome, the last act (of a play) [SC/N]
jiélùn	結論	summary, conclusion [SC/N]
jiéqīn	結親	to unite in marriage [V-O]
jiéshè	結社	to form a club [V-O]
jiéshéng	結繩	to tie knots on cords as means of reckoning or recordkeeping before the invention of writing [V-O]
jiéshì	結識	to make the acquaintance of, to become friends with [CC/V]
jiésù	結束	to wind up, to end (war, quarrel, etc.) [CC/V]
jiésuàn	結算	=*jiézhàng* [CC/V]
jiéyè	結業	to graduate [V-O]; graduation
jiéyuàn	結怨	to become deadly enemies [V-O]
jiéyuán	結緣	to lay the basis for future relationship or intimacy [V-O]
jiéyuē	結約	to sign a treaty or agreement [V-O]
jiézhàng	結賬	to clear or close account [V-O]
bājie	巴結	to fawn on, to toady
gōujie	勾結	to conspire, to work in collusion with

jiěcháo 解嘲	to justify one's action, to answer criticism [V-O]
jiěchú 解除	to relieve, to eliminate, to annul: *jiěchú hūnyuē*, to annul an engagement (to marry) [CC/V]
jiědá 解答	to answer (questions), to solve (problems) [CC/V]
jiěfàn 解犯	to deliver a prisoner under guard [V-O]
jiěfàng 解放	to liberate, to set free: *jiěfàng hēinú*, to set the Negro slaves free [CC/V]
jiěhèn 解恨	to quench hatred, to get even with the enemy [V-O]
jiějiù 解救	to save [CC/V]
jiějué 解決	to settle, to solve (problems), to put an end to the difficulties, to kill a person off: *xiān bǎ tā jiějué le.* Take care of him first. [CC/V]
jiěkāi 解開	to untie, to solve (a riddle) [VC]
jiěmènr 解悶兒	to dispel sadness, to kill time [V-O]
jiěnáng 解囊	to loosen the purse string/to donate money for worthy cause [V-O]
jiěquàn 解勸	to exhort, to calm down [CC/V]
jiěsàn 解散	to scatter, to breakup, to dissolve (Parliament): *jiěsàn yìhuì* [CC/V]
jiěshì 解釋	to explain, to clarify, to expound [CC/V]; an explanation
jiěshuō 解說	to explain [CC/V]; an explanation
jiěshǒur 解手兒	to relieve oneself, to urinate [V-O]
jiětǐ 解體	to disintegrate, to fall to pieces [V-O]
jiětuō 解脫	to set free, to liberate from worldly cares [CC/V]; such liberation, freedom [CC/V]
jiěwéi 解圍	to raise seige, to save someone from embarrassment [V-O]
jiěyōu 解憂	to allay grief or sorrow [V-O]
jiěyuē 解約	to annul a contract [V-O]

jìnbī	進逼	to press hard [CC/V]
jìnbīng	進兵	to dispatch troops, to order an attack on the enemy [V-O]
jìnbù	進步	to make progress, to be progressive, to improve [VO/SV]; an improvement
jìnchū	進出	entrance and exit, receipt and expenditure [CC/N]; to go in and out [V]
jìngōng	進攻	to mount an attack on (the enemy) [CC/V]
jìnhuà	進化	to evolve, to develop [CC/V]; evolution
jìnkǒu	進口	an entrance, imports: *jìnkǒuhuò*, imported goods [SC/N]
jìnkuǎn	進款	income, revenue, receipts [SC/N]
jìnqián	進錢	to receive money [V-O]; money received [SC/N]
jìnqǔ	進取	to make progress, to advance further and further, to be aggressive: *jìnqǔxīn*, enterprising mind [CC/V]
jìnqu	進去	to go in [VC], also used as complement to other verbs
jìnshēn	進身	to gain entrance or to be admitted to some exclusive circle [VO]
jìntuì	進退	to go forward or retreat/decision to do or not to do: *jìn tuì liǎng nán*, equally difficult to go on or retreat [CC/N]
jìnxiāng	進香	to offer incense [V-O]
jìnxiàng	進項	=*jìnkuǎn* [SC/N]
jìnxíng	進行	to proceed, to advance, to make moves for an office: *jìnxíng gōngzuò* [CC/V]
jìnxiū	進修	to pursue further studies, to take an advanced course [CC/V]
jìnxué	進學	to go to school [V-O]
jìnyán	進言	to offer suggestions, to make recommendations [V-O]
jìnyè	進謁	to see (superior) [CC/V]
jìnyì	進益	progress, improvement [SC/N]
jìnzhǎn	進展	to advance, to make progress [CC/V]; advance, progress

進

to advance, to enter, to present

---

jìnzhàng 進賬   to enter into account [V-O]; money income, receipts [SC/N]

tīngbujìnqu 聽不進去   can't stand listening to (something boring) [VC]

jǔ
to raise, to start   舉

jǔbàn	舉辦	to initiate, to undertake, to sponsor [CC/V]
jǔbīng	舉兵	to take up arms [V-O]
jǔchū	舉出	to enumerate, to itemize, to elect [VC]
jǔcuò	舉措	an act, action, any measure taken [CC/N]
jǔdòng	舉動	an act, a move, activity: *yì jǔ yí dòng*, every move [CC/N]
jǔfā	舉發	to expose (the wrongdoing of someone), to accuse publicly [CC/V]
jǔlì	舉例	to give examples [V-O]; an example, illustration
jǔ mù wú qīn	舉目無親	to be stranded in a foreign land, far away from one's kin
jǔ qí bú dìng	舉棋不定	to hesitate about a chess move/shilly-shally
jǔqǐlai	舉起來	to raise up (hands, flags, etc.) [VC]
jǔshì	舉世	all the world: *jǔshì wén míng*, known all over the world, internationally famous [SC/N]
jǔshì	舉事	to raise the standard of revolt (=*jǔyì*) [V-O]
jǔshǒu	舉手	to raise hands: *jǔshǒu zànchéng*, to show approval by raising hands (for voting) [V-O]
jǔxíng	舉行	to put into operation, to hold (meeting, ceremony) [CC/V]
jǔ yì fǎn sān	舉一反三	to learn by analogy
jǔzhǐ	舉止	behavior, conduct: *jǔzhǐ dàfāng*, to carry oneself in a graceful manner [CC/N]
jǔzhòng	舉重	to lift weight [V-O]; weightlifting
jǔzǐ	舉子	to give birth to a son: *yì jǔ dé zǐ* [VO]; a successful candidate of old provincial examinations (=*jǔrén*)
jǔ zú qīng zhòng	舉足輕重	to play decisive role
duō cǐ yì jǔ	多此一舉	action unnecessarily taken
gāo jǔ hóng qí	高舉紅旗	to raise the red flag high (PRC)
xuǎnjǔ	選舉	to elect, an election [CC]
yì jǔ liǎng dé	舉兩得	one action two gains/to kill two birds with one stone

76

---

kāibukāi 開不開   can't open [VC]

kāicǎi 開彩   to draw the lottery [V-O]

kāi chéng bù gōng 開誠布公 to act with honesty and justice

kāichú 開除   to expel (a student from school, a person from party member-ship) [CC/V]

kāi dānzi 開單子   to make out a list [V O]

kāidāo 開刀   to operate (surgical); to be operated on; to punish [V O]

kāi fángjiān 開房間   to rent a hotel room (often for illicit love)

kāiguān 開關   open-close/a switch [CC/N]

kāihuà 開化   to be civilized: *wèikāihuà guójiā*, uncivilized country[CC/V]

kāi huǒ 開火   to start a boarding arrangement [V-O]

kāi huǒr 開火兒   to open fire (in a battle) [V-O]

kāi kǒu 開口   to open mouth/to speak up: *kāikǒu dà xiào*, to laugh broadly; to break (dam) or (dam) breaks [V-O]

kāikǒuxiào 開口笑 open-mouth-smile/a kind of pastry

kāiluó 開鑼   to begin beating the gong/to begin an opera [V-O]

kāi mén jiàn shān 開門見山 to open the door to see the mountain/to speak without beating around the bush

kāimíng 開明   liberal, enlightened, progressive [CC/SV]

kāishǐ 開始   to begin, a beginning [CC]

kāi shuǐ 開水   boiled water [SC/N]; to turn on the water [V O]

kāitōng 開通   to break through obstructions [VC]; liberal, modern-minded: *Tā fùmǔ hěn kāitōng*. His parents are modern-minded. [CC/SV]

kāitōur 開頭兒 to begin [VO]; the beginning

kāi wánxiào 開玩笑   to poke fun at

kāi wèi 開胃	to be appetizing [VO/SV]; to tease: *Bié ná wǒ kāiwèi.* Don't tease me. [V-O]	
kāixiāo 開消	expenses: *Kāixiāo hěn dà.* The operating expenses are heavy. [CC/N]	
kāixīn 開心	to make fun of somebody: *Bié ná wǒ kāixīn.* Don't make fun of me. [V-O]; to be happy [SV]	
dǎkāi 打開	to open [VC]	
nákāi 拿開	to take something away [VC]	

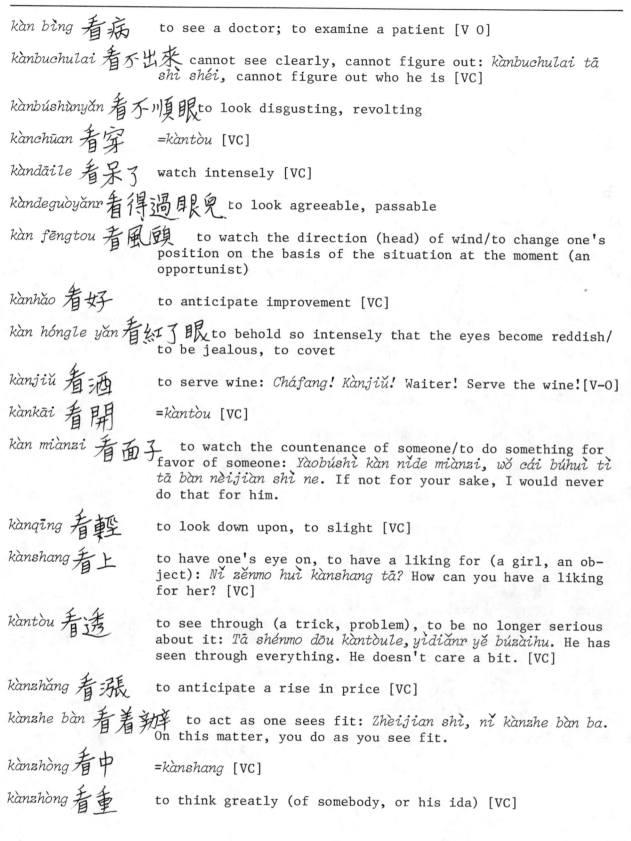

kàn bìng 看病   to see a doctor; to examine a patient [V O]

kànbuchulai 看不出來 cannot see clearly, cannot figure out: *kànbuchulai tā shì shéi*, cannot figure out who he is [VC]

kànbúshùnyǎn 看不順眼 to look disgusting, revolting

kànchūan 看穿   =*kàntòu* [VC]

kàndāile 看呆了   watch intensely [VC]

kàndeguòyǎnr 看得過眼兒 to look agreeable, passable

kàn fēngtou 看風頭   to watch the direction (head) of wind/to change one's position on the basis of the situation at the moment (an opportunist)

kànhǎo 看好   to anticipate improvement [VC]

kàn hóngle yǎn 看紅了眼 to behold so intensely that the eyes become reddish/ to be jealous, to covet

kànjiǔ 看酒   to serve wine: *Cháfang! Kànjiǔ!* Waiter! Serve the wine![V-O]

kànkāi 看開   =*kàntòu* [VC]

kàn miànzi 看面子   to watch the countenance of someone/to do something for favor of someone: *Yàobúshì kàn nǐde miànzi, wǒ cái búhuì tì tā bàn nèijiàn shì ne.* If not for your sake, I would never do that for him.

kànqīng 看輕   to look down upon, to slight [VC]

kànshang 看上   to have one's eye on, to have a liking for (a girl, an object): *Nǐ zěnmo huì kànshang tā?* How can you have a liking for her? [VC]

kàntòu 看透   to see through (a trick, problem), to be no longer serious about it: *Tā shénme dōu kàntòule, yìdiǎnr yě búzàihu.* He has seen through everything. He doesn't care a bit. [VC]

kànzhǎng 看漲   to anticipate a rise in price [VC]

kànzhe bàn 看着辦   to act as one sees fit: *Zhèijian shì, nǐ kànzhe bàn ba.* On this matter, you do as you see fit.

kànzhòng 看中   =*kànshang* [VC]

kànzhòng 看重   to think greatly (of somebody, or his ida) [VC]

79

kàngdí	抗敵	to resist the enemy [VO]
kànggào	抗告	to sue somebody at court [CC/V]
kàng jié bú fù	抗節不附	to maintain moral integrity and not to depend on others
kàngjù	抗拒	to resist: *Wǒmen děi kàngjù dírénde qīnlüè.* We must resist the enemy's aggression. [CC/V]
kànglùn	抗諭	to make brave defense against opposite views [SC/V]
kàng mǐ	抗米	to carry rice on shoulders [V O]
kàngmìng	抗命	to defy order: *Sīlìng yào nǐ qù, nǐ kě bùnéng kàngmìng búqù.* The commander wants you to go. You shouldn't defy his order. [V-O]
kàng mìng jù dí	抗命拒敵	to defy the order and to oppose the enemy
kàngqilai	抗起來	to hide away: *Bǎ zhèbāo dōngxi kàngqilai ba.* You'd better hide this package away.[VC]
kàngshēngsù	抗生素	anti-biotics
kàngshīzhǐ	抗濕紙	water-proof paper
kàngshuì	抗稅	to refuse to pay tax [V-O]
kàngwèi	抗衛	to fight to defend [CC/V]
kàngyì	抗議	to protest [V-O]; a protest; *Nǐ yīngdāng tíchū kàngyì cái duì.* It won't be right if you don't lodge a formal protest.
kàngyù	抗禦	=*kàngwèi* [CC/V]
kàngzhàn	抗戰	war of resistance (from *kàng rì zhànzhēng*, war of resisting Japan) [SC/N]; *Wǒmen kàngle bānián de zhàn cái bǎ Rìběn dǎbài le.* Not until we fought eight years of war did we defeat Japan [V-O]
kàng zhì bù qū	抗志不屈	to maintain moral integrity and never submit to the crooked/to be a man of lofty ambition and high virtue
fēn tíng kàng lǐ	分庭抗禮	to meet as equals: *Nǐ shì shéi? Zěnmo gǎn gēn tā fēn tíng kàng lǐ ne?* Who are you? How dare you meet with him as equals?

kǎochá	考察	to inspect [CC/V]; an inspection
kǎodìng	考訂	to study and settle problems of age, authoriship, edition, and textual differences [CC/V]
kǎogǔ	考古	to work as an archaeologist: *Wǒ míngnian yào dào Zhōngguo qù kǎogǔ.* I am going to China to do some archaeological work next year. [VO]; archaeology (also *kǎogǔxué*)
kǎojiù	考究	to be exquisite: *Tāde yīshang zhēn kǎojiù.* Her dresses are really exquisite; to be fastidious about: *Tā zhēn kǎojiù chuān.* She is really fastidious about clothing. [CC/SV]; to examine carefully: *Bǎ yuányīn kǎojiùchūlai jiù zhīdao shì zěnmo huí shì le.* When we find out the reasons (we) will know what it is all about. [CC/V]
kǎojù	考據	to do research (particularly on textual criticism), to seek proofs for data [CC/V]
kǎojuàn(r)	考卷兒	examination paper [SC/N]
kǎolǜ	考慮	to consider, to think over: *Zhèjian shì, nǐ děi hǎohāorde kǎolǜkaolü.* Regarding this matter, you must think it over carefully. [CC/V]
kǎoqiú	考求	to examine and search for (conditions, origin, relations, etc.): *kǎoqiú bìngyuán*, to search for the cause of disease [CC/V]
kǎoqǔ	考取	to pass an examination (=*kǎoshàng*) [VC]
kǎoshàng	考上	to pass an examination: *Táidàde rùxué kǎoshì nǐ kǎoshàngle méiyou?* Did you pass the entrance examination for Taiwan University? [VC]
kǎoshì	考試	to examine, to take an examination [VO]; examination
kǎo shū	考書	to examine on books studied [V O]
kǎowèn	考問	to interrogate [CC/V]
kǎo xuéxiào	考學校	to take a school entrance examination
kǎoyàn	考驗	to test: *Shídài kǎoyàn qīngnian.* This age is putting (our) youth to the test. [CC/V]; a test: *Tā quēdiǎn tài duō, shì jīngbùqǐ kǎoyàn de.* He has too many shortcomings. He just cannot stand the test.
kǎoyǔ	考語	remark giving opinion on test paper, written comments [SC/N]

kǎo
to examine, to take a test

考

kǎozhèng	考證	=*kǎojù* [CC/V]
kǎozhòng	考中	to pass an examination (=*kǎoshàng*) [VC]
dàkǎo	大考	big examination/final examination
yuèkǎo	月考	monthly examination

---

kèdāng 克當   to be worthy of: *kèdāng zhòngrèn*, to be worthy of an important appointment

kè dāng yí miàn 克當一面   to have the qualifications to head up an office

kèfú 克服   to overcome: *kèfú kùnnán*, to overcome difficulties [VC]

kèfù 克復   to recover: *kèfù shīdì*, to recover the lost terribory [VC]

kèjǐ 克已   to overcome selfishness, to be unselfish [VO/SV]

kè jiā lìng zǐ 克家令子   a son who is efficient to take charge of the family affairs

kè jìn jué zhí 克盡厥職 to perform fully the functions of an office

kè jìn xiào yǎng 克盡孝養   to discharge all the filial duties to one's parents

kènàn 克難   to overcome difficulties: *kènàn yùndòng*, movement to overcome difficulties (during time of war, etc.); *kènàn chéngguǒ*, accomplishments as a result of work done to overcome difficulties; *kènàn fángwū*, shed used as living quarters during time of difficulty or a crisis [VO]

kè qín kè jiǎn 克勤克儉 to have capacity for industry and thrift: *Lǎo Wáng kè qín kè jiǎn, rìzi guòde yìtiān bǐ yìtiān hǎo.* Old Wang is both industrious and thrifty. His life is better everyday.

kèsī 克私   to overcome selfishness: *kèsī wèi gōng*, to repress the private for the public [VO]

kèxiǎng 克享   can enjoy: *kèxiǎng tiānnián*, can enjoy long life

kèyù 克慾   to overcome desires [VO]

kè yù xiū xíng 克慾修行 to subdue the passions and cultivate moral conduct

kèzhì 克制   to control: *kèzhì qínggǎn*, to control one's emotions; to rule over (territory) [CC/V]

róu néng kè gāng 柔能克剛 softness can overcome strength: *Nǐ róu néng kè gāng shuō jǐjù hǎohuà bú jiù wánle ma?* Since softness can overcome strength, you say a few nice words (to apologize) and the matter will end there.

kuān
to be lenient, to extend deadlines   寬

kuān dà bāo róng 寬大包容 to be broadminded and tolerant

kuān dà fàng zòng 寬大放縱 to be permissive

kuān dà rén ài 寬大仁愛 to be generous and merciful

kuān dà shū chàng 寬大舒暢 with broad and enlightened mind/to be cheerful
and liberal

kuān dà yǒu yú 寬大有餘 abundance and wealth/well-to-do

kuān guǎng bó dà 寬廣博大 vast and extensive in scope and field of
knowledge, etc.

kuān hǎi dà liàng 寬海大量 to be broadminded and magnanimous (as open as
the sea)

kuān hóng dà liàng 寬洪大量 to be liberal minded, tolerant, magnanimous:
*Tā yíxiàng kuān hóng dà liàng cái búhuì gēn nèixie xiǎorén
yì bān jiàn shì ne.* As a magnanimous person, he will never
behave like those hypocrites.

kuānmiǎn 寬免 to forgive (fines, taxes, etc.), to pardon (offense)[SC/V]

kuānróng 寬容 to pardon (offenses, person), to tolerate: *kuānróng zhèngcè*,
tolerant policy [SC/V]

kuānshù 寬恕 to pardon (person, wrongdoing): *Kàn zai tā fùqinde
miànshang, bǎ tā kuānshùle ba.* For his father's sake, let's
forgive him.[SC/V]

kuānwèi 寬慰 to comfort (person): *Yào kuānwèi fùmǔ, jiù děi hǎohāor
niànshū.* In order to comfort one's parents, one has to
study hard. [CC/V]; to be happy: *Nǐ hǎohāorde niànshū cái
néng ràng fùmǔ gǎndào kuānwèi.* Only by studying hard can
you make your parents feel happy. [SV]

kuānxiàn 寬限 to extend date (of delivery, etc.): *kuānxiàn yíge yuè*, to
extend the time-limit with a month's grace [VO]

kuānxīn 寬心 to.relax [V-O]; not worried: *Tā zǒngshi hěn kuānxīn.* He is
always very relaxed. [SV]

kuān yī jiě dài 寬衣解帶 to remove the upper clothing and loosen the belt

kuān yǐ dài rén, yán yǐ zé jǐ 寬以待人嚴以責己 to be lenient in treating
others, to be strict in treating oneself.

kuānzhǎi 寬窄 broad and narrow/width [CC/N]

lā cháng liǎn 拉長臉 to pull a long face

lā cháng xiàn(r) 拉長線兒 to draw a long line/to leave something for future decision

lāche 拉扯 to involve others by loose talk: *Qǐng bié bǎ wǒ lāche jìnqu.* Please don't involve me. [CC/V]

lādǎo 拉倒 to pull down: *Tā bǎ shù lādǎole.* He pulled down the tree. to forget it: *Zhèjian shì wǒ kàn háishi lādǎo ba.* I think we should forget about this matter. [RC/V]

lā dùzi 拉肚子 to have loose bowels [V O]

lā guānxi 拉關係 to draw relations with someone/to try to draw close to influential people: *Gēn tā lābushang guānxi.* Can't draw close to him.

lā húqinr 拉胡琴兒 to play a Chinese fiddle

lājià 拉架 to mediate between two parties quarreling or fighting [V-O]

lā jiāoqing 拉交情 =*la guanxi*

lā kè 拉客 to solicit customers (esp. streetwalkers) [V O]

lālong 拉攏 to draw to one's side: *Nǐ lālong tā zuò shénmo?* Why do you draw him to your side? to draw people with different views together: *Nǐ tì tāmen liǎngge lālonglalong.* You do something to get those two together. [CC/V]

lā mǎimai 拉買賣 =*lā shēngyi*

lā pítiaor 拉皮條 =*lā mǎ*, to act as a pimp

lā shēngyi 拉生意 to solicit business

lā shétou 拉舌頭 to draw the tongue/to gossip [V O]

lā shǐ 拉屎 to move bowels [V O]

lāta 拉遢 to be untidy, dirty [SV]

lā yìnggōng 拉硬弓 to draw a stiff bow/to force someone to do something against his will

lā yìpigu zhài 拉一屁股債 to owe a mountain of debts

lāza 拉雜 to be untidy, disorganized: *lālazazade shuōle bàntiān,* talked in a confused way for a long time

lái
to come, to do, to bring 來

láibīn 來賓	guest [SC/N]
láide 來得	the manner in which one does something: *Nǐ zhèju huà láide lìhai.* Your words are most telling.
láidejí 來得及	(There is) enough time to do something [VC]
láihuí(r) 來回	a round trip: *láihuí piào,* a roundtrip ticket [CC/N]
láilì 來歷	origin, background, source: *Láilì bùmíng.* The origin is not known. [SC/N]
lái lóng qù mò 來龍去脈	a sequence of events, cause and effect
láilù huò 來路貨	imported goods
láinián 來年	next year [SC/TW]
láirén 來人	a messenger; a call for someone to come (usually servants): *lái rén a*; a call to get attention to someone coming: *Lái rén la!* Someone is coming! [SC/N]
láishēng 來生	next life [SC/TW]
lái shì xiōngxiōng 來勢洶洶	to break in in full fury, to come to look for trouble
láitou(r) 來頭	position or social status: *Tāde láitou bùxiǎo.* He is very influential socially, something worth doing: *Zhèzhong yóuxì hái yǒu shénmo láitou ne.* This kind of game is not worth playing.
láiwǎng 來往	to come and go/to exchange visits: *Wǒmen zǎo jiu bùláiwǎng le.* We don't see each other anymore. [CC/V]; friendly intercourse: *Nǐ gēn tā yǒu láiwǎng ma?* Do you have any dealings with him? [CC/V]
láixìn 來信	your letter: *Láixìn shōudàole.* Your letter has been received. [SC/N]; to write a letter (to someone): *Nǐ hěn jiǔ méi gěi wǒ lái xìn le.* You haven't written me a letter for a very long time. [V-O]
láiyì 來意	Intention of one's coming: *Tāde láiyì búshàn.* His intention is not good. [SC/N]
láizhe 來着	marker to indicate action that occurred a short while ago: *Tā shuō tā xìng shénmo láizhe?* What did he say his surname was?
méi lái yǎn qù 眉來眼去	to exchange glances, to communicate with eyes

離

líbié 離別 to take leave of: *Wǒmen líbié yǐhòu méi tōngguo xìn.* We have not written to each other since we said goodbye. [CC/V]

líbùliǎo 離不了 cannot be separated from: *Tā nèizhong rén líbùliǎo nǚrén.* His kind of people can't live without women. [VC]

lí chóu bié hèn 離愁別恨 grief of parting

lígér 離格兒 to deviate from standard: *Shuōhuà bié lígér.* Talk must be within limit. [V-O]

lígǔr 離股兒 (of the joints of furniture, etc.) to become loose [V-O]

líhūn 離婚 to divorce: *Tāmen lǎo zǎo líhūnle.* Those two were divorced a long time ago. [V-O]

líjiàn 離間 to sow dissention between or among: *Nǐ děi xiǎoxin xiǎorén líjiàn wǒmen.* You must watch the wicked person's sowing dissention between us. [CC/V]

líkāi 離開 to depart from (place, person): *Xiǎoháir líbùkāi fùmǔ.* Children can't leave their parents. [VC]

lípǔ(r) 離譜兒 to be off or below standard, to be irregular: *Zhèjian shì zuòde yǒu diǎnr lípǔ le.* This matter was handled a little irregularly. [V-O]

líqí 離奇 to be unbelievably strange, to be mysterious [CC/SV]

lí qún suò jū 離群索居 to live the life of a recluse

lísàn 離散 to be scattered about, to be separated from one another: *Yìjiā rén yīnwei zhànzhēng dōu lísànle.* The whole family was separated from one another because of the war. [CC/V]

lí xiāng bèi jǐng 離鄉背井 to be away from one's native place

líxīnlì 離心力 centrifugal force

lí zhèr hěn jìn 離這兒很近 very close to here

bēi huān lí hé 悲歡離合 sorrows and joys, separations and reunions/facts of life

fēnlí 分離 to be separated: *Tāmen búyuànyi fēnlí.* They don't want to be separated. [CC/V]

pànlí 叛離 to rebel [CC/V]

lǐ
to take notice of, to manage, to realize

理

lǐcái 理財	to administer financial affairs [VO]
lǐcǎi 理睬	to heed the presence of (someone), to take notice of: *Tā bùlǐcǎi wǒ*. He doesn't take notice of me. [CC/V]
lǐfǎ 理髮	to cut hair, to have a haircut [V-O]
lǐ fán zhì jù 理繁治劇	to manage difficulties and regulate the trouble
lǐhuì 理會	to realize, understand (a situation, an explanation), to pay attention to: *Tā chángchang bùlǐhuì rén*. He doesn't often pay attention to people. [CC/V]
lǐjiā 理家	to manage domestic affairs: *Zhāng Tàitai zhēn huì lǐjiā*. Mrs. Chang is really a good housekeeper. [V-O]
lǐjiě 理解	to comprehend [CC/V]; comprehension
lǐjiělì 理解力	ability to comprehend: *Tāde lǐjiě lì hěn gāo*. His ability to comprehend is very high.
lǐ luàn jiě fēn 理亂解紛	to control the chaos and mediate disputes
lǐlùn 理論	theory [SC/N]; to discuss, to argue [V]
lǐsāng 理喪	to manage the funeral ceremony [V-O]
lǐshì 理事	to attend to a matter [VO]; director (of a firm, organization, etc.)
lǐshū 理書	to revise a book [V-O]
lǐxiǎng 理想	to be ideal [SC/SV]; an idea
dàilǐ 代理	to act in place of [CC/V]: *Zhǔrèn bìng le. Shéi dàilǐ tāde zhíwù?* The chairman is sick. Who acts in his place?
xiūlǐ 修理	to repair; to punish (Taiwan slang): *Nèige bùliáng shàonian zuótian bèi jǐngchá hǎohāor xiūlǐ le yícì*. That juvenile dilenquent was punished well by the police yesterday. [CC/V]

連 *lián běn dài lì* 連本帶利 both principal and interest

liánbì 連璧 to join the jade/to combine two good things [V-O]

liánchuànr 連串兒 a series of (disasters, mishaps, etc.): *yì liánchuànrde bùxìng shìjian*, a series of unfortunate incidents [VO/N]

lián dǎ dài mà 連打帶罵 with both beating and cursing

liándàiguānxi 連帶關係 the relationship or connection (between two things)

liánhào 連號 consecutive numbers, firms of the same owner, the hyphen [SC/N]

liánhé 連合 to join (efforts, pieces together) [CC/V]

liánhuán 連環 a chain of rings linked together: *liánhuántú*, comic strips [SC/N]

liánjiē 連接 continuously: *Wǒ liánjiē kànle sānge bìngren.* I saw three patients in succession. [CC/Adv]

liánlèi 連累 to cause or bring trouble to another: *Wǒ liánlèi nǐ le.* I have caused you trouble. [CC/V]

liánlián 連連 continuously: *liánlián diǎntóu*, to nod repeatedly [Adv]

liánluò 連絡 to get in touch with: *Nǐ gēn tā liánluò-yixia.* You get in touch with him. [CC/V]; *Liánluò chù*, Liaison office.

liánmáng 連忙 quickly, without hesitation: *Tā kànjian shàngsi láile, jiù liánmáng guòqu dǎ zhāohu.* As soon as he saw his boss coming, he quickly went over to greet him. [Adv]

liánnián 連年 year after year: *liánnián hànzāi*, famine year after year [VO/TW]

liánpiān 連篇 page after page: *liánpiān cuò zì*, wrong characters all over the essay [VO/Adv]

liánqìr 連氣兒 in a fit of determination: *Yì liánqìr pǎole sānlǐ lù.* Ran for a mile (three li) at one stretch [VO/Adv]

liánrèn 連任 to serve another term of office [V-O]

liánshū 連書 to write syllables together to form words [SC/V]

liánxù 連續 continuously: *liánxù xiàle sāntiān yǔ*, rained continuously for three days [CC/Adv]

聯

liánbāng 聯邦 federation, confederate [VO/N]

liánbāng zhèngfǔ 聯邦政府 federal government

liánbǎo 聯保 to serve as a guarantor for one another [SC/V]

liándà 聯大 abbreviation for *Liánhéguó Dàhuì*, United Nations General Assembly

liándān 聯單 duplicate or joint forms for receipt, etc. [SC/N]

liánhé 聯合 to unite: *Wǒmen liánhéqilai shéi yě búpà.* When we unite, we will not be afraid of anyone. [CC/V]

liánhéguó 聯合國 United Nations

liánhé zhèngfǔ 聯合政府 coalition government

liánhuānhuì 聯歡會 a get together party

liánjūn 聯軍 allied troops [SC/N]

liánluò 聯絡 =*liánluò* (p. 81) [CC/V]

lián mèi ér lái 聯袂而來 to come together

liánmíng 聯名 to sign together: *Wǒmen liánmíng shēnqǐng.* We apply with joint signatures. [VO/Adv]

liánpiào 聯票 connection tickets for journey [SC/N]

liánqilai 聯起來 to unite, to connect [VC]

liánshū 聯書 to sign jointly [SC/V]

liánxi 聯系 to make connection (with someone): *Wèile zhèjian shì de chénggōng, nǐ yīngdāng gēn tā liánxilianxi.* You ought to contact him for the success of this venture. [CC/V]

liánxiǎng 聯想 to remind one of something or someone [SC/V]

liányìhuì 聯誼會 social, fellowship party

liányīn 聯姻 to be related by marriage [V-O]

liányíng 聯營 to manage jointly: *gōng sī liányíng*, to manage jointly between government and private citizens [SC/V] *liè biǎo* 列表   to prepare a chart, table, schedule, etc. [V O]

lièchē 列車   a train of wagons/railroad train [SC/N]

lièdān 列單   to draw up a list [V-O]

lièdǎo 列島   archipelago [SC/N]

lièguó 列國   the different countries: *chūnqiū lièguó*, the city-states at the time of Confucius [SC/N]

lièjǔ 列舉   to give list of (names, crimes): *lièjǔ rénmíng, zuìzhuàng* [CC/V]

lièmíng 列名   to enter or appear on a list of names of persons [V-O]

lièqiáng 列強   a group of strong nations/the Great Powers [SC/N]

lièrù 列入   to enter as an item (of agenda, list, etc.): *Qǐng bǎ zhèjian shì lièrù yìchéng.* Please include this matter in the agenda. [RC/V]

Lièwèi 列位   Gentlemen! or Ladies and Gentlemen! [SC/N]

lièxí 列席   to be present at meeting, to be observers at conference [V-O]

lièzhuàn 列傳   biographies, especially section on biographies in different dynastic histories [SC/N]

bìngliè 並列   to be listed side by side [SC/V]

bìnglièshì 並列式   parallel style

hángliè 行列   row or column [CC/N]

kāiliè 開列   to draw up a list: *Nǐ bǎ yào mǎi de dōngxi kāiliè yíge dānzi ba.* You ought to draw up a list of the things you want to buy. [CC/V]

xiàliè 下列   the following: *Qǐng jiěshì xiàliè gè míngcí.* Please explain the following terms. [SC/V]

91

lǐng
to lead, to receive, to understand   領

---

lǐngbān 領班   foreman [VO/N]

lǐng bīng 領兵   to command troops [V O]

lǐngdài 領帶   to lead troops [CC/V]; necktie [SC/N]

lǐngdān 領單   receipt on delivery [SC/N]

lǐngdì 領地   territory under jurisdiction [SC/N]

lǐngháng 領航   to pilot (navigation, aviation, etc.) [V-O]

lǐnghuí 領回   to get back [VC]

lǐnghuì 領會   to understand, to comprehend: *Zhège wèntí tài fùzá, xiǎoháizi kǒngpà bùnéng lǐnghuì.* This problem is too complicated, I'm afraid that children cannot understand. [CC/V]

lǐngjiào 領教   to receive instructions/to get someone's opinion, to pay a visit; *Míngtian wǒ zài lái lǐngjiào.* I will come to see you again tomorrow. [V-O]

lǐnglüè 領略   to grasp, to understand [CC/V]

lǐngqíng 領情   to accept with thanks, to accept the sentiment but not the gift: *Nǐde hǎoyì wǒ lǐngqíng jiùshi le.* I accept your thoughtfulness with thanks (but I can't accept the gift). [V-O]

lǐngqǔ 領取   to receive [CC/V]

lǐngshòu 領受   to receive formally (awards, baptism, etc.) [CC/V]

lǐngtóu(r) 領頭   to lead the way, to be first [V-O]

lǐngwù 領悟   to comprehend (truth, doctrine, significance) [CC/V]

lǐngxǐ 領洗   to receive baptism, to be baptized [V-O]

lǐngxiān 領先   to head the list (of sponsors, actors, etc.) [VO]

lǐngxiè 領謝   to show appreciation [V-O]

lǐngyǎng 領養   to adopt: *lǐngyǎng yíge xiǎoháir*, to adopt a child [CC/V]

lǐngzuì 領罪   to offer apology [V-O]

rènlǐng 認領   to claim (lost property, dog, etc.) [CC/V]

màolǐng 冒領   to make false claim on (lost property, etc.) [SC/V]

流

liúbì	流弊	defects that have been passed down/malpractice, shortcoming [SC/N]
liúbiàn	流變	flowing and change/the development [CC/N]
liúchǎn	流產	to have a miscarriage; to fail to materialize: *Tāde jìhuà búxìng liúchǎn le.* Unfortunately, his plan did not materialize. [V-O]
liúdòng	流動	to drift, to move about [CC/V]; mobile, liquid (assets): *liúdòng cáichǎn* [SV]
liúfāng	流芳	to leave a good name: *wànshì liúfāng*, to leave a good name to posterity [VO]
liúfàng	流放	to exile, to send to: *Tā bèi liúfàng dào xīnjiāng qù le.* He was exiled to Hsinchiang. [CC/V]
liú hàn	流汗	to perspire [V O]
liúhuá	流滑	to be slippery, to be cunning [CC/SV]
liúlǎn	流覽	to glance over (books) [SC/V]
liúlàng	流浪	to travel freely, to drift from one place to another [CC/V]
liú lèi	流淚	to shed tears [V O]
liúlì	流利	to be fluent: *Tāde Zhōngguohuà shuōde hěn liúlì.* His Chinese is really fluent·[CC/SV]
liúlí shī suǒ	流離失所	to wander about lost or homeless
liúlián	流連	to loiter, to linger; *liúlián wàng fǎn*, to indulge in pleasures and forget to return [CC/V]
liúluò tā xiāng	流落他鄉	to drift about in strange places (other than native place)
liúlù	流露	to reveal, to show unintentially: *zhēnqíng liúlù*, true sentiments were revealed [CC/V]
liú shuǐ	流水	flowing water [SC/N]; to flow [V O]
liútōng	流通	to circulate (air, currency, etc.) [CC/V]; to flow through [VC]
liúwáng	流亡	to live as a refugee (abroad): *liúwáng hǎiwài* [CC/V]

liú
to flow, to drift

流

liúxiànxíng 流線型 streamlined style: *liúxiànxíng huǒchē*, streamlined train

liúxíng 流行 to be fashionable, to be generally accepted [CC/SV]

liú xuě 流血 to shed blood

liúyán 流言 rumors, hearsay (especially malicious) [SC/N]

lùndiǎn 論點 point of discussion [SC/N]

lùndiào 論調 tone of discussion [SC/N]

lùnduàn 論斷 judgement, opinion [CC/N]

lùn gōng xíng shǎng 論功行賞 to reward on merit

lùnjià 論價 to discuss price [V-O]

lùn jiāoqing 論交情 to consider friendship: *Lùn jiāoqing, nǐ bùyīnggāi fǎndui ta.* Considering your friendship with him, you should not have opposed him.

lùnjù 論據 grounds for discussion [SC/N]

lùnlǐ 論理 according to reason [VO/Adv]; logic

lùnshuō 論說 a treatise, essay [SC/N]

lùnwén 論文 thesis, dissertation: *bóshì lùnwén*, doctoral dissertaion [SC/N]

lùnzhàn 論戰 war of discussion/controversy in journals, papers, etc.[SC/N]

lùnzhèng 論證 evidence, proof [SC/N]

lùnzhù 論著 published works [CC/N]

lùnzuì 論罪 to consider one's guilt, to sentence (according to offense) [V-O]

biànlùn 辯論 to debate [CC/V]; a debate

búlùn 不論 regardless of: *búlùn nǐ zěnmo yàng*, regardless of what you do [SC/Adv]

tǎolùn 討論 to discuss [VO]

wúlùn 無論 =*búlùn* [VO/Adv]

yánlùn 言論 published statements: *Zǒngtǒng yánlùn*, President's speeches [CC/N]

yǐ shì lùn shì 以事論事 to consider the matter itself (not to involve personalities)

yúlùn 輿論 public opinion [SC/N]

zuò wéi bàlùn 作為罷論 to consider (the matter) closed

luòbǎng	落榜	to fail to pass the examination (one's name not appearing on the roster) [V-O]
luòcǎo	落草	to join the bandits [V-O]
luòchéng	落成	to be completed (of buildings): *luòchéng diǎnlǐ*, dedication ceremony [VC]
luòdì	落地	to touch the ground: *luòdì chuāng*, French window; *luòdìshì diànshì*, console television set [VO]
luòfǎ	落髮	to cut off the hair/to become a Buddhist monk or nun [V-O]
luò huā liú shuǐ	落花流水	thoroughly, whole-heartedly: *Bǎ dírén dǎde luò huā liú shuǐ*. Route the enemy completely.
luòhòu	落後	to be backward: *luòhòu guójiā*, underdeveloped countries [VO/SV]
luòkōng	落空	to end up with nothing [V-O]
luòlèi	落淚	to shed tears, to weep [V-O]
luòluò dàfāng	落落大方	to be very poised and dignified
luòpò	落魄	to be down and out, to be a failure [V-O]
luòshí	落實	to realize, to put into effect: *Nèi shi luòshí Máo Zhǔxí zhǐshì de zhòngyào cuòshī*. That is an important measure to realize Chairman Mao's instructions.(PRC) [VC]
luòshuǐ	落水	to fall into the water, to become a prostitute [V-O]
luòshuǐgǒu	落水狗	a dog that falls into the water/a defeated person: *Dǎ luòshuǐgǒu*, to hit a person who has been defeated
luòtāngjī	落湯鷄	chicken drenched and about to be feathered/a person drenched through
luòwǔ	落伍	to drop behind others, to become outdated: *sīxiǎng luòwǔ*, thinking is backward [V-O]
luòxialai	落下來	to drop down, to fall (as leaves from the tree) [VC]
luòxuǎn	落選	to fail in election or competition [V-O]
luòyǔ	落雨	to rain [V-O]
línglíng luòluò	零零落落	in piecemeal fashion

mǎibàn 買辦 compradore [CC/N]

mǎibuqǐ 買不起 can afford to buy [VC]

mǎifāng 買方 the buying party in a contract [SC/N]

mǎiguān 買官 to buy official post/to pay bribe to obtain official post [V-O]

mǎihǎo 買好 to try to secure goodwill, friendship, etc. (of person), to try to please: *mǎi tāde hǎo*, to please him [V-O]; to be through buying: *Mǎihǎole jiu zǒu.* Will leave after buying is done. [VC]

mǎijìn 買進 to buy in (goods) [VC]

mǎikè 買客 customer at shops [SC/N]

mǎi kōng mài kōng 買空賣空 buy empty sell empty/to speculate on stocks, to cheat by empty talk

mǎiliǎn 買臉 to buy face/to show off [V-O]

mǎilín 買鄰 to buy neighbors/to choose neighbors in buying property [V-O]

mǎilùqián 買路錢 blackmail money paid for immunity for robbers, money demanded by robbers

mǎimài 買賣 to buy and sell, to trade [CC/V]; *mǎimai*, business: *Mǎimai hǎo ma?* Is business good? [CC/N]

mǎimíng 買名 to buy fame/to cater to publicity by sordid methods (V-O)

mǎi rénxīn 買人心 to buy people's hearts/to win people's hearts through favors [V O]

mǎitōng 買通 to pay bribe to: *Nǐ bǎ tā mǎitōngle jiù méi wèntí le.* There will be no problem if you have bribed him. [VC]

mǎixiào 買笑 to buy smiles/to visit prostitutes [V-O]

mǎizhǔ 買主 customer, buying party [SC/N]

mǎizuì 買醉 to buy drink/to have a drinking spree [V-O]

bùmǎizhàng 不買賬 won't do others a favor, won't yield to pressure *mài běnshi* 賣本事 to sell ability/to show off skill [V O]

màibǔ 賣卜 to be a fortune teller [V-O]

màichàng 賣唱 to sell singing/to be a professional singer [V-O]

màichū 賣出 to sell out [VC]

màidāi(r) 賣呆 to sell ignorance/to pretend not to understand [V-O]

màidǐ 賣底 to sell the bottom/to betray the secret [V-O]

màiguāi 賣乖 to sell good behavior/to show off cleverness, good behavior, etc. [V-O]

màiguó 賣國 to sell the country/to be a traitor: *màiguózéi*, a traitor [V-O]

màijì 賣技 to sell skill/to be a professional artist [V-O]

màijià 賣價 the selling price [SC/N]

màilì 賣力 to sell strength/to put in extra energy in work [V-O]; to be hard-working [SV]

màiliǎn 賣臉 to sell face/to disregard the loss of face, to sell looks: *Chànggērde mài liǎn búmài shēn.* The singsong girls sell their looks, but not their bodies. [V-O]

màilòng 賣弄 to show off: *màilòng wénmò*, to show off one's writings [CC/V]

màiqiào 賣俏 to sell cuteness/to flirt [V-O]

mài rénqing 賣人情 to sell fellowship/to do favor

mài wén wéi shēng 賣文為生 to sell writing for a living

màixiào 賣笑 to sell smiles/to be a prostitute [V-O]

mài yǎnréntóu 賣野人頭 to sell savage heads/to exaggerate for showing off

màiyì 賣藝 to sell art/to be an acrobat [V-O]

màiyín 賣淫 to sell lewdness/to be a prostitute [V-O]

mài yǒu qiú róng 賣友求榮 to betray friends to obtain promotion

màizuǐ 賣嘴 to sell mouth/to show off forensic skill, to indulge in clever talk [V-O] *mǎn buzàihu* 滿不在乎 to be totally unconcerned: *Tā duì nèijian shì mǎn buzàihu.* He is totally unconcerned with that matter.

mǎn chéng fēng yǔ 滿城風雨 the city is full of wind and rain/the city is full of rumors: *Tāmen liǎngge de shì nàode mǎn chéng fēng yǔ.* Rumors about the two of them have spread all over town.

mǎn fù láo sāo 滿腹牢騷 to have a grudge against everything

mǎn kǒu dāying 滿口答應 to make profuse promises

mǎn kǒu hú yán 滿口胡言 to be full of stupid talk

mǎn miàn chūn fēng 滿面春風 spring wind fills the face/to radiate happiness: *Tā jìnlai mǎn miàn chūn fēng déyìde hěn.* Recently he radiates happiness and is having a ball.

mǎnqī 滿期 to expire [V-O]

mǎnyì 滿意 to satisfy, to be satisfied [V-O/SV]

mǎn yǐwéi 滿以為 to be fully convinced (but...): *Wǒ mǎn yǐwéi tā huì dāngxuǎn, méixiǎngdào huì shūde zhème cǎn.* I was fully convinced that he would win the election. Unexpectedly, he suffered a big loss.

mǎnyuè 滿月 full moon [SC/N]; to be one month old [V-O]; celebration of baby's first full month.

mǎn zài ér guī 滿載而歸 to come back loaded (with honors, profit, etc.)

mǎnzú 滿足 to be satisfied [CC/SV]; to satisfy [V]

mǎn zuǐ rén yì dàodé, mǎn dùzi nán dào nǚ chāng 滿嘴仁義道德 滿肚子男盜女娼 mouth full of humanity, righteousness, and moral principles; stomach full of being thieves for a male and a prostitute for a female/to be a hypocrite

mǎn zuǐ yīngwén 滿嘴英文 mouth filled with English/to keep on speaking English

mǎnzuò 滿座 to have a full house: *Jīntian xìyuánzi yídìng mǎnzuò.* Today the theatre will certainly have a full house. [SC/V]

bǎomǎn 飽滿 to be vigorous: *Tāde jīngshen zǒng shì hěn bǎomǎn.* He is always full of vigor. [CC/SV]

yuánmǎn 圓滿 to be satisfactory: *Jiéguǒ yuánmǎn.* The result is satisfactory. [CC/SV]

mídèng 迷瞪	to become infatuated with something; *mímidèngdengde yàngzi*, to look infatuated [CC/V]	
míguǎi 迷拐	to drug and kidnap [CC/V]	
míhu 迷糊	to be unclear, blurred; *mímihuhu*, in a daze, difficult to make out [CC/SV]	
míhún 迷魂	to infatuate the soul/to be infatuated, to be bewildered: *míhúntāng*, soup of infatuation/enticing words [V-O]	
míhuò 迷惑	to tempt, to confuse, to mislead [CC/V]	
míle xīn 迷了心	to be thoroughly infatuated	
míliàn 迷戀	to love blindly: *Tā jìngran huì míliàn yíge jìnǚ*. He went so far as to blindly love a prostitute. [SC/V]	
mílù 迷路	to lose one's way: *Wǒ yīnwèi míle lù, zěnmo yě zhǎobuzháo tāde jiā.* Because I lost the way, I simply couldn't find his home. [V-O]	
míluàn 迷亂	to be bewildered [CC/SV]	
míméng yào 迷蒙藥	an aesthetics	
mínǐ 迷你	transliteration of mini-: *mínǐqún*, miniskirt [VO]	
mírén 迷人	to charm, to be charming: *mírénjīng*, charmer, enchanter [VO/SV]	
míshī fāngxiàng 迷失方向	to lose one's bearings	
míwǎng 迷罔	to be lost, confused [CC/SV]	
míxìn 迷信	to believe blindly [SC/V]; superstition: *pòchú míxìn*, to eradicate superstition [SC/N]	
mízuì 迷醉	to be fascinated by (new ideas, etc.): *mízuì xīn sīxiǎng* [CC/V]	
cáimí 財迷	one who is crazy for wealth [SC/N]	
hūnmí zhuàngtài 昏迷狀態	in a comatose state	
sèmí 色迷	one who is infatuated with women [SC/N]	
xìmí 戲迷	one who is an avid opera fan [SC/N]	
zhí mí bùwù 執迷不悟	to be obstinately foolish, to be hopelessly confused	

拿

nábàn	拿拌	to purposely embarrass others [CC/V]
nábàn	拿辦	to arrest and punish [CC/V]
nábuqilai	拿不起來	cannot lift, (figuratively) cannot handle: *Tā zhēn wúnéng. Shénmo shì dōu nábuqilai.* He is really incompetent. He can't handle anything.[VC]
nábuzhù rén	拿不住人	can't keep people under control: *Nábuzhù rén, bié xiǎng dāng zhǔguǎn.* If one can't keep people under his control, he shouldn't think of becoming boss.
nádà	拿大	to pretend to be superior [VO]
nádàdǐng	拿大頂	to stand on one's head [V-O]
náding zhǔyi	拿定主意	to make up one's mind
náhuá	拿滑	to hold fast: *Zhèzhǒng píxié bùnáhuá.* This pair of shoes slips easily. [VO]
nájiàzi	拿架子	to put on airs: *Tā ná shénmo chòu jiàzi. Shéi bùzhīdao tā shi shéi.* What smelly airs is he putting on? Who doesn't know who he is? [V-O]
námáo	拿毛	to look for trouble: *námáo dǎjià,* to look for trouble and engage in fisticuffs [VO]
nánie	拿捏	to purposely put obstacles in the way of someone, to pretend to conform to the rules of propriety [CC/V]
ná qián búdàng qián huā	拿錢不當錢花	to spend money recklessly
ná qiāng zuò shì	拿腔作勢	to pretend to be important
náqiáo	拿喬	to put on airs [VO]
náquán	拿權	to get control of [V-O]
náshì	拿勢	to have the power [V-O]
náshǒu	拿手	to be good at, to excel in: *Tā duì zúqiú hěn náshǒu.* He is very good at football. [VO/SV]
nátáng	拿糖	to put on airs [VO]
názéi	拿賊	to capture the thief [V-O]
ná zéi dàng hǎorén	拿賊當好人	to treat a thief as a good person

niàn
to read, to remember, to think of

niànbáile zì 念白了字 to read a character incorrectly

niàndao 念叨 to remember someone by talking: *Tā chángcháng niàndaozhe ni.* She often remembers you in her talks; *niànniandaodao,* to grumble: *Tā lǎo shi zài ner niànniandaodao.* He is always grumbling.

niànfó 念佛 to chant Buddhist scriptures, to say prayers to Buddha [V-O]

niàn jiāoqing 念交情 to care about friendship

niànjīng 念經 to chant religious scriptures

niànjiù 念舊 to remember old friends, old times, etc. [VO/SV]

niàn něiyìxì 念那一系 to study in which department

niànniànbúwàng 念念不忘 never to forget

niànniàn yǒu cí 念念有辭 to mumble: *Tā zǒng shi niànniàn yǒu cí, bùzhīdao shuō xie shénmo.* He is always mumbling. Nobody knows what he is talking about.

niàn shū 念書 to read books, to study [V O]

niàntou 念頭 idea, thought, intention: *Wèile yíge nǚren, tā bùzhīdao zhuǎnle duōshao niàntou.* For a woman he has tried many things (in order to win her).

niàn xiǎoxué 念小學 to study in an elementary school

niànzhū 念珠 rosary [SC/N]

búniàn 不念舊惡 to forget and forgive old grudges

huíniàn 回念 to recall the past [SC/C]

jìniàn 紀念 to commemorate: *Zhèkē shù shi wèile jìniàn wǒ mǔqin zhòng de.* This tree was planted to commemorate my mother.[CC/V] commemoration: *jiéhūn jìniàn,* wedding momentos, wedding anniversary

liúniàn 留念 to keep as a memento (used in sending a picture, etc.): *Dàgē liúniàn,* To my brother (oldest) [CC/V]

xiǎngniàn 想念 to think of, to miss: *Tā hěn xiǎngnian tā mùqin.* He misses his mother a lot.[CC/SV]

pàbu 怕不   to be afraid: *Pàbu yě hái yào sānsì shí tiān de gōngfu.* I am afraid it will take 30 to 40 days yet.

pàde shi 怕的是   What I am afraid of is: *Pàde shi míngtian xiàxuě bùnéng kāichē.* What I am afraid of is that it will snow tomorrow and we won't be able to drive.

pà dézuì rén 怕得罪人   to be afraid of offending people

pà guǐ 怕鬼   to be afraid of ghosts [V O]

pà guǐ jiào mén 怕鬼叫門   to be afraid that a ghost may knock on the door: *Búzuò kuīxīn shì, búpà guǐ jiào mén.* If one has not done anything discreditable, he is not afraid that a ghost may knock on his door.

pà jiàn rén 怕見人   to be afraid of seeing people, bashful

pà lǎopó 怕老婆   to be henpecked

pà qián pà hòu 怕前怕後   to be afraid of front and back/to be afraid of everything, to worry too much

pàrén 怕人   to be shy: *Zhège xiǎoháir pàrén.* This child is shy. to be terrifying, shockingly bad: *Zhèzhang huàr zhēn pàrén.* This picture is really terrifying. [VO/SV]

pàsào 怕臊   to be bashful: *Nǚháir duōbànr pàsào.* Most girls are bashful. [VO/SV]

pà shénmo 怕什麼   What are you afraid of? Don't be afraid.

pàshì 怕事   to be afraid of getting involved, don't want to be bothered: *Zhège rén pàshìde budeliǎo. Nǐ zuìhǎo bié zhǎo ta.* This man hates to be bothered. You'd better not disturb him. [VO]

pà sǐ 怕死   to be afraid of death [V O]

pàxiū 怕羞   to be bashful [VO/SV]

hàipa 害怕   to fear, to be afraid of, to be scared [VO]

kǒngpà 恐怕   perhaps: *Tā kǒngpà búhuì láile.* Perhaps he will not come. [CC/Adv]

pǎobīng	跑冰	to ice skate [V-O]
pǎochāi	跑差	to run errands [V-O]
pǎochē	跑車	a race car, sports car [SC/N]
pǎodānbāng	跑單幫	to travel back and forth with profit making goods
pǎodào	跑道	runway, athletic track [SC/N]
pǎodiàole	跑掉了	to have escaped, to have run away [VC]
pǎodùzi	跑肚子	to have loose bowels [V-O]
pǎogǒu	跑狗	to have a dog race [V-O]; dog race
pǎojiē	跑街	to run errands [V-O]; errand boy
pǎo jǐngbào	跑警報	to run for air raid shelter
pǎo lái pǎo qù	跑來跑去	to run around

pǎo lóngtào 跑龍套   to act insignificant roles in Chinese opera, to serve in a supporting role: *Wǒ zhǐ néng tì rénjia pǎopao lóngtào éryi.* What I can do is only serving a supporting role for others.

pǎomǎ	跑馬	to have a horse race; to have a wet dream [V-O]; horse race

pǎo mǎtóu 跑碼頭 to travel from one port to another/to make a living in wandering around (magicians, singers, etc.)

pǎotángde	跑堂的	waiter in a restaurant
pǎotīngde	跑廳的	servant in a brothel
pǎotuǐ	跑腿	to run on errand [V-O]; footman, messenger
pǎo xīnwén	跑新聞	to run around to gather news (reporter)
pǎozhàngde	跑賬的	debt collector
dǎpǎole	打跑了	to chase somebody (or a dog) away by beating [VC]
gēn rén pǎole	跟人跑了	to run away with someone
sàipǎo	賽跑	to run a race [V-O]

平

píng'ān	平安	to be peaceful, safe: *yílù píng'ān*, all the way peaceful/ bon voyage [CC/SV]
píngděng	平等	to be equal [CC/SV]; equality: *nán nǚ píngděng*, equality between male and female
píngdìng	平定	to subjugate (rebels) and restore peace [VC]; to be peaceful: *Dìfangshang hěn píngdìng.* This place is peaceful.[SV]
píngfán	平凡	to be commonplace: *yíjian hěn píngfánde shì*, a commonplace thing; *Nèige rén kě bùpíngfán.* That person is really unusual. [CC/SV]
píngfēn	平分	To divide equally: *Wǒmen píngfēn zhèxie dōngxi.* We will divide these things equally. [SC/V]
pínghé	平和	to be moderate [CC/SV]
pínghéng	平衡	to be evenly balanced [CC/SV]
pínghuá	平滑	to be smooth and even [CC/SV]
píngjìng	平静	to be peaceful and quiet: *Zhège dìfang hěn píngjìng.* This place is very quiet and peaceful. [CC/SV]
píngjūn	平均	to be evenly distributed, on the average: *Píngjūn yíge rén zhuàn duōshao qián?* On the average how much does a person earn? [CC/SV]
píngmín	平民	common people [SC/N]
píngpíng	平平	to be so-so, nothing special: *jìnlai yíqiè píngpíng. Méiyou shénmo kěshuōde.* Recently everything is so-so. There is nothing worth saying. [CC/SV]
píngshí	平時	usually: *Píngshí wǒ búshuì wǔjiào.* Usually I don't take a noon-nap. [SC/TW]
píngtǎn	平坦	to be level: *Dàolù píngtǎn.* The road is level. [CC/SV]
píngwěn	平穩	to be steady, safe [CC/SV]
píngxìn	平信	ordinary mail [SC/N]
píng xīn jìng qì	平心静氣	to be calm, cool
píng yì jìn rén	平易近人	to be personable and accessible
píngyǔn	平允	to be fair and objective [CC/SV]

105

pòchǎn	破產	to declare bankruptcy [V-O]; bankruptcy
pòchú	破除	to overcome, to eradicate (prejudices, obstacles, super-stition): pòchú míxìn, to eradicate superstition [CC/V]
pòfèi	破費	to spend money (used by guests to host after dinner or re-ceipt of gifts): Pòfèi, pòfèi! Jīntian ràng nín pòfèi le. Today you spent too much money. [V-O]
pògé	破格	to take exception [V-O]
pòguā zhī nián	破瓜之年	age sixteen (girl), age 64 (women)
pò guànzi	破罐子	a broken jar/unchaste woman, a physical wreck [SC/N]
pòhuài	破壞	to damage: pòhuài míngyù, to damage the reputation; to destroy: pòhuài jiāting, to destroy a family [CC/V]
pòlàn	破爛	torn and rotten/torn-down, ragged [CC/SV]
pòlànr	破爛兒	junk: jiǎn pòlànr guòhuó, to make a living by picking up junk
pòliè	破裂	to break, to be broken: gǎnqíng pòliè, friendship is broken [CC/V]
pòluò	破落	to decline [CC/V]
pòsǎngzi	破嗓子	broken voice, lost voice [SC/N]
pòshāngfēng	破傷風	tetanus infection
pòsuì	破碎	to be piecemeal, to be broken up [CC/SV]
pòtiānhuāng	破天荒	to be unprecedented: Tā pòtiānhuāng dìyícì lái. He breaks all precedents to come for the first time.
pòtír	破題兒	the opening sentence of essay in civil examinations defin-ing the theme; (figuratively) the first thing [VO/N]
pòtǔ	破土	to break ground (for construction)
pòxiǎo	破曉	daybreak [VO/N]
pòzhàn	破綻	a flaw (secret, argument) [SC/N]
shì rú pò zhú	勢如破竹	It's like splitting bamboo/with irresistible force
yì yǔ dào pò	語道破	to hit the point with one remark

106

qǐbīng	起兵	to raise troops/to go to war [VO]
qǐcǎo	起草	to prepare a draft [V-O]
qǐchéng	起程	to start the journey [VO]
qǐchū	起初	at the beginning [Adv]
qǐchuáng	起床	to get out of bed [V-O]
qǐfēi	起飛	to take off (airplane, economy): *Jīngjì qǐfēi.* The economy took off. [CC/V]
qǐgōng	起工	to start work [VO]
qǐhòng	起閧	to make an uproar [V-O]
qǐjiā	起家	to raise the fortunes of the family, to be prosperous in one's career: *Tā shi zuò shēngyi qǐjiā de.* He raised the fortunes of his family by doing business. [V-O]
qǐjiàn	起見	motive, purpose: *wèile shěng qián qǐjiàn,* for the purpose of saving money
qǐjìn(r)	起勁兒	to be energetic: *Tā zuòshì zhēn qǐjìnr.* He is really energetic when he does things. [VO/SV]
qǐjū	起居	rising and resting/one's everyday life style: *Tā jìnlai qǐjū hěn zhèngcháng.* His recent behavior is very normal. [CC/N]
qǐlai	起來	to rise, to get up; as a verbal complement in neutral tone, it indicates the beginning of an action: *shuōqǐhuàlai méiyou wán.* When one starts talking, there will be no end. *Shuōqǐlai, huà cháng.* It's a long story when one starts to talk about it. [VC]
qǐmíng	起名	to give a name [V-O]
qǐsè	起色	improvement: *Tāde bìng yǒu diǎnr qǐsè.* His illness is improving/He is a little better. [SC/N]
qǐshēn	起身	to start a journey [V-O]
qǐshǒu	起手	to start [VO]
qǐshì	起誓	to take an oath, to swear [V-O]
qǐtóu(r)	起頭兒	to begin: *Shéi qǐde tóur?* Who started it? [V-O]

qǐ
to rise; to begin

起

qǐyì 起義	to raise a righteous revolt [V-O]	
kànbuqǐ 看不起	to look down upon (somebody or something) [VC]	
mǎideqǐ 買得起	can afford to buy [VC]	

qiángbào 強暴   to violate: *qiángbào shàonǚ*, to rape a young girl [CC/V]

qiángbiàn 強辯   to argue forcefully; to call white black, refuse to admit one's mistake: *Tā cuòle hái yào qiángbiàn.* Even when he has made a mistake, he still won't admit it. [SC/V]

qiáng cí duó lǐ 強辭奪理 to exaggerate by rhetoric

qiángdào 強盜   a robber [SC/N]

qiángdiào 強調   to emphasize, to reiterate: *Tā yìzhí qiángdiào tā fǎnduì de lǐyóu.* He constantly reiterates the reasons for his opposition. [SC/V]

qiánggàn 強幹   to do something by force [SC/V]

qiánghàn 強悍   to be powerful, brutal [CC/SV]

qiánghéng 強橫   to be arrogant, brutal [CC/SV]

qiángjiān 強姦   to rape [SC/V]

qiángjiàn 強健   to be physically strong [CC/SV]

qiǎngpò 強迫   to force, coerce (somebody to do something) [SC/V]

qiǎngpò jiàoyù 強迫教育 compulsory education

qiángshèng 強盛   to be strong and prosperous (nation): *Zhōngguó xiànzài kě qiángshèngqilai le.* China is now really strong and prosperous. [CC/SV]

qiángshuǐ 強水   strong acids like sulphuric acid [SC/N]

qiángyìng 強硬   to be unyielding: *Dírende tàidu hěn qiángyìng.* The enemy's attitude is very unyielding. [CC/SV]

qiángyǒulì 強有力   to be powerful: *yíge qiángyǒulìde guójiā*, a powerful country

qiǎngzhì zhíxíng 強制執行 to carry it out by force

qiángzhuàng 強壯   to be powerful, strong [SC/SV]

miǎnqiǎng 勉強   to do something against one's will: *Nǐ yàoshi búyuànyi, qǐng bié miǎnqiǎng.* If you are not willing, please don't force yourself; to strive to do one's best: *Wǒ shízài zuòbuliǎo, nǐ yídìng yào wǒ zuò, wǒ zhǐhǎo miǎnqiǎng shìshi.* I really can't do it. Since you insist, I will try my best.

qièchǐ 切齒	to grind one's teeth in hatred: *qièchǐ zhī hèn* [VO]	
qièdàng 切當	to be very appropriate, to the point [SC/SV]	
qiēduàn 切斷	to cut in two, to amputate [VC]	
qièfū zhī tòng 切膚之痛	sorrow close to the skin/heartfelt sorrow	
qiègǔ zhī hèn 切骨之恨	hatred to the bones	
qièhé 切合	to be fitting; to fit: *qièhé shìshí*, to correspond to the facts [SC/SV]	
qièjì 切記	be sure to remember	
qièjìn 切近	to be close to (reality), to be close at (home) [CC/SV]	
qièqiè 切切	be sure to: *qièqiè jìzhù*, be sure to remember [Adv]	
qièquàn 切勸	to advise firmly	
qièshēn 切身	to be close, personal, intimate: *qièshēn wèntí*, personal problem to be taken care of immediately; *qièshēn zhī tòng*, sorrow that hits close to home [VO/SV]	
qièshí 切實	to be practical: *qièqieshíshí*; in earnest: *qièqieshíshíde zuòshì*, to work in earnest [SV]	
qièzhòng shíbì 切中時弊	to hit closely the shortcomings of the day	
búqiè shíjì 不切實際	to be unrealistic, not practical: *Tāde huà yìdiǎnr dōu búqiè shíjì*. His words are not practical at all.	
guānqiè 關切	to be concerned about: *Tā duì wǒde shìqing yíxiàng hěn guānqiè*. He has always been very concerned about my affairs. *Tā hěn guānqiè wǒ*. He is very concerned about me. [CC/SV]	
mìqiè 密切	to be close, intimate: *Tāmen liǎ de guānxi hěn mìqiè*. The relationship between the two of them is very close. to pay close attention to: *Qǐng nǐ mìqiè zhùyì tāde xíngdòng*. Please pay close attention to his activities. [CC/SV]	
qīnqiè 親切	to be warm and sincere: *Tāde tàidu hěn qīnqiè*. His attitude is very warm and sincere. [CC/SV]	
pòqiè 迫切	to be urgent: *Zhèjian shì hěn pòqiè*. This matter is very urgent. [CC/SV]	

親

to love, to be close to, to be related by blood

qīn'ài	親愛	to be affectionate, dear: *qīnàide mǔqin*, my dear mother [CC/SV]
qīngjia	親家	relatives by marriage (note special pronunciation for *qīn*) [SC/N]
qīnjìn	親近	to associate closely with: *qīnjìn xiǎorén*, to associate closely with dishonorable men [CC/V]; to be close, intimate [SV]; close friends or relatives
qīnkǒu	親口	personally: *qīnkǒu dāying*, to promise personally [SC/Adv]
qīnmì	親密	to be very intimate [CC/SV]
qīnniáng	親娘	one's own mother [SC/N]
qīnqǐ	親啓	letter writing form used after addressee's name: *Wáng Dànián Xiānsheng qīnqǐ*, "personal" for Mr. Wang Tanien [SC/V]
qīnrè	親熱	to be warm and affectionate (with people) [CC/SV]
qīnrén	親人	a relative [SC/N]
qīnshàn	親善	to be friendly: *Zhōng Měi qīnshàn*. China and the U.S. are friendly. [CC/SV]
qīnshēn	親身	personal: *qīnshēn jīngyàn*, personal experience [SC/Adj]
qīnshēng	親生	one's own (children, parents): *qīnshēng zǐnǚ*, *qīnshēng fùmǔ* [SC/Adj]
qīnshì	親事	wedding [SC/N]
qīnsuí	親隨	personal attendant [SC/N]
qīnxìn	親信	confidant, right-hand man [CC/N]
qīnzì	親自	personally: *qīnzì chūmǎ*, to deal with something personally [CC/Adv]
qīnzuǐ	親嘴	to kiss: *qīn tāde zuǐ*, kiss her or him, or *gēn tā qīnle ge zuǐ* [V-O]
chéngqīn	成親	to marry [V-O]
jiéqīn	結親	to unite by marriage [V-O]

xiāng qīn xiāng ài 相親相愛　to be deeply attached to each other: *Tāmen shì qīn xiōngdì, dāngran yīnggāi xiāng qīn xiāng ài*. They are blood brothers. Of course they should love each other dearly.

111

qǐng'ān	請安	to inquire after someone's health, to wish the best of health [V-O]
qǐngbiàn	請便	please make yourself at home, do as you please
qǐng cáishen	請財神	to call upon the god of wealth
qǐng chá	請茶	to invite to tea
qǐngjià	請假	to ask for leave: *qǐng bìngjià*, to ask for sick leave; *qǐng shìjià*, to ask for business leave [V-O]
qǐngjiǎn	請柬	invitation card or letter [SC/N]
qǐngjiào	請教	to ask for advice [V-O]
qǐng jìn	請進	Please come in.
qǐngkè	請客	to give a party, to be host: *Jīntian wǒ qǐngkè.* Today I am the host. *Wǒ qǐng nǐde kè.* I invite you (You are my guest). [V-O]
qǐngqiú	請求	to beg, request, to demand [CC/V]
qǐngshì	請示	to beg for instructions: *Nǐ yàoshi búxiàng shàngsī qǐngshì, zuòcuòle shì shéi fùzé?* If you don't get instructions from your superior, who is going to be responsible if something is done wrong? [V-O]
qǐngtiē	請帖	invitation card [SC/N]
qǐngtuō	請託	to request another's help: *qǐngtuō rén zuò yíjian shì*, ask someone to do something [CC/V]
qǐngwèn	請問	May I ask: *Qǐngwèn nǐ guìxìng?* May I ask what your surname is? *Qǐng wèn ba.* Please ask.
qǐng yīsheng	請醫生	to call a doctor
qǐngyuàn	請願	to demand (usually at popular demonstration) [V-O]
qǐngzuì	請罪	to confess guilt and ask for punishment [V-O]
kěnqǐng	懇請	to beg earnestly [SC/V]
pìnqǐng	聘請	to appoint: *pìnqǐng jiājiào (jiāting jiàoshī)*, to hire a home tutor [CC/V]
shēnqǐng	申請	to make application: *shēnqǐng gōngzuò*, to apply for a job [CC/V]

112

qiúcái	求才	to look for talent [V-O]
qiúdài	求貸	to ask for a loan [V-O]
qiúhé	求和	to beg for peace by offering surrender [V-O]
qiúhūn	求婚	to ask for a girl's hand [V-O]
qiújiàn	求見	to seek an interview [CC/V]
qiújiào	求敎	to ask for advice [V-O]
qiújiù	求救	to ask for help [V-O]
qiúmíng	求名	to set one's mind to obtain fame [V-O]
qiúqǐ	求乞	to beg for (help, pardon, forgiveness, etc.) [CC/V]
qiúqīn	求親	to ask for marriage between two families; to ask for help from relatives [V-O]
qiúqíng	求情	to ask for special consideration, to make an appeal on friendship [V-O]
qiúráo	求饒	to ask for pardon [V-O]
qiú rén	求人	to ask others for help: *Wǒ shì méishì jué bù qiú rén de.* If I don't have anything important, I will never ask others for help. [V O]
qiú shì	求事	to seek a job [V O]
qiúxué	求學	to seek knowledge, to go to school or college for studies [V-O]

qiú zhī bù dé 求之不得   just what one wished for: *Nà zhēn shi yíjian qiú zhī bù dé de shì.* That is just what one wished for.

bù qiú yǒu gōng, zhǐ qiú wú guò 不求有功只求無過   to seek no rewards for accomplishment, but only to be free from mistakes.

kě yù ér bù kě qiú 可遇而不可求 something unique that may come only by chance

lì qiú shàng jìn 力求上進   to try to get ahead (in studies, career, etc.)

yǒu qiú bì yìng 有求必應   (of god, gentlemen) never refuses a request

qǔ
to take, to obtain, to aim for 取

qǔbǎo	取保	to ask somebody to act as guarantor [V-O]
qǔcái	取材	to get material for a writing assignment [V-O]
qǔdào	取道	to go by way of: *Wǒmen qǔdào Xiānggǎng dào Zhōngguó qù.* We go to China by way of Hong Kong. [V-O]
qǔdé	取得	to obtain (consent, degree, wealth, etc.) *qǔdé xuéwèi,* to receive a degree [CC/V]
qǔdēngr	取燈兒	matches
qǔdì	取締	to ban (publications, etc.); to deprive (person) of certain rights [CC/V]
qǔ dōngxi	取東西	to fetch things
qǔfǎ	取法	to copy somebody as example: *Wǒmen dōu yào qǔfǎ Yuè Fēi àiguóde jīngshen.* We must follow the example of Yüeh Fei in patriotism.
qǔjué	取決	to make decision: *Wǒmen jiā de shì yóu tàitai qǔjué.* In our family, the wife makes the decision. [VO]
qǔlè(r)	取樂兒	(to do something) to have fun: *Tā zhuānmen màren qǔlè(r).* He especially enjoys scolding people. [V-O]
qǔmíng(r)	取名兒	to give or to be given a name: *Tā qǔmíng dàqiáng.* He was given the name Ta Ch'iang. *Dàqiáng shi tā bàba gěi ta qǔ de míngr.* Ta Ch'iang is the name his father gave him. [V-O]
qǔ qí biàn	取其便	choose it for its convenience: *Wǒmen zhèyang juédìng búguò shì qǔ qí biàn éryi.* We made such a decision only because of its convenience.
qǔ qián	取錢	to get money [V O]
qǔqiǎo	取巧	to take short cut, to choose the easy way: *Xǐhuan tóujī qǔqiǎo de rén chángcháng huì shīwàng.* Those who enjoy speculation and shortcuts are often disappointed. [V-O]
qǔ rén zhī shàn	取人之善	to take a person's good points
qǔshě	取捨	the power of judgement in taking or rejecting [CC/N]
qǔshèng	取勝	to win victory [V-O]
qǔxiāo	取消	to cancel (appointment, treaty, contract, etc.) [CC/V]

取

qǔxiào(r) 取笑兒　to make fun, to make fun of (somebody): *Bié qǔxiào ta.* Don't make fun of him. [VO/TV]

yì wú kě qǔ 一無可取　nothing worth mentioning: *Zhège rén zhēn shi yì wú kě qǔ.* This person really has nothing to offer.

qù
to go, past, gone

去

qùbìng	去病	to drive away illness [V-O]
qùchu	去處	a place to go: *méiyǒu ge qùchu*, there is no place to go (for visits, recreation, etc.); whereabouts: *bùzhī qùchu*, whereabouts unknown [SC/N]
qùde	去得	to be worth a visit; *qùbude*, to be unfit to go
qùdú	去毒	(Chinese medicine) to reduce poison in the body system [V-O]
qùguó	去國	to depart from one's own country [V-O]
qùhú(r)	去核兒	to remove the stone of fruits, pitted: *qùhú(r) hóng zǎo(r)*, pitted red dates [V-O]
qùhuǒ	去火	(Chinese medicine) to reduce combustion in body system [V-O]
qùjiù	去就	to resign or to stay in office (an important Confucian moral principle) [CC/N]
qùliú	去留	the question of leaving or staying, resigning or continuing (position), dismissing or retaining [CC/N]
qùpí	去皮	to remove the skin, to exclude the packing (net weight) [V-O]
qù sāncùn	去三寸	to shorten by three inches
qùshēng	去聲	falling tone [SC/N]
qùshì	去世	to depart from the world/to pass away [V-O]
qù Wáng Bǎo-chuān	去王寶釧	to play the role of Lady Precious Stream in Chinese opera
qùxiàng	去向	direction: *bùzhī qùxiàng*, don't know the direction or destination [SC/N]
qùxiàng(r)	去項兒	items of expense [SC/N]
qùxié	去邪	to ward off evil spirits [V-O]
qùzhí	去職	to leave an official position [V-O]
guòdequ	過得去	to be able to cross; to be presentable [VC]
shuō lái shuō qù	說來說去	to talk about something over and over again
xìn kǒu shuō qu	信口說去	reckless talking

116

讓

ràngbù 讓步　　to make concessions [V-O]

ràng fènliang 讓分量　to give the customer a little more of what he is buying

rànggei 讓給　to yield (One's rights) to

ràngguò(r) 讓過兒　to yield, to give in: *Nèi liǎngge rén yì chǎoqilai, shéi yě búràngguòr.* When these two men start to quarrel, neither will give in to the other. [V-O]

ràngjià(r) 讓價兒　to reduce the price: *Yàoshi nǐ búràng diǎnr jià, wǒ jiù bùmǎi.* If you don't reduce the price a little, I won't buy it. [V-O]

ràng jiǔ 讓酒　to offer wine: *Kèren dōu zuòhǎole, zěnmo hái búràngjiǔ?* The guests have all been seated. Why don't you offer them a drink? [V O]

ràngkāi 讓開　to make way for someone: *Qìchē lái le; qǐng ràngkāi.* A car is coming; please make way. [VC]

ràng lí 讓梨　to show fraternal affection (allusion to the story of K'ung Yung, who let his elder brother have the bigger pear) [V O]

ràng lù 讓路　to step aside to let other people pass [V O]

ràngrang 讓讓　to make a polite gesture: *Ràngrang jiu shi le. Lái bulai zài tā.* We made a polite gesture to invite him. It's up to him whether he comes or not.

ràngrén 讓人　to yield to others [V-O]

Ràng tā qu shìshi 讓他去試試 Let him try it.

ràngwèi 讓位　to abdicate the throne in favor of someone else; to give up one's seat or position to another [V-O]

ràngyú 讓與　to cede (one's rights to someone else): *Bǎ fángchǎn quán ràngyú Lǐ Sì.* To cede one's right to a property to Li Ssu.

ràngzhàng 讓賬　to pay a bill for another [V-O]

ràngzhe 讓着　to give (someone) the better of an argument: *Tā niánji xiǎo, nǐ jiu ràngzhe ta diǎnr.* Since he is younger, you just give him the better of the argument.

ràngzuò(r) 讓座　to give one's seat to a lady or an older person, to invite someone to take a seat [V-O] *rèài* 熱愛   to love ardently: *Luóměiōu rèài Zhūlìyè.* Romeo loves Juliet ardently. [SC/V]

rèchéng 熱誠   to be earnest, enthusiastic [CC/SV]

rèhōnghōngde 熱烘烘的 red-hot

rèhūhūde 熱呼呼的 very hot (of food)

rèhuo 熱和   to be warm (person or temperature), friendly, affectionate [CC/SV]

rèliè 熱列   (of feelings) to be warm, passionate, fervent, ardent: *Tāde qíngxu hěn rèliè.* His emotion is very fervent. [CC/SV]

rèmén(r) 熱門兒   hot door/any commodity in great demand [SC/N]; popular: *rè-ménr rénwù,* persons who make frontpage news [Adj]

rè'nào 熱鬧   to be jolly, noisy, boisterous: *rère'naonāo,* very jolly; *rè'naore'nao,* to have fun, merry-making [CC/SV]

rè'nàor 熱鬧兒   noisy fun in which many people take part, stage shows and stunts, merry-making: *rénjia bàn shēngrì, zámen qù còu ge rè'nàor ba.* They are celebrating a birthday. Let's go have some fun together.

rèqíng 熱情   to be passionate [SC/SV]; passionate feelings or love

rèsǐ 熱死   to be unbearably hot: *Zhèzhong tiānqi néng bǎ rén rèsǐ.* This kind of weather can really kill people with the heat. [VC]

rè tāng 熱湯   hot soup [SC/N]; to heat the soup [V-O]

rèxiàn 熱線   hot line (telephone line between the White House and Kremlin) [SC/N]

rèxīn 熱心   to be enthusiastic, ardent, zealous, earnest: *Zhège rén bànshì hěn rèxīn.* This man does things very enthusiastically. *Tā rèxīn gōngyì.* He is enthusiastic about public wellbeing. [SC/SV]

rè xīnchang 熱心腸   to be enthusiastic, sincere, zealous: *Zhège rén rè xīnchang. Shéide máng tā bùbāng?* This person is enthusiastic. He will help anybody.

rèzhao 熱着   to fall victim to heat stroke [VC]

rèzhòng 熱中   to be restless, impatient; to hanker for (official prefer-ment). *Tā duì dǔbo hěn rèzhòng.* He likes to gamble. *Tā rè-zhòng mínglì.* He hankers for fame and fortune. [CC/SV]

認

rèn búshì 認不是　to apologize: *Bàba zài shēng nǐde qì. Hái bu kuài qù rèn ge búshì.* Father is mad at you. Why don't you go over and apologize.

rèncuò 認錯　to admit one's fault, to mistake someone (or thing) for another: *Tā rèncuòle rén le.* He mistook one person for another. [V-O]

rènde 認得　to be able to recognize (character, person); *Wǒ rènde zhège zì (or rén).* I know this character (or person).

rènding 認定　to affirm, to put one's finger on [VC]

rèn gāndiē 認乾爹　to recognize one as godfather

rènkě 認可　to approve, to endorse, to give legal force to [VO]

rènle 認了　to accept without protest: *wǒ shū duōshao qián yě rènle.* No matter how much I have lost, I accept the loss (not going to try to win it back)

rènlǐng 認領　to adopt (a child), to claim a lost article [CC/V]

rènmìng 認命　to accept one's fate [VO]

rènqīn 認親　to recognize relatives, especially first meeting on wedding day between both sides [V-O]

rènshēng 認生　to recognize strangers/to be shy (said of children) [VO]

rènshi 認識　to recognize, to know (=*rènde*) [CC/V]

rènshū 認輸　to admit defeat (gambling, fighting, etc.) [V-O]

rènwéi 認為　to consider to be, to consider that..., to think: *Wáng Tóngzhì bú zhèyang rènwéi.* Comrade Wang doesn't think this way. (PRC) [CC/V]

rènxǔ 認許　to approve, to acknowledge [CC/V]

rènzhēn 認真　to make earnest effort to do something, to take seriously [VO]

rènzì 認字　to recognize characters, to be literate (=*shì zì*) [V-O]

rènzéi zuò fù 認賊作父　to take a thief as one's father/unfilial, disloyal

liù qīn bú rèn 六親不認　to be unfeeling toward everybody, to be utterly devoid of human feelings

róngbuxià	容不下	can't take it (because of limited capacity) [VC]
rónghuò	容或	perhaps, maybe, possibly [Adv]
róngjī	容積	volume as measured in cubic units [SC/N]
róngjiē	容接	to welcome, receive (guests) [CC/V]
róngliàng	容量	capacity [SC/N]
róngliàng	容諒	to forgive and forget [CC/V]
róngnà	容納	to accept (ideas, views, suggestions): *Zhèngfǔ guānyuán dōu yào yǒu néng róngnà dàzhòng yìjian de yǎliàng.* Government officials should all have the capacity to accept opinions from the masses. [CC/V]
róngqí	容乞	to ask permission for, request
róngqíng	容情	to be lenient, to make special allowance for [V-O]
róngrěn	容忍	to tolerate [CC/V]
róng rén zhī guò	容人之過	to tolerate other's mistakes
róngshēn	容身	to have somewhere to stay: *wú dì róng shēn*, nowhere to live, ashamed to show one's face [V-O]
róngshòu	容受	to endure, to put up with [CC/V]
róngshù	容恕	to forgive, to pardon [CC/V]
róng wǒ jǐ tiān	容我幾天	Please give me a few days' grace
róngxī	容膝	to accept the knee/a tiny spot [V-O/N]
róngxiàn	容限	limitation, limit of capacity [SC/N]
róngxǔ	容許	to permit [CC/V]; perhaps, maybe [Adv]
róngyi	容易	to be easy [CC/V]
róngyǐn	容隱	to try to cover up [CC/V]

入

rùchāo 入超	import over/to have an unfavorable balance of trade [SP/V]
rùěr 入耳	to be pleasant to hear [VO/SV]; house centipede, popular name for *yóuyan* (because of its fondness for creeping into the ear)
rùgǎng 入港	to enter port [V-O]; to be harmonious, in full agreement: *Tāmen shuōde rùgǎng.* They got along very affably in their conversation. [V-O]
rùjí 入籍	to be naturalized: *Tā yǐjing rùle Měiguo jí le.* He has already been naturalized as an American. [V-O]
rùjìng 入境	to enter country [V-O]
rùkǒu 入口	entrance, imports [SC/N]
rùkòur 入扣兒	to be completely engrossed, fascinated: *Tā kàn wǔxiá xiǎoshuō kànde rùkòur.* He is entirely absorbed in reading kungfu novels. [VO]
rùmǎ 入馬	to enter horse/to make progress in courtship [VO]
rùmén(r) 入門	to be initiated into a subject [V-O]; a primer or introduction (of a subject): *Guóyǔ Rùménr,* <u>Mandarin Primer</u>
rùmí 入迷	to be enchanted, enraptured: *Tā xiàqí xiàde rùmíle, shénmo shì dōu bùguǎn le.* He is so much interested in playing chess that he doesn't tend to any other business. [V-O]
rùmó 入魔	to be completely bewitched; to go the way of the devil [V-O]
rùshǒu 入手	to commence, to start [V-O]; a start
rùtǔ 入土	to be buried [V-O]
rùwéi 入闈	to live incommunicado during period of examination (of official in charge of government examinations) [V-O]
rùwèir 入味	to be interesting, to be tasteful [V-O]
rùwǔ 入伍	to enter military service [V-O]
rùxuǎn 入選	to be selected (for a job, contest, etc.) [V-O]
rùyǎn 入眼	to be pleasing to the eye [V-O]
rùyuàn 入院	to enter the hospital/to be hospitalized [V-O]

sàichē 賽車　　　to race cars [V-O]

sàichuán 賽船　　to run a boat race [V-O]

sàidēng 賽燈　　to show off lanterns (as at the lantern festival) [V-O]

sàigǒu 賽狗　　to have a dog race [V-O]

sàiguo 賽過　　to excell: *Zhāngjiāde sānge nǚháizi, zhǎngde yíge sàiguo yíge.* As for the Changs' daughters, each is prettier than the last. (VC)

sàihuì 賽會　　a religious festival (with parades of idols, stilts, floats, etc.); an exposition [SC/N]

sàilùluò 賽璐珞　(transliteration) celluloid

sàimǎ 賽馬　　to hold a horse race [V-O]; horse race

sàiměi 賽美　　to hold a beauty contest [V-O]

sàipǎo 賽跑　　to hold a race [V-O]

sàiqiú 賽球　　to play a ball game [V-O]

sàiquán 賽拳　　to match fingers (drinking game) [V-O]

sàishè 賽社　　a village festival of offerings of thanks to the gods, esp. after the harvest [SC/N]

sàishén 賽神　　=*sàihuì* [V-O/N]

sài tiānxiān 賽天仙　　to rival the beauty of a fairy

sài xishì 賽西施　to rival the beauty of Hsi Shih (an historical beauty)

sài yīngtao 賽櫻桃　to rival a cherry (as to size and color of a girl's mouth)

sài yuàn 賽願　　to give offerings of thanks for wish granted [V-O]

bǐsài 比賽　　to have a contest: *Jīntian wǒmen bǐsài xiězì.* Today we will have a contest for writing characters. [CC/V]; a contest; *xiězì bǐsài,* writing contest

商

shāngbàn	商辦	to consult and take action [CC/V]
shāngdìng	商定	to decide after discussion [VC]
shāngliang	商量	to discuss: shānglaingshangliang, to discuss a bit [CC/V]; shāngshangliangliangde, indecisive
shānglüè	商略	to discuss (situation) [CC/V]
shāngmíng	商明	to come to a clear understanding after discussion [VC]
shāngquè	商榷	to discuss together (problems, business, etc.) [CC/V]
shāngtán	商談	to discuss, to confer [CC/V]
shāngtǎo	商討	to discuss (from shāngliang and tǎolùn) [CC/V]
shāngtóng	商同	to confer with, to deliberate jointly: Zhèjian shì wǒmen děi shāngtóng Wáng Xiānsheng yíkuàir qù bàn. So far as this matter is concerned, we must do it in consultation with Mr. Wang. [CC/V]
shāngyì	商擬	to propose to, to suggest [CC/V]
shāngyì	商議	to discuss [CC/V]
shāngyuē	商約	to decide (together to do something) [CC/V]
shāngzhǔn	商準	to agree to after discussion [CC/V]
shāngzhuó	商酌	to discuss (situation, etc.), (from shāngliang and zhēnzhuó) [CC/V]
cóngshāng	從商	to go into business as a career [V-O]
cuòshāng	搓商	to deliberate, to discuss [CC/V]
jīngshāng	經商	to engage in business [V-O]
miànshāng	面商	to discuss personally [SC/V]
xiéshāng	協商	to discuss together (terms, procedures, etc.) [SC/V]

shàngcāo 上操   to go to drill [V-O]

shàngchǎng 上場   to appear on scene, market, or stage [V-O]

shàngdàng 上當   to fall into a trap, to be cheated: *Jīntiān wǒ shàngle ge dà dàng*. I was badly cheated today. [V-O]

shàngdiào 上吊   to hang oneself [V-O]

shàngdòng 上凍   to freeze (of river, lake, etc.) [V-O]

shànggǎnzhe 上趕着   to hurry forward to please: *shànggǎnzhe jiào lǎo bó*, hurried forward and called "Uncle!"

shànggōng 上工   to report for work (usually labor work) [V-O]

shànghuǒ(r) 上火兒   to be inflamed with anger, to get angry [V-O]

shàngjǐn 上緊   to affix tightly: *Bǎ luósī shàngjǐn*, to affix the screw tightly [VC]

shàngjìn 上勁   to do something energetically; to encourage: *Tā jīntiān guāng gěi wǒ shàngjìn*. She has encouraged me all day today. [V-O]

shàngjìn 上進   to make progress (esp. in studies) [SC/V]

shàngkǒu 上口   easy to read [V-O]

shànglai 上來   to come up [VC]; also used as complement to other verbs

shàngliè 上列   above-mentioned [SC/Adj]

shàngshēng 上升   to go up (skyward) [SC/V]

shàngshǒu 上手   to get in one's hand [V-O]

shàngsuàn 上算   it pays to (do something): *Zuò fēijī bǐjiǎo shàngsuàn*. Comparatively, it pays to go by plane. [VO/SV]

shàngtiān 上天   to go up to the heavens, to die [V-O]; the sky above [SV/N]

shàngxiāng 上香   to offer incense at temple [V-O]

shàngxiàng 上相   to be photogenic [VO/SV]

shàngyǎn 上眼   to appeal to the eye: *kàn búshàngyǎn*, to disdain, to hold in contempt [V-O]

shàngyìng 上映   to show, to be shown, now showing

shēngbìng	生病	to fall ill [V-O]
shēngcài	生菜	raw vegetable, salad [SC/N]
shēngchǎn	生產	to produce, to give birth to children: *Nǐ tàitai shénmo shíhou shēngchǎn?* When is your wife going to have the baby? [CC/V]
shēng huā miào bǐ	生花妙筆	gifted pen
shēng huāyàng	生花樣	to make difficulties
shēnghuo	生活	to live; *chī shēnghuo*, (Shanghai dialect) to get a beating [CC/V]
shēnghuǒ	生火	to build a fire [V-O]
shēngjì	生計	to plot [V-O]; means of livelihood [SC/N]
shēnglì	生利	to bear interest, to make profit [V-O]
shēng lóng huó hǔ	生龍活虎	live dragon and live tiger/extremely vivid or forceful
shēnglù	生路	way out, ways to make a living [SC/N]
shēngmìng	生命	life [CC/N]
shēngqì	生氣	to get angry [V-O]; vitality [SC/N]
shēngshì	生事	to cause trouble [V-O]
shēngsǐ	生死	life and death: *shēngsǐ guāntou*, a grave crisis between life and death; *shēngsǐ zhī jiāo*, lifetime friendship [CC/N]
shēngxí	生息	to bear interst [V-O]
shēngxìng	生性	one's born nature [SC/N]
shēngyǎng	生養	to give birth to and bring up (children) [CC/V]
shēngyi	生意	business: *zuò shēngyi*, to do business; *shēngyì*, will to live [SC/N]
shēngzhǎng	生長	to grow, to grow up: *shēngzhǎngde piàoliang*, to grow up pretty [CC/V]
shēngzhí	生殖	to grow, multiply, to reproduce: *shēngzhíqì*, sexual organs [CC/V]

shēngzǐ 生子   to give birth to a son [V-O]

shēngzì 生字   new characters, new words [SC/N]

wú shì shēng fēi 無事生非 to make uncalled for trouble

shèbǎi	設擺	to lay out (for occasion, alter, dinner, etc.) [CC/V]
shèbèi	設備	to provide (facilities) [CC/V]; facilities, equipment: *Zhège xuéxiào shèbèi búcuò.* The facilities of this school are not bad.
shèdìng	設定	to set up (laws, regulations, etc.) [CC/V]
shèfǎ	設法	to think of ways to, to try to: *Wǒmen děi shèfǎ shěng qián.* We have to try to save money. [V-O]
shèfáng	設防	to set up defense [V-O]
shèguǎn	設館	to give private tutoring [V-O]
shèhuò	設或	if [CC/Conj]
shèjì	設計	to design, to draw up a blueprint, to contrive [CC/V]
shèjiào	設教	to set up as teacher, to found a religion [VO]
shèjǐng	設穽	to lay a trap [VO]
shèjú	設局	to set up a situation: *shè piànjú*, to lay a plan for swindle [V-O]
shèlì	設立	to establish: *shèlì xuéxiào*, to establish a school [CC/V]
shèrú	設如	if [CC/Conj]
shèruò	設若	if [CC/Conj]
shèshī	設施	arrangement, provisions, facilities [CC/N]
shèshǐ	設使	if [CC/Conj]
shèxí	設席	to set up banquet at [V-O]; or *xíshè*, banquet at [SP/V]
shèxiǎng	設想	to conjecture, to consider: *wèi rén shèxiǎng*, to be considerate of others [CC/V]
shèzhì	設置	to arrange [CC/V]; arrangement
shèzuò	設座	to set up seats/to give dinner at: *shèzuò Huáguó Fàndiàn*, to give a dinner at the Huakuo Restaurant [V-O]
chénshè	陳設	display, arrangement (of furniture, etc.) [CC/N]

shībài 失敗	to fail, to be defeated [CC/V]	
shīcháng 失常	to be abnormal [VO]	
shīdàng 失當	to be inappropriate: *chǔzhì shīdàng*, badly handled [VO]	
shīhé 失和	to quarrel, to have differences of opinion, do not get along [VO]	
shīhuǒ 失火	to have fire: *Fángzi shīhuǒle.* The house is on fire. [V-O]	
shījiǎo 失腳	to slip on the ground [VO]	
shījìng 失敬	to fail in courtesy or etiquette [VO], also *shīlǐ*	
shīkǒu 失口	to say something carelessly [V-O], also *shīyán*	
shīliàn 失戀	to be disappointed in love [V-O]	
shīmián 失眠	to suffer from insomnia [V-O]	
shīmíng 失明	to become blind [VO]	
shīsàn 失散	to scatter, to disperse [CC/V]	
shīshēn 失身	to lose virginity [V-O]	
shīshì 失事	to run into trouble, to have an accident: *Fēijī shīshì le.* The plane crashed. [V-O]	
shīwàng 失望	to lose hope, to be disappointed [V-O]	
shīxiào 失效	to become invalid [V-O]	
shīxìn 失信	to fail to keep promise [V-O]	
shīxué 失學	to be forced to drop out of school [V-O]	
shīyè 失業	to be unemployed [V-O]	
shīyì 失意	to be disappointed: *qíngchǎng shīyì*, disappointed in love [VO/SV]	
shīyuē 失約	to fail to meet appointment, to break promise [V-O]	
shīzōng 失蹤	to lose traces/to be missing [V-O]	
wàn wú yì shī 萬無一失	complete success assured	

shìbá 識拔   to recognize (a person's ability) and promote (him) [CC/V]

shìbié 識別   to know the difference, to distinguish [CC/V]

shìbiélì 識別力 power of discrimination

shìhuò 識貨   to know the goods/to have good judgement for goods [VO]

shìjiàn 識見   definite views gained from superior knowledge [CC/N]

shìjīng 識荊   (courtesy) to make your esteemed acquaintance [VO]

shìqiào 識竅   to be tactful [VO/SV]

shìqù(r) 識趣兒 to know the subtleties/to be tactful, know the right thing to do [VO/SV]

shìrén 識人   to know people/to be able to distinguish between good and bad people [VO]

shìxiàng 識相   to be able to read the countenance/to know what is right to do, to be tactful: *Tā yàoshi shāowéi shìxiàng diǎnr yě búhuì ràng rénjia xiàohua ta.* If he is a little tactful, he will not be laughed at by people. [VO/SV]

shìyě 識野   (psychology) field of awareness [SC/N]

shìyù 識閾   =*shìyě* [SC/N]

shìzhě 識者   the one who knows/experts: *wéi shìzhě suǒ xiào*, to be laughed at by the experts [SC/N]

shìzì 識字   to know characters/to be able to read [V-O]

cáishì 才識   ability and insight (from *cáinéng* and *jiànshì*) [CC/N]

jiànshì 見識   insight, intellectual discrimination [CC/V]

mù bú shì dīng 目不識丁 eyes cannot read the character *dīng*/to be completely illiterate

shǎngshì 賞識   to appreciate (a person's ability): *Lǎo Wáng de shàngsī hěn shǎngshì tāde gōngzuò.* Lao Wang's superior appreciates his work very much. [CC/V]

xiāngshì 相識   to know each other [SC/V]

xuéshì 學識   knowledge and insight (from *xuéwèn* and *jiànshì*) [CC/N] *shǐbèi* 使婢　maidservant [SC/N]

shǐbude 使不得　cannot be used: *Zhèbǎ dāozi shǐbude.* This knife cannot be used. [VC]

shǐbuliǎo 使不了　cannot use (so much): *Mǎi shū shǐbuliǎo zhèmo duō qián.* One doesn't need so much money for buying books. [VC]

shǐde 使得　will do: *Zuór mǎide nèijian dàyī shǐde ma?* Is that coat (that you) bought yesterday all right? [VC]

shǐ guāi nòng qiǎo 使乖弄巧　to play tricks

shǐ guǐjì 使詭計　to play tricks

shǐ huài 使壞　to willfully make someone suffer, to hurt, to destroy [VC]

shǐhuan 使喚　to order servants, children) about: *Tā huì shǐhuan rén.* He knows how to order people around. [CC/V]

shǐhuanrén 使喚人　servant, attendant

shǐjin(r) 使勁兒　to exert effort, to put out strength: *shǐjinr niànshū*, to study hard [V-O]

shǐmìng 使命　official mission: *Shàngcì tā méiyou wánchéng shǐmìng.* Last time he didn't complete his mission. [SC/N]

shǐnǚ 使女　a maidservant [SC/N]

shǐqì 使氣　to act on impulse or in fit of anger [V-O]

shǐ rén nánshòu 使人難受　to make people feel bad

shǐ shǒuduàn 使手段　to use strategy to maneuver

shǐtú 使徒　(Christian) disciples [SC/N]

shǐ xìngzi 使性子　to be tempermental: *Tā xǐhuan shǐ xìngzi shì yīnwèi fùmǔ bǎ tā guànhuàile.* She is tempermental because her parents spoiled her. [V O]

shǐ xīnyǎnr 使心眼兒　to use holes of intelligence supposed to be in the heart to act intelligently

shǐ yǎnsè 使眼色　to ogle, to make signs with the eyes

shǐyòng 使用　to use, to employ: *Wàiguo rén búhuì shǐyòng kuàizi.* Foreigners do not know how to use chopsticks. [CC/V]

shìdēng 試燈	to hold the lantern contest on the 15th day of the first lunar month [V-O]
shìér 試兒	to test baby's inclinations on its first birthday by having different objects displayed within its reach to see what it grabs. See *zhuāzhōu* [V-O]
shìgōng(r) 試工兒	to try out a workman or employee [V-O]
shìhūn 試婚	to try out a marriage [V-O]; a trial marriage [SC/N]
shìjīnshí 試金石	a touch stone
shìjuàn 試卷	examination paper [SC/N]
shìshi 試試	to have a try
shìtàn 試探	to explore [CC/V]
shìtí 試題	examination questions or topics [SC/N]
shìwèn 試問	May I ask, formula in asking questions, especially in class-room exercises [CC/V]
shìyǎn 試演	to rehearse [V-O]; a rehearsal [SC/N]
shìyàn 試驗	to experiment [CC/V]; an experiment: *shìyànguǎn*, test tube
shìyòng 試用	to try out (person, utensil); to be on probation: *shìyòng qījiān wǒ bùgǎn qǐngjià*. During probation, I dare not ask for leave. [CC/V]
shìzhǐ 試紙	Litmus paper [SC/N], also *shìyànzhǐ*
shìzhōu 試周	=*shìér* [V-O]
bǐshì 筆試	written examination [SC/N]
chángshì 嘗試	to try out [CC/V]; an attempt, a trial
jiānshì 監試	to monitor an examination [V-O]
kǎoshì 考試	to take an examination, to examine [CC/V]; an examination
kǒushì 口試	oral examination [SC/N]
yìngshì 應試	to go to take an examination [V-O]

shōubīng 收兵   to withdraw troops [V-O]

shōucáng 收藏   to collect (curios, rare books, etc.) [CC/V]

shōuchǎng 收場   to wind up [V-O]; end, ending (of a play): *Shōuchǎng tài lìng rén nánshòu le.* The ending makes people very sad.

shōuchéng 收成   harvest: *Jīnniánde shōuchéng tèbié hǎo.* This year's harvest is especially good. [SC/N]

shōufù 收復   to recover (lost territory): *shōufù shīdì* [CC/V]

shōugōng 收工   to wind up work [V-O]

shōugòu 收購   to buy for business or collection [CC/V]

shōuhuí 收回   to take back, to rescind (order) [VC]

shōuhuò 收穫   harvest, results (of study, exploration, etc.) [CC/N]

shōujù 收據   a receipt, also *shōutiáor* [SC/N]

shōulǎn 收攬   to win over (people's support): *shōulǎn mínxīn* [CC/V]

shōulèi 收淚   to stop weeping [V-O]

shōuliú 收留   to accept (orphan, relative) for care [CC/V]

shōumǎi 收買   =*shōugòu*; to win (popular support): *shōumǎi rén xīn* [CC/V]

shōuróng 收容   to provide housing for (refugees): *shōuróng nànmín* [CC/V]

shōurù 收入   to receive [CC/V]; income

shōushi 收拾   to tidy up, to manage: *bùkě shōushi*, unmanageable; to punish: *Hǎohāo shōushishoushi nèige huàidàn.* Take good care of that rascal. [CC/V]

shōusuō 收縮   to shrink up, to curtail (business, deals) [CC/V]

shōuwěi 收尾   ending (of story, affair) [VO/N]

shōuyǎng 收養   to keep and raise (orphan) [CC/V]

shōuyì 收益   income, profit [VO/N]

shōuyīn 收音   to receive radio message: *shōuyīnjī*, a radio [V-O]

shōuzhī 收支   receipt and expenditure [CC/N]

受

shòubuliǎo	受不了	can't stand it [VC]
shòuchǒng	受寵	to receive favor from superior: *shòuchǒng ruò jīng*, to be overwhelmed by superior's favor [V-O]
shòuhài	受害	to suffer, to be murdered [V-O]
shòuhuì	受賄	to accept bribe [V-O]
shòujīng	受精	to conceive, to be fertilized [V-O]
shòukàn	受看	to be good to look at [VO/SV]
shòukǔ	受苦	to suffer [V-O]
shòulěi	受累	to be involved on account of others: *shòulèi*, to suffer hardship [V-O]
shòulǐ	受理	(of court) to accept a complaint [CC/V]
shòunàn	受難	to suffer hardship, to die a martyr [V-O]
shòupiàn	受騙	to be cheated [V-O]
shòuqì	受氣	to suffer petty annoyances: *shòuqì bāor*, person subjected to daily persecutions [V-O]
shòuqū	受屈	to suffer an injustice [V-O]
shòuròu	受辱	to be humiliated [V-O]
shòushāng	受傷	to be injured [V-O]
shòutīng	受聽	to be good to hear [VO/SV]
shòutuō	受託	to be entrusted to do something by a friend [V-O]
shòuxǐ	受洗	to be baptized [V-O]
shòuyòng	受用	to be physically comfortable, enjoyable: *Tiān rè hē bēi bīngchá hěn shòuyòng.* On a hot day, it is very enjoyable to drink a cup of ice tea. [VO/SV]
shòuyùn	受孕	to become pregnant
shòuzuì	受罪	to suffer: *shòu yáng zuì*, to suffer something difficult to explain [V-O]
nánshòu	難受	to feel unhappy, to be uncomfortable. [SC/SV]

shǔbuguòlai 數不過來 cannot reckon how many: *Rén tài duō, wǒ shǔbuguòlai.* There are so many people that I can't count them. [VC]

shǔbuqīng 數不清 cannot reckon how many [VC]

shǔbushàng 數不上 cannot be counted as one: *Hǎo xuésheng lǐtou zěnmo yě shǔbushàng tā.* No matter how you do it, he can't be counted as one of the good students. [VC]

shǔdiǎn 數點 to count up [CC/V]

shǔ diǎn wàng zǔ 數典忘祖 to count the records but forget the ancestors/to forget one's ancestral traditions

shǔ dōngguā dào qiézi 數東瓜道茄子 to enumerate melons and talk about eggplants/to gabble, to twaddle

shǔguò 數過 to enumerate faults [VO]

shǔluò 數落 to scold: *Chéngtiānjia shǔluò tā, nǐ yǒu méiyou ge wán ne?* Scolding him day in and day out, don't you have an end?

shǔmà 數罵 to enumerate faults and scold/to scold [CC/V]

shǔ mǐ ér cuī 數米而炊 to count grains before cooking/to be extremely poor

shǔ pínzuǐ 數貧嘴 to count poor mouths/to gabble, to twaddle

shǔshuō 數說 to enumerate faults [CC/V]

shǔshu shùr 數數數兒 to make an account of the amount: *Nǐ shǔshu shùr bújiù zhīdao tā gěi nǐ duōshǎo le ma?* If you've made an account of the amount, you'll know how many he has given you.

shǔshùr 數數兒 to count the number [V-O]

shǔsuàn 數算 to count and reckon [CC/V]

shǔ tā cōngming 數他聰明 to count him as the intelligent one

shǔ yī shǔ èr 數一數二 to count at the top (number one or number two): *Tā shì Měiguo shǔ yī shǔ èr de kēxuéjiā.* He is a top American scientist.

shǔzhe 數着 to count as (the best, the ablest, etc.): *Péngyoulǐtou, shǔzhe tā zuì yǒuqián le.* Among friends, count him as the richest.

134

shuōbuguòqu 說不過去 to be unreasonable: *Tā zhèzhǒng zuòfēng zhēn shuōbuguòqu.* His way of doing things is really unreasonable. [VC]

shuōbulái 說不來 hard to say; cannot get along: *bǐcǐ shuōbulái,* cannot get along with each other [VC]

shuōbushàng 說不上 cannot be considered: *Zhèzhang huà shuōbushàng jiézuò.* This painting cannot be considered a masterpiece. [VC]

shuōchuān 說穿 to expose (a secret): *Shuōchuānle yì qián bùzhí.* When the secret is exposed, it is worth nothing. [VC]

shuō dōng dào xī 說東道西 to speak of East and West/to engage in random talk, also *shuō cháng dào duǎn, shuō tiān dào dì, shuō sān dào sì*

shuō fāngbian 說方 to speak in favor of someone or something (=*shuō hǎohuà*)

shuōfú 說服 to convince (another) [VC]

shuōkāi 說開 to explain, to allay fears; to have become current [VC]

shuōliūle zuǐ 說溜了嘴 to make a slip of the tongue: *Wǒ běnlái bùxiǎng gàosong ta. Kěshi wǒ shuōliūle zuǐ le.* I didn't want to tell him, but I made a slip of the tongue.

shuōpò 說破 to expose (secret) [VC]

shuōpòzuǐ 說破嘴 to talk oneself hoarse (in futile long persuasion)

shuōqilai 說起來 to mention, in regard to: *shuōqilai huà cháng,* if one starts talking, it will be a long story. *Shuōqihuàlai méiyou wán.* There will be no end when one starts talking. [VC]

shuō rénqing 說人情 to plead for leniency because of friendship

shuō shi ne 說是呢 You said it (in response to someone's remarks)

shuōshū 說書 to tell stories (of professional story-tellers): *shuōshūde,* story-teller [V-O]

shuōzhe wánr 說着玩兒 do not mean what one says: *Wǒ shì shuōzhe wánr de.* I didn't mean what I said.

shuōzuǐ 說嘴 to boast [V-O], also *shuō dàhuà,* to talk big

---

sǐbǎn 死板   to be inflexible, rigid [SC/SV]

sǐbié 死别   to part and never see each other again [SC/V]

sǐ búyào liǎn 死不要臉 to be devoid of shame

sǐchóu 死仇   eternal enemy [SC/N]

sǐdǎng 死黨   partisans sworn to the death [SC/N]

sǐděng 死等   to wait forever [SC/V]

sǐduìtou 死對頭 deadly foe: *Tā shì wǒde sǐduìtou.* He is my deadly foe. [SC/N]

sǐguǐ 死鬼   (abuse) devil: *Nǐ zhège sǐguǐ.* You devil! [SC/N]

sǐ hútongr 死胡同兒 dead alley

sǐjié 死結   a tightly-tied knot; a long-standing grudge [SC/N]

sǐkěn 死啃   to work hard on eating from a piece of bone, to read without digesting [SC/V]

sǐlù 死路   dead end, fatal route [SC/N]

sǐ pí lài liǎn 死皮賴臉 shamelessly: *Tā sǐ pí lài liǎn chiúle yìtiān.* He shamelessly begged for a whole day.

sǐ qù huó lái 死去活來 to be half dead: *Tā bèi dǎde sǐ qù huó lái.* He was beaten half to death.

sǐrén 死人   (abuse) a dunce, a dead person [SC/N]

sǐshuǐ 死水   stagnant water [SC/N]

sǐwáng 死亡   to die [CC/V]

sǐxiàng 死相   a teasing remark in disgust: *kàn nǐ nèige sǐxiàng!* Take a look at yourself! [SC/N]

sǐxīn 死心   to give up hope [V-O]

sǐxīnyǎnr 死心眼兒 single-minded

sǐ yào qián 死要錢   to be dead set on getting money

sǐyìng 死硬   to be irreconcilable [SC/SV]; *sǐyìngpài*, diehard faction

sǐzuì 死罪   death penalty [SC/N]

èsǐ 餓死   *to die* to die of hunger, to be extremely hungry [VC]
kěxiàosǐle 可笑死了   to be extremely funny, laughable [VC]

sòngbié 送別 to send off [V-O]

sòngbìn 送殯 to attend funeral [V-O]

sòng hányī 送寒衣 to send winter clothing/to burn paper clothing for the dead at the end of the 10th lunar month

sònghuà 送話 to send words; to give opponent grounds for attack by using ill advised statement [V-O]

sòng jiù yíng xīn 送舊迎新 to send off the old and welcome the new (year or friend)

sònglǎo 送老 to give burial ceremony to deceased parents (=*sòngzhōng*)[V-O]

sònglǐ 送禮 to give gift [V-O]

sònglù 送路 to send off [V-O]

sòngmìng 送命 to risk one's life [V-O]

sòngqián 送錢 to send money, to waste money [V-O]

sòngqīn 送親 to accompany bride to groom's family on wedding day: *sòngqīn tàitai*, woman selected by bride's family for this purpose[V-O]

sòngrénqíng 送人情 to do a favor for friendship; to give a present

sòngsāng 送喪 to attend funeral [V-O]

sòngshén 送神 to send spirits away after offering sacrifice [V-O]

sòngsǐ 送死 to walk into a trap [VO]

sòng wǎng yíng lái 送往迎來 to send off the going and welcome the coming/ to meet and send off visitors

sòng xìn 送信 to deliver a letter [V O]

sòng xìnr 送信兒 to send message through third party [V O]

sòngxíng 送行 to send off [V-O]

sòngzàng 送葬 to attend funeral [V-O]

sòngzào 送竈 to send off kitchen god for New Year holiday, on the 23rd day of the 12th lunar month [V-O]

sòngzhōng 送終 =*sònglǎo* [V-O]

算

suànbude 算不得 cannot be considered as (unusual, rare, etc.) [VC]

suànbuliǎo 算不了 cannot be reckoned as: *Suànbuliǎo yìhuí shì*. This is nothing. [VC]

suànfǎ 算法 arithmetic [SC/N]

suànguà 算卦 to practice divination, to tell fortune [V-O]

suànjì 算計 to calculate, to plot ruin or injury (of someone): *Xiǎoxīn bèi rénjia suànjì*. Be careful about another's plot against you. [CC/V]

suànle 算了 let it be, do not bother anymore: *Búqù suànle*. If you don't go, forget it.

suànmìng 算命 to tell fortune; *suànmìngde*, fortune-teller [V-O]

suànqilai 算起来 all counted or considered: *suànqilai háishi zhège hǎo*. All considered, this one is still better. [VC]

suànshang 算上 to include, to count in: *Nǐ zǔzhī lǚxuétuán bié wàngle bǎ wǒ suànshang*. If you are organizing a study tour, don't forget to include me. [VC]

suànshù 算術 arithmetic [SC/N]

suànshùr 算數兒 to count, to be taken seriously: *Nǐ shuōde huà suànshùr bu-suànshùr*? Are you serious about what you say? [V-O]

suànxué 算學 mathematics [SC/N]

suànzhàng 算賬 to reckon accounts, to ask for bill to pay; to get even (for revenge): *Huítóu wǒ gēn nǐ suànzhàng*. I'll get even with you later. [V-O]

bǐsuàn 筆算 to calculate with a pen [SC/V]

dǎsuàn 打算 to plan, to intend to [CC/V]

dǎ suànpan 打算盤 to calculate on abacus; to calculate costs and benefits: *Tā jiù huì dǎ rúyì suànpan*. He always indulges himself in wishful thinking.

jìsuàn 計算 to reckon, to compute: *jìsuànjī*, calculator [CC/V]

pánsuàn 盤算 to ruminate in mind [SC/V]

xīnsuàn 心算 to calculate mentally [SC/V]

tán
to talk   談

tánbǐng	談柄	butt of jokes [SC/N]

tándelái 談得來 can make conversation with: *Tāmen liǎngge hěn tándelái.* The two of them can talk to each other. [VC]

tánfēng 談鋒 ability to talk: *tánfēng shèn jiàn*, very good talker [SC/N]

tán hé róngyi 談何容易 It's so easy to talk and criticize. (It imples that it isn't so easy to do.)

tán hǔ sè biàn 談虎色變 to turn pale at the mere mention of a tiger/to get scared easily

tánhuà 談話 to talk [V-O]; conversation, talk: *Tā zuótiānde tánhuà zhēn yǒuyìsi.* His talk yesterday was really interesting.

tánlùn 談論 to discuss [CC/V]; a discussion

tán qíng shuō ài 談情說愛 to talk love

tánpàn 談判 to negotiate [CC/V]; a negotiation

tántiān(r) 談天兒 to chat, to gossip idly (V-O)

tán tiān shuō dì 談天說地 to talk of anything under the sun

tántǔ(r) 談吐兒 way of talking: *Tántǔ hěn fēngyǎ.* His way of talking is very cultured. [CC/V]

tán xiào fēng shēng 談笑風生 to talk in a fascinating and lively manner

tán xiào zì ruò 談笑自若 to be completely at ease while talking

tánxīn 談心 to have a heart-to-heart talk [V-O]

tán yán wéi zhòng 談言微中 talk sparingly but to the point

tán zhèngzhì 談政治 to talk politics

tánzhù 談助 material for gossip (SC/N)

jiē tán xiāng yì 街談巷議 street gossip

lǎoshēng cháng tán 老生常談 moral platitudes

xiántán 閒談 to have a leisurely talk [SC/V]

yántán 言談 a person's style or ability of conversation [CC/N]

逃

táobēn	逃奔	to flee [CC/V]
táobì	逃避	to shirk (duty): *táobì zérèn*; to refuse to face (reality): *táobì xiànshí* [CC/V]
táobīng	逃兵	a deserter [SC/N]
táo bīngyì	逃兵役	to avoid military service
táocuàn	逃竄	(of bandits, rebels) to flee elsewhere [CC/V]
táodiào	逃掉	to get away with: *Zhè cì ràng nǐ táodiào le.* This time you got away. [VC]
táofàn	逃犯	escaped convict [SC/N]
táohuāng	逃荒	to flee from famine [V-O]
táohūn	逃婚	to run away from a wedding [V-O]
táomìng	逃命	to flee for one's life [V-O]
táonàn	逃難	to run away from disaster, to become a refugee [V-O]
táonì	逃匿	to escape and to hide, to keep oneself out of sight [CC/V]
táopǎo	逃跑	to escape, to flee, to steal away [CC/V]
táoshēng	逃生	to flee for one's life (=*táomìng*) [V-O]
táoshuì	逃稅	to evade tax [V-O]
táotuō	逃脫	to succeed in escaping [VC]
táowáng	逃亡	to flee from home: *táowáng zài wài* [CC/V]
táoxué	逃學	to play truant: *Wǒ cónglái méi táoguo xué.* I have never played truant. [V-O]
táo zhī yāoyāo	逃之夭夭	to have escaped and is nowhere to be found
táozǒu	逃走	to run away [VC]
táozuì	逃罪	to escape from the law [V-O]

---

tǎochiú 討求   to ask, beg, demand [CC/V]

tǎofá 討伐   to make war on (country, rebels) to vindicate authority [CC/V]

tǎofàn 討飯   to beg for food: *tǎofànde*, a beggar [V-O]

tǎo fánnǎo 討煩惱   to ask for trouble

táohǎo 討好   to ingratiate oneself, to toady [V-O]

tǎo jià huán jià 討價還價   to haggle over price

tǎojiào 討教   to seek instruction [V-O]

tǎo lǎopó 討老婆   to get a wife

tǎolùn 討論   to discuss [CC/V]; discussion

tǎo piányi 討便宜   to seek advantage: *Ràng tā tǎo ge piányi.* Let him get a bargain.

tǎoqián 討錢   to ask for money [V-O]

tǎoqiǎo 討巧   to try to get something for nothing [V-O]

tǎoqin 討親   to marry a wife [V-O]

tǎoqíng(r) 討情兒   to ask for leniency [V-O]

tǎoráo 討饒   to beg for pardon, forgiveness [V-O]

tǎo shēnghuó 討生活   to seek a living

tǎo tóulù 討頭路   to seek a job

tǎoxián 討嫌   to ask for unpleasant treatment: *tǎo rénxián*, to annoy people [V-O]

tǎo xífu 討媳婦   to get a wife

tǎoyàn 討厭   to incur dislike, to be annoying [V-O/SV]; to dislike [TV]

tǎozhàng 討賬   to ask for payment of debt [V-O]

zì tǎo kǔ chī 自討苦吃   to walk into trouble oneself

zì tǎo méi qù 自討沒趣   to do something that will result in a rebuke or embarrassment

提   *tí*

to carry or lift by hand, to mention, to promote

---

tíbǐ 提筆   to take up pen/to write: *Wǒ hěn jiǔ méi tíguo bǐ le.* I have not written for a long time. [V-O]

tíchū 提出   to bring up (opinion): *tíchū yìjian* [VC]

tídào 提到   to mention, refer to: *Shūshang tídào nǐ méiyou?* Does the book mention you? [VC]

tífáng 提防   to guard against (enemy attack): *tífáng dírén jìngōng* [CC/V]

tí gāng xié lǐng 提綱挈領 to give main outline (of facts, principles, etc.)

tígāo 提高   to elevate, to heighten (vigilance): *tígāo jǐngjué* [VC]

tígōng 提供   to contribute: *Zhège jiémù shì Fútè Gōngsī tígōng de.* This program is brought to you by the Ford Company. [CC/V]

tíkuǎn 提款   to withdraw money [V-O]

tíliàn 提煉   to refine, extract (oil, chemicals) [CC/V]

tímíng 提名   to nominate (person for election, awards, etc.) [V-O]

tíqilai 提起來   to lift up; mentioning (someone or something): *Tíqilai tāde nǚ'er jiù diào lèi.* At the mention of her daughter, she sheds tears.[VC]

tíqīn 提親   to bring up proposal of marriage [V-O]

tíqín 提琴   a violin [SC/N]

tíshén 提神   to refresh oneself, to put on one's guard [V-O]

tíshì 提示   to point out, to give advice (to younger people) [CC/V]

títóur 提頭兒 worth mentioning: *Zhège rén méi shénmo dà títóur.* This person is not worth talking a great deal about.

tí xīn diào dǎn 提心吊膽 to worry a great deal

tíxǐng 提醒   to remind, to alert [CC/V]

tíyào 提要   brief summary [VO/N]

tíyì 提議   to propose [V-O]; a proposal

tíyùn 提運   to transport [CC/V]

ěr tí miàn mìng 耳提面命 (teacher, parent) give personal advice constantly

調

diào (tiáo)
to transfer; to blend, to mediate

diàochá 調查	to investigate [CC/V]
diàodòng 調動	to transfer (troops, personnel) [CC/V]; *diàobúdòng*, cannot transfer [VC]
diào hǔ lí shān 調虎離山	to lure tiger to leave mountain/to lure enemy out of position
diàorén 調人	to transfer (someone) to a new post [V-O]
diàoshēng 調升	to transfer and promote [CC/V]
diàozǒu 調走	to transfer away [VC]
tiáohé 調和	to blend (flavors), to mediate [CC/V]
tiáohuo 調貨	food ingredients (salt, pepper, etc.) [SC/N]
tiáojì 調劑	to set right proportions, to make adjustments: *Zhěngtiān gōngzuò, zhōumò dào xiāngxia qù wánrwanr, tiáojìtiaoji shēnghuó.* We work all day. We should go to the country for a change. [VO]
tiáojiě 調解	to mediate, to reconcile [CC/V]
tiáolòng 調弄	*tiáoxì*, to flirt, and *wánlòng*, to make fun/to make fun of; to play (musical instrument) [CC/V]
tiáopí 調皮	to be naughty, to be tricky
tiáoqíng 調情	to flirt with, to court [V-O]
tiáorén 調人	a mediator [SC/N]
tiáoting 調停	to settle dispute amicably [CC/V]
tiáowèi 調味	to blend flavors: *tiáowèipǐn*, seasoning [V-O]
tiáoxì 調戲	to flirt with (a girl) [CC/V]
tiáoxiào 調笑	to ridicule, to tease [CC/V]
tiáoyǎng 調養	to recuperate [CC/V]
tiáozhěng 調整	to make adjustment, to reorganize: *tiáozhěng gōngjiào rényuán dàiyù*, to make adjustments in salary and fringe benefits for civil servants and teachers [CC/V]
tiáozhì 調治	to receive medical treatment [CC/V]

tiàocáo 跳槽　to change profession (=*tiàoháng*) [V-O]

tiàochóng 跳蟲　flea [SC/N]

tiàochū huǒkēng 跳出火坑　to jump out of fire/to pull oneself out of a bad situation

tiàodòng 跳動　to jump about [CC/V]

tiàogāo 跳高　to do high jump [VC]

tiàoháng 跳行　to skip a line in reading; to change profession (=*tiàocáo*) [V-O]

tiào jiāguān 跳加官　scene to open opera performance, invoking blessings

tiào jǐng 跳井　to jump into well (to commit suicide) [V O]

tiàolán 跳欄　to jump hurdles [V-O]

tiào lóu 跳樓　to jump off a building [V O]

tiàosǎn 跳傘　to parachute [V-O]; a parachute; also *jiànglò sǎn*

tiàoshén(r) 跳神　to dance before the gods to exorcise evil spirits [V-O]

tiào shéng 跳繩　to skip rope [V O]

tiàoshī 跳蝨　flea [SC/N]

tiàotiao bengbeng 跳跳蹦蹦　to jump and skip about

tiàowǔ 跳舞　to dance [V-O]

tiàoyuǎn 跳遠　to do broad jump [VC/V]

tiàoyuè 跳躍　to jump, hop for joy [CC/V]

gǒu jí tiào qiáng 狗急跳牆　a desperate dog jumps over a wall/take desperate measures if pushed to the wall

xiàle yitiào 嚇了一跳　to give one a start (from fright)

xīn jīng ròu tiào 心驚肉跳　to be jumpy with fear

xīntiào 心跳　heart palpitates: *Wǒ yǒu diǎnr xīntiào.* My heart palpitates a little. [SP/V]

yǎnpí tiào 眼皮跳　eyelids twitch

tìngbiàn	聽便	to let someone have his own option [V-O]
tīngchāi	聽差	to serve as a servant [V-O]; a servant
tīngcóng	聽從	to obey, to heed [CC/V]
tīngguān	聽官	the sense of hearing [SC/N]
tīnghuà	聽話	to listen to someone's advice; to obey: *Zhège xiǎoháir bù-tīnghuà.* This child doesn't obey. [V-O]
tīnghòu	聽候	to await (arrival, decision, etc.) [CC/V]
tīngjian	聽見	to hear [VC]
tīngjiǎng	聽講	to hear said, to attend lectures [V-O]
tīngjué	聽覺	sense of hearing (=*tīngguān*) [SC/N]
tīngmìng	聽命	to let fate take its course [V-O]
tīngnéng	聽能	the power, function of hearing [SC/N]
tīng qí zìrán	聽其自然	to let things take their natural course
tīngqǔ	聽取	to listen and hear (opinion): *tīngqǔ yìjian* [CC/V]
tīngshěn	聽審	(of judge) to sit on a trial [CC/V]
tīngshū	聽書	to attend a recitation by storytellers [V-O]
tīngshuō	聽說	to hear, it is said [CC/V]
tìng tiān yóu mìng	聽天由命	to resign to fate, to be fatalistic
tīngtǒng	聽筒	earphone [SC/N]
tīngtou	聽頭	what is worth listening to
tīngwén	聽聞	to hear (story, news, etc.) [CC/V]
tīngxì	聽戲	to go to opera [V-O]
tīngxiě	聽寫	to listen and write/to dictate [CC/V]; dictation
tīngxìn	聽信	to listen and to believe [CC/V]; to wait for news, *tīngxìnr* [V-O]
tīngzhòng	聽眾	the audience [SC/N]

tíngbàn	停辦	to stop operation, to close up [VO]
tíngbó	停泊	to lie at anchor [VO]
tíngchē	停車	to stop driving, to park a car: *tíngchēchǎng*, parking lot [V-O]
tíngdang	停當	all set, all arranged [CC/SV]
tíngdiàn	停電	to stop electric supply [V-O]
tíngdùn	停頓	to bog down, to be at a standstill [CC/V]
tíngfù	停付	to stop payment [VO]
tínggōng	停工	to stop work [V-O]; a stoppage of work
tínghuǒ	停伙	to stop cooking [V-O]
tínghuǒ	停火	to cease fire (=*tíngzhàn*) [V-O]
tíngkān	停刊	to cease publication (of periodical) [V-O]
tíngkè	停課	to suspend classes [V-O]
tíngliú	停留	to stop over during journey, to delay for a rest [CC/V]
tíng qī zài qǔ	停妻再娶	to divorce wife and remarry
tíng shuǐ	停水	to stop water supply [V 0]
tíngtíng(r)	停停兒	by and by, after a while
tíngxué	停學	to give up schooling, to suspend schooling [V-O]
tíngyòng	停用	to stop using [VO]
tíngzhàn	停戰	to cease fire [V-O]; a cease fire, armistice
tíngzhí	停職	to suspend appointment, to dismiss [V-O]
tíngzhǐ	停止	to stop [CC/V]
tíngzhì	停滯	to be held up, to be blocked up [CC/V]
tíngzhu	停住	to come to a stop [VC]
bùtíngde	不停的	continuously: *bùtíngde dòng*, to move about continuously [Adv]

tōng
to get through, to master, to understand 通

tōngbiàn	通便	to help bowel movement [V-O]
tōngcái	通才	one who has received a liberal education [SC/N]
tōngchē	通車	through train or bus, to begin operation [V-O]
tōngdá	通達	to be well versed, experienced and understanding [CC/SV]
tōngfēng	通風	to ventilate; to send secret message [V-O]
tōngguò	通過	to go through; carried as a motion [VO]
tōnghóng	通紅	to flush red all over [SC/V]
tōngjiān	通姦	to commit adultery [V-O]
tōnglì hézuò	通力合作	to work together with everybody pitching in for a common cause
tōnglùn	通論	a general introduction (to a subject): *Zhèngzhìxué Tōnglùn*, A General Introduction to Political Science [SC/N]
tōngqì(r)	通氣	to be in touch with each other; to ventilate [V-O]
tōngrén	通人	profound scholar [SC/N]
tōngrong	通融	to relax or circumvent regulations to accomodate: *Qǐng tōngrong yixia*. Please make an accommodation. [CC/V]
tōngshāng	通商	to trade, to have commercial intercourse [V-O]
tōngshùn	通順	(of writing) good and clear [CC/SV]
tōngsú	通俗	to be common, popular [CC/SV]
tōngtōng	通通	all, altogether, entirely
tōngxìn	通信	to correspond: *Nǐ cháng gēn jiāli rén tōngxìn ma?* Do you correspond with your family often? [V-O]
tōngzhī	通知	to notify [CC/V]
bùtōng rénqíng	不通人情	to be unreasonable in dealing with people
shuōbutōng	說不通	cannot get (person) to understand or agree; (of argument) unconvincing: *Zhèyang shízài shuōbutōng.* This is really unconvincing. [VC]
Zhōngguó tōng	中國通	a China hand, an expert on China

同

tóngbān	同班	to go to the same class [V-O]; classmate
tóngbàn	同伴	companion [CC/N]
tóngbāo	同胞	brothers of the same mother; compatriots [VO/N]
tóngbèi	同輩	persons of the same generation [SC/N]
tóng bìng xiānglián	同病相憐	fellow sufferers (of same sickness) understand one another
tóngchuāng	同窗	to share the same window/schoolmate, classmate [V-O]
tóng chuáng yì mèng	同牀異夢	same bed different dreams/persons thrown together but having different problems or ambitions
tóngdào	同道	person of same belief or conviction [SC/N]
tóngděng	同等	to be equal, same [SC/V]
tóngfáng	同房	to share the same room [V-O]; roommate
tóng guī yú jìn	同歸於盡	to perish together
tóngháng(r)	同行兒	fellow craftsman, person of the same profession [SC/N]
tónghào	同好	same taste or hobby [SC/N]
tónghuà	同化	to assimilate [SC/V]
tónghuǒ	同夥	fellow worker in same shop, member of group or gang [SC/N]
tóngjū	同居	to live together, especially common law husband and wife [SC/V]
tóng liú hé wù	同流合污	to associate oneself with undesirable elements or trend
tónglùrén	同路人	fellow travelers
tóngqíng	同情	to sympathize; *tóngqíngxīn*, sympathy [SC/V]
tóngshì	同事	to work in the same firm; a colleague, coworker [V-O]
tóngxiāng	同鄉	a fellow provincial, a person from the same area [VO]
tóngxíng	同行	to travel together [SC/V]
tóngxué	同學	to go to the same school; a schoolmate [V-O]

tóng
to share, together, in common

同

tóngzhì 同志 comrade [SC/N]

tóng zhōu gòng jì 同舟共濟 people in the same boat help each other in distress

bùtóng 不同 to be different [SC/SV]

偷

tōuān 偷安　　　to get by without trying [VO]

tōu gōng jiǎn liào 偷工減料. (contractors) to save illegally on materials and labor

tōu hànzi 偷漢子 =*tōurén* [V O]

tōu jī mò gǒu 偷鷄摸狗 to steal chickens and dogs/small burglar

tōukàn 偷看　　　to watch without permission, to peep [SC/V]

tōukòng(r) 偷空　　to manage a little time (to do something): *tōukòngr kàn péngyou*, to manage a little time to see friends [V-O]

tōulǎn(r) 偷懶　to be idle or negligent at work [V-O]

tōu lóng zhuǎn fèng 偷龍轉鳳　　to steal a dragon and replace with a phoenix/ to steal a male child and substitute a female child

tōuqiǎo 偷巧　　to do something as a shortcut [V-O]

tōuqiè 偷竊　　to steal [CC/V]; a thief, thievery

tōuqíng 偷情　　to have illicit relations with men or women [V-O]

tōurén 偷人　　(of women) to have illicit relations with men (=*tōu hànzi*) [V-O]

tōushēng 偷生　　to live on without meaning or purpose [VO]

tōushuì 偷稅　　to evade tax, to smuggle [V-O]

tōu tiān huàn rì 偷天換日 to steal heaven and replace the sun/ audacious scheme of cheating people

tōutōur(de) 偷偷兒地 stealthily [Adv]

tōuxí 偷襲　　to make a surprise attack [SC/V]

tōuxián 偷閒　　to spare a few moments from work to do something else [VO]

tōuyǎnr 偷眼　　to steal a hole/to act like a Peeping Tom [VO]

tōuyíng 偷營　　to steal camp/to attack a camp at night [V-O]

tōuzuǐ 偷嘴　　to steal mouth/to steal food, to eat without permission [V-O]

xiǎo tōur 小偷兒 a petty thief [SC/N]

tuī
to push, to promote, to make excuse

推

tuī bō zhù làng 推波助浪 to follow and hasten movement of waves/ to aggravate dispute by third party

tuībúdiào 推不掉 can't shove off (duty) [VC]

tuīcè 推測 to calculate, to conjecture [CC/V]; a conjecture

tuī chén chū xīn 推陳出新 to make renovations

tuīcí 推辭 to decline (offer) [CC/V]

tuīdǎo 推倒 to push down, to overthrow [VC]

tuīdòng 推動 to move by pushing, to initiate [VC]

tuīduàn 推斷 to predict [CC/V]

tuīgù 推故 to give as reason or pretext [VO]

tuī jǐ jí rén 推己及人 to place oneself in another's place/to do to others what you would do to yourself

tuījiàn 推薦 to recommend [CC/V]

tuī lái tuī qù 推来推去 to push back and forth; to make all sorts of excuses

tuī páijiǔ 推牌九 to play dominoes

tuīqiāo 推敲 to try to find out, to weigh words [CC/V]

tuīràng 推讓 to yield to others [CC/V]

tuītóu 推頭 to push the head/to cut the hair [V-O]

tuī xián yú néng 推賢與能 to select the capable and put them in power

tuīxiǎng 推想 to imagine, to reckon [CC/V]

tuīxiè 推卸 to evade, to shove off (duty): *tuīxiè zérèn* [CC/V]

tuī xīn zhì fù 推心置腹 to show the greatest consideration or confidence, to treat someone as oneself

tuīxuǎn 推選 to elect [CC/V]

bàn tuī bàn jiù 半推半就 (of women) half refusing and half yielding

shùn shuǐ tuī zhōu 順水推舟 to go with the current, to take advantage of favorable trend

152

tuōbìng	託病	to use sickness as excuse [V-O]
tuōcí	託辭	to make excuse [CC/V]; an excuse [SC/N]
tuōérsuǒ	託兒所	a day nursery
tuōfú	託福	to have blessings: *Tuō nǐde fú* or *tuōfútuōfú*. All because of your blessings. [V-O]
tuōfu	託付	to entrust: *Bǎ zhèjiàn shì jiù tuōfu gei nǐ le.* I will entrust this matter to you. [CC/V]
tuōgù	託顧	to entrust orphan to someone's care [V-O]
tuōgù	託故	to use some pretext: *tuōgù búqù*, will not go on pretext [V-O]
tuōguǎn	託管	trusteeship [CC/V]
tuōmèng	託夢	(spirit of deceased) appear in a dream to give a message [V-O]
tuōmíng	託名	to do something in someone's name, to assume false name [V-O]
tuōqíng	託情	to ask someone to put in a nice word for one [V-O]
tuō rén	託人	to entrust someone [V O]
tuōshēn	託身	to take abode in some place [V-O]
tuōshēng	託生	to be reincarnated: *Tā shì niú tuōshēng de.* He was reincarnated from an ox. [VO]
tuō yǐ tā cí	託以他詞	to evade by making excuses
tuōyùn	託運	to have something shipped [CC/V]
bàituō	拜託	to request (of someone): *Bàituō nǐ yíjiàn shì.* Please do one thing for me. *Bàituō bàituō!* Thanks! [CC/V]
shòu rén zhī tuō	受人之託	I am entrusted (with something by someone)
wěituō	委託	to commission (someone), to ask someone to be reasonable for something: *wěituō háng*, a second-hand shop [CC/V]

wán'àn 完案   To close a case at court [V-O]

wánbèi 完備   to be complete, well provided: *Zhège xuéxiàode yíqiè dōu hěn wánbèi.* This school is well equipped in every respect.[CC/SV]

wánbì 完畢   to come to an end, to end: *Gōngzuò wánbì.* The work has been finished. [CC/V]

wánchéng 完成   to complete (project, mission, etc.): *wánchéng rènwù*, to complete mission [CC/V]

wándàn 完蛋   done for

wángōng 完工   to complete work: *Wǒmende chúfáng, shénmo shíhou wángōng?* When is our kitchen going to be completed? [V-O]

wánhǎo 完好   complete and good/intact, not cracked [CC/SV]

wánhūn 完婚   to get married [V-O]

wánjié 完結   to close account; closed [CC/V]

wánjuàn 完卷   to finish an examination paper [V-O]

wánjùn 完竣   to be completed [CC/V]

wánle 完了   to have expired; to be done; It's finished! *Yíqiè dōu wánle!* an expression of despair after fire, flood, or defeat

wánmǎn 完滿   to be satisfactory, to be happy: *Hūnyīn hěn wánmǎn.* The marriage is satisfactory. [CC/SV]

wánměi 完美   to be happy; to be beautiful [CC/SV]

wánpiān 完篇   to complete a written piece [V-O]

wánqīng 完清   to clear off (account) [VC]

wánquán 完全   to be complete [CC/SV]; completely [Adv]

wánrén 完人   a perfect person [SC/N]

wánshàn 完善   to be perfect, excellent [CC/SV]

wánshì(r) 完事   to be done, (work) is finished [V-O]

wánshuì 完稅   to pay tax [V-O]

wánzhěng 完整   (=*wánhǎo*) [CC/SV]

玩　　　　　　　　　　　　　　　　　　　　　　　　　　　　　　　　*wán*
to play, to have fun with, to fool with

wán bǎxi 玩把戲 to play magic

wánfǎ 玩法　　　to juggle the law [V-O]

wánhào 玩好　　　favorite pastime, hobby [CC/N]

wánhū 玩忽　　　to ignore [CC/V]

wánhuà 玩話　　　a joke, an empty promise [SC/N]

wánjù 玩具　　　toy [SC/N]

wánlòng 玩弄　　　to toy with, to play tricks on people: *wánlòng rén* [CC/V]

wán'ǒu 玩偶　　　a toy figurine [SC/N]

wánr 玩兒　　　to play, to amuse oneself: *Tā shì shuōzhe wánr de. Nǐ búyào rènzhēn.* He was joking. Don't take it seriously.

wánr gǔpiào 玩兒股票 to buy stocks as a side investment

wánr huāyàngr 玩兒花樣兒 to play tricks: *Bié wánr huāyàngr. lǎolǎoshishíde zuò zuì hǎo.* Don't play tricks. It is best to do it honestly.

wánrhuǒ 玩兒火　to play with fire, to do something dangerous [V-O]

wánrmìng 玩兒命　to do something that endangers life [V-O]

wánr nǚren 玩兒女人 to enjoy women

wánr pái 玩兒牌　to play cards [V O]

wán(r)piào 玩票　to sing Chinese opera as amateur, to sing without pay [V-O]

wánshǎng 玩賞　　to enjoy (flowers, moon, etc.) [CC/V]

wán shì bù gōng 玩世不恭 to live dangerously or in defiance of conventions

wánshuǎ 玩耍　　to play to relax [CC/V]; relaxation, pastime

wánwèi 玩味　　to appreciate slowly (a profound saying, etc.) [CC/V]

wánwù 玩物　　things for people to enjoy or play with [SC/N]

wánxiào 玩笑　　something done for fun: *kāi wánxiào*, to play jokes upon (person) [CC/N]

wányìr 玩意兒　a toy, something interesting, a trifle

---

wǎngcháng 往常   usually, in the past: *Wǎngcháng tā bùhējiǔ.* Usually he doesn't drink. [CC/Adv]

wǎngchū 往初   formerly [CC/Adv]

wàngdōng 往東   towards the east: *wàngdōng zǒu*, to go towards the east [VO/Adv]

wǎngfǎn 往返   back and forth [CC/Adv]

wǎngfù 往復   repeatedly, back and forth [CC/Adv]

wǎnghòu 往後   henceforth; *wànghòu*, backward: *wànghòu zǒu liǎng bù*, to go backward a couple of steps [VO/Adv]

wǎnghuán 往還   back and forth; to have social dealings (with people): *Wǒmen chángcháng wǎnghuán.* We have social dealings quite often [CC/V]

wǎnglái 往來   to go and to come/to have social dealings [CC/V]; social intercourse: *Wǒmen méiyou wǎnglái.* We don't have any social intercourse.

wǎngnián 往年   in former years [SC/TW]

wǎngrì 往日   in former days: *Wǎngrì wǒ yǒu hěn duō péngyou.* In the past I had many friends. [SC/TW]

wǎngshí 往時   formerly [SC/TW]

wǎngshì 往事   things of the past: *Wǎngshì hái tí ta zuò shénmo?* Why do you still mention things of the past? [SC/N]

wǎngwǎng(r) 往往兒   oftentimes, frequently: *Tā wǎngwǎngr bǎ rén jìcuòle.* He often mixes people up. [Adv]

wǎngwǎng rú cǐ 往往如此 It is often like this.

gǔ wǎng jīn lái 古往今來   old go present come/all the time

jì wǎng bù jiū 既往不究 what is past do not blame/let bygones be bygones

láilái wǎngwǎng 來來往往   frequent social dealings; traffic is heavy: *Zhètiao lùshang láilái wǎngwǎngde chēzi zhēn duō.* This road has many cars driving back and forth.

wàng chén mō jí 望塵莫反 to see the dust but can't reach/to fall far behind

wàng fēng dǎo 望風倒 to see the wind and fall/unable to maintain one's determination

wàng fēng zhuǎn duò 望風轉舵 to watch the wind and turn the rudder/to be an opportunist

wàng méi zhǐ kě 望梅止渴 to look at plums to quench thirst/imagined satisfaction.

wàngxiāngtái 望鄉台 terrace in hell where deceased can see their homes in the distance

wàng yǎn yù chuān 望眼欲穿 wishing eyes about to bore through/to hope for something earnestly

wàng yáng xīng tàn 望洋興歎 to see the ocean and sigh/to view with despair something difficult to do

wàngyuǎnjìng 望遠鏡 telescope, binoculars

wàng zǐ chéng lóng 望子成龍 to hope one's son becomes a dragon/to hope one's son becomes a high official in the government

wàng zǐ chéng niú 望子成牛 to hope one's son becomes an ox/to hope one's son works hard or becomes a worker (PRC)

wàngzú 望族 respected clan [SC/N]

juéwàng 絕望 to despair, to give up hope [V-O]

míngwàng 名望 *míngyù*, reputation, and *rénwàng*, prestige [CC/N]

pànwàng 盼望 to long for, to hope for [CC/V]

qīwàng 期望 expectation [CC/N]

rénwàng 人望 *wéirén*, as a person, and *shēngwàng*, reputation [CC/N]

shēngwàng 聲望 *míngshēng*, reputation, and *rénwàng*, prestige [CC/N]

shīwàng 失望 to give up hope, to be disappointed [VO/SV]

wúwàng 無望 to be hopeless [VO]

xīwàng 希望 to hope [CC/V]

yuànwàng 願望 *xīnyuàn*, wish, and *xīwàng*, hope [CC/N]

157

---

wěiguò 委過　　to shift blame [VO]

wěijī 委積　　to accumulate, to pile up [CC/V]

wěi juě bú xià 委決不下 to delay decision

wěi mí bú zhèn 委靡不振 to be weak

wěimìng 委命　　to entrust to fate, to take fatalistic attitude [VO]

wěipài 委派　　to appoint (someone): *Zhèngfǔ wěipài shéi qu tánpàn?* Who is going to be sent by the government to negotiate? [CC/V]

wěiqì 委棄　　to abandon, to cast away on the ground [CC/V]

wěiqū 委屈　　to wrong (someone): *wěiqū nǐ le*, to have wronged you [CC/V]; injustice, grievance: *Nǐde wěiqū wǒ zhīdao*. I know your grievances.

wěi qū qiú quán 委曲求全 to stoop in order to accomplish something, to do the best possible under the circumstances.

wěirèn 委任　　to appoint (someone to a post) [CC/V]; also used for a lower grade in Chinese civil service as in *wěirèn guān* or *zhí*, a post in the *wěirèn* grade

wěishí 委實　　really (not bad): *wěishí búcuò*; truthfully (confess): *wěishí zhāogōng* [Adv]

wěisuǒ 委瑣　　being a stickler for forms, details

wěituō 委託　　to entrust (person, task): *wěituō nǐ tì wǒ zuò yíjiàn shì*, to entrust you to do one thing for me [CC/V]

wěiwǎn 委婉　　to be tactful in telling the truth that may hurt: *Tā huà shuōde hěn wěiwǎn, yàoburán zěnmo chīdexiāo.* He spoke very tactfully, otherwise how can the one spoken to have stood it? [CC/SV]

wěiwōzi 委窩子　 person fond of keeping to his bed

wěiyuán 委員　　a committee member; *wěiyuánhuì*, committee [SC/N]

wěizuì 委罪　　to shift blame [VO]

wēnbao	温飽	warm and full/to have enough to wear and eat [CC/N]
wēncun	温存	to be kind and attentive: *wēncún huàr*, comforting words
wēndai	温帶	temperate zone [SC/N]
wēndu	温度	degree of temperature: *wēndùjì*, thermometer [SC/N]
wēn gu zhi xin	温故知新	to review the old and learn something new
wēnhé	温和	mild (weather): *qìhou wēnhé*; gentle (temperament): *píqi wēnhé* [CC/SV]
wēnhòu	温厚	*wēnhé*, gentle, and *hòudao*, generous [CC/SV]
wēn jiùqíng	温舊情	to renew old friendship, to talk over old times
wēnjū	温居	to give a house-warming party [VO]
wēnkè	温課	to review lessons, from *wēnxí gōngkè* [V-O]
wēnliáng	温良	*wēnhé*, gentle, and *shànliáng*, good [CC/SV]
wēnnuǎn	温暖	warm (sun, fellowship) [CC/SV]; warmth: *rénjiān wēnnuǎn*, warmth between people
wēnqíng	温情	warm feeling [SC/N]
wēnquán	温泉	hot springs [SC/N]
wēnróu	温柔	*wēnshùn*, obedient, and *róuhé*, gentle/gentle and affectionate (particularly between lovers) [CC/SV]
wēnróuxiāng	温柔鄉	love nest, a brothel
wēnshì	温室	hothouse [SC/N]
wēnshū	温書	to review lessons (in a book) [V-O]
wēnshùn	温順	*wēnhé*, gentle, and *xiàoshùn*, filial/filial, obedient [CC/SV]
wēnwén	温文	*wēnhé*, gentle, and *wényǎ*, cultured/cultured in manners [CC/SV]
wēnxí	温習	to review [CC/V]
wēnyǎ	温雅	to be refined [CC/SV]
chóng wēn jiù mèng	重温舊夢	to relive an old dream/to have a reunion with lover

159

---

wèn'ān 問安　　to ask about health, to give greeting: *Tā yào wǒ xiàng nǐ wèn'ān.* He asked me to remember him to you.[V-O]

wèn cháng wèn duǎn 問長問短　to ask all sorts of questions

wèndá 問答　dialogue: *wèndá tí,* question and answer topics in examination [CC/N]

wèndǎo 問倒　to stymie someone in questions: *Nǐ bǎ wǒ wèndǎole.* Your question stymied me.[VC]

wèn dào yú máng 問道於盲　to ask the way from a blind person/to approach the wrong person

wènhǎo 問好　to give greeting (=*wèn'ān*) [V-O]

wènhou 問候　to greet people: *Tā yào wǒ wènhou nǐ.* He asked me to remember him to you. [CC/V]

wènhuà 問話　to ask questions [V-O]; a question

wènmíng 問明　to find: *Zhèjian shì yídìng děi wènmíng shì shéi gǎo de.* We must find out who did this. [VC]

wènshì 問世　to be published: *Nǐde shū shénmo shíhou wènshì?* When is your book going to be published? [V-O]

wèntí 問題　questions, problems [SC/N]

wèn xīn wú kuì 問心無愧　to have no regrets upon self-examination/to feel at ease

wènxùn 問訊　to inquire [VO]; *wènxùnchù,* information desk

wènzhu 問住　(=*wèndǎo*) [VC]

wènzuì 問罪　to condemn, to sentence [V-O]

bù chǐ xià wèn 不恥下問　(Confucius) was not ashamed to ask from common people

bù wén bú wèn 不聞不問　neither ask nor hear/to show no interest in

bú wèn hǎo dǎi 不問好歹　without first asking about what happened

fǎngwèn 訪問　to interview and study (person, country)

rù jìng wèn jìn 入境問禁　to ask about taboos and bans upon entering a foreign country

xǐbǐ	洗筆	to wash the brush [V O]; a small water container for painting, also *bǐxǐ*
xǐchén	洗塵	to wash off the dust/to give a welcome dinner to friend on return from a trip [VO]
xǐchéng	洗城	to wash the city/to kill everybody in the city [V-O]
xǐ ěr bùwén	洗耳不聞	to wash one's ears not to listen/to shut one's ears to happenings around him
xǐ ěr gōng tīng	洗耳恭聽	to wash one's ears to listen respectfully/to listen respectfully
xǐlǐ	洗禮	baptism: *Tā jīntian shòu xǐlǐ le.* He received baptism today. [SC/N]
xǐ'nǎo	洗腦	to wash brain/to brainwash: *Tā bèi xǐ'nǎo le.* He was brainwashed. [V-O]; brainwash
xǐpái	洗牌	to wash the cards/to shuffle the cards [V-O]
xǐ shǒu	洗手	to wash hands; to leave the gang and reform: *Tā xǐ shǒu bú gàn le.* He has reformed himself and doesn't do that anymore. To go to the toilet [V O]
xǐshuā	洗刷	to wash and brush; to clear one's name of criminal charges [CC/V]
xǐtóu	洗頭	to wash head/to shampoo [V O]
xǐ xīn gé miàn	洗心革面	to wash one's heart and to change one's face/to reform: *Tā yǐjing xǐ xīn gé miàn búzài zuò huài shì le.* He has reformed and does not do anything bad anymore.
xǐxuě	洗雪	to right a wrong, to clear charges [CC/V]
xǐyǎn	洗眼	to wash eyes/to watch attentively [V-O]
xǐyuān	洗冤	to right a wrong [V-O]
tiào dào Huáng Hé xǐbùqīng	跳到黃河洗不清	to jump into the Yellow River and not be able to wash oneself clean/impossible to clear oneself of charges even with the water of the Yellow River
xuě xǐ quán cūn	血洗全村	to bathe the whole village with blood/to kill everybody in the village

161

xǐ'ài	喜愛	to like, to love (children, swimming, detective stories, etc.) [CC/V]
xǐbìng	喜病	joy sickness/pregnancy [SC/N]
xǐ chī lǎn zuò	喜吃懶做	to enjoy eating but lazy about work
xǐ chū wàng wài	喜出望外	to be pleased beyond expectation
xǐ dài gāo màozi	喜帶高帽子	to like to wear high hat/to enjoy vain compliments
xǐguǒ	喜果	eggs painted red to be presented to friends and relatives on birth of a child or on wedding [SC/N]
xǐhào	喜好	to love (sports, etc.) [CC/V]
xǐjiǔ	喜酒	wine served at wedding: *Shénmo shíhou chī nǐde xǐjiǔ?* When (can we) drink your wedding wine?/When are you going to get married? [SC/N]
xǐ nù wú cháng	喜怒無常	joy and anger have no norm/to be unpredictable in mood: *Zhège rén xǐ nù wú cháng, búshì kū jiù shì xiào.* This person's mood is unpredictable. If he doesn't cry, he laughs.
xǐ qì yáng yáng	喜氣洋洋	to be filled with gayety
xǐshì	喜事	happy occasions (birthdays, weddings, etc.) [SC/N]
xǐ xīn yàn jiù	喜新厭舊	to like the new and dislike the old/to abandon the old for the new
xǐ zhú yán kāi	喜逐顏開	to beam with happy smiles
bàoxǐ	報喜	to report on birth of a son, getting a degree, promotion, etc. [V-O]
dàoxǐ	道喜	to congratulate: *Tā shēngguānde shì, nǐ gěi tā dàoguoxǐle meiyou?* Concerning his promotion, have you congratulated him? [V-O]
gōngxǐ	恭喜	to congratulate [VO/TV]; Congratulations! (usually in reduplicated form: *gōngxǐ! gōngxǐ!*
hàixǐ	害喜	to show symptoms of pregnancy (morning sickness) [V-O]
huān tiān xǐ dì	歡天喜地	to be overjoyed

xiàbǐ	下筆	to set down pen on paper/to write [V-O]
xià běnqián	下本錢	to put up capital
xià bù liǎo tái	下不了台	cannot find a way out of an embarrassing situation: *Tā dāngzhe nèimo duō ren kāi wǒde wánxiào. Zhēn jiào wǒ xià bù liǎo tái.* He made fun of me in front of so many people, it caused unending embarrassment for me.
xiàdàn	下蛋	to lay eggs [V-O]
xià dìngyì	下定義	to give a definition: *Qǐng nǐ gěi mínzhǔ xià ge dìngyì.* Please define democracy.
xiàfàng	下放	to reassign from urban to rural areas (PRC) [SC/V]
xià fēijī	下飛機	to disembark a plane
xià gōngfu	下功夫	to put forth effort: *Bùguǎn zuò shénmo shì dōu děi xià gōngfu.* No matter what one does, he has to put forth effort.
xiàguō	下鍋	to put raw food into cooking pan [V-O]
xiàhǎi	下海	to put out to sea; to get into a profession from status as amateur [V-O]
xiàhuò	下貨	to unload the goods [V-O]
xiàjiǔ	下酒	to go with wine: *Zhèixie dōu shì xiàjiǔde hǎo cài.* These are all good dishes with wine. [V-O]
xià juéxīn	下決心	to take a firm resolve
xiàlèi	下淚	to shed tears: *Wǒ nánguòde dōu xiàlèi le.* I felt so bad that I cried. [V-O]
xià pìnshū	下聘書	to send a letter of appointment
xiàqí	下棋	to play chess [V-O]
xiàshǒu	下手	to start (work, to take action) [V-O]
xiàtái	下台	to get off stage (theatrical or political): *Wǒmende zhōuzhǎng shénmo shíhou xiàtái?* When does our governor get off the stage (leave office)? [V-O]
xià xiāng	下鄉	to go to the country [V O]
xiàzuo	下作	to be low and contemptible [SC/SV]

xiànchǎng 現場 location of what actually happened: *Chūle shì qiānwàn bié gǎibiàn xiànchǎng*. When something happened, by all means, don't change anything on the spot. [SC/N]

xiànchéng(r) 現成兒 ready-made, immediately available: *chī xiànchéngr fàn*, to have a living without doing any work; *shuō xiànchéngr huà*, to speak with stock phrases [SC/Adj]

xiàn chī xiàn zuò 現吃現作 to prepare food as it is ordered (col. pron. *xuan*)

xiànchu(lai) 現出來 to show, to reveal: *Máobìng xiànchulaile*. The defects have been revealed. [VC]

xiànkuǎn 現款 cash: *Nǐ yǒu duōshao xiànkuǎn?* How much cash do you have? [SC/N]

xiànnòng 現弄 to show off [CC/V]

xiànrèn 現任 incumbent: *Shéi shì xiànrèn shìzhǎng?* Who is the incumbent mayor? [SC/Adj]

xiàn shēn shuō fǎ 現身說法 to set an example by one's own conduct, to appear personally (at meetings, etc.)

xiànshí 現實 practical, realistic: *Zhège rén zhēn xiànshí a*. This person is really practical. [CC/SV]

xiànshì 現勢 current situation: *guójì xiànshì*, current international situation [SC/N]

xiànshìbào 現世報 retribution in present life: *Lǎo Wángde qīzi pǎole yòu sǐle érzi. Nà cái zhēn shì xiànshìbào ne*. Lao Wang's wife ran away and his son died. That is really a retribution in his present life. Also, *xiànbào*

xiànxià 現下 =*xiànzài* [SC/TW]

xiànyǎn 現眼 to make a fool of oneself: *Nǐ qǐng huíqu ba. Bié zài xiànyǎn le*. Please go back. Don't make a fool of yourself any longer. [V-O]

xiàn yòng xiàn mǎi 現用現買 to buy as one needs for the day (col.pron. *xuàn*)

xiànzài 現在 at present, the present: *Dào xiànzài wéi zhǐ wǒ hái méi kànjian tā ne*. Up to the present, I have not seen him. [SC/TW]

xiànzhuàng 現狀 status quo: *wéichí xiànzhuàng*, to maintain status quo [SC/N]

xiànbǎo 獻寶	to present valuables/to show off one's valuables [V O]
xiàncè 獻策	to offer a plan or strategy (=*xiànjì*) [V-O]
xiàncí 獻辭	to offer a dedication speech [V-O]; a dedication speech, a written dedication
xiànchǒu 獻醜	(self-depreciating) to reveal awkwardness/to present a show or performance [V-O]
xiànfú 獻俘	to present prisoners of war to emperor or commander [VO]
xiàngōng 獻功	to report one's accomplishment, contributions, etc. [V-O]
xiànjì 獻計	to present a plan or strategy [V-O]
xiàn jìcè 獻計策	to offer a plan or strategy (=*xiànjì*, *xiàncè*)
xiànjié 獻捷	to announce victory [VO]
xiànjiǔ 獻酒	to offer wine [V-O]
xiànmèi 獻媚	to curry favor, to fawn upon, to cater to: *Tā jiù huì xiàng shàngsī xiànmèi.* The only thing he knows how to do is to curry favor from his superior. [VO]
xiànshēn 獻身	to dedicate oneself to (cause, career, etc.): *Zhōng Shān Xiānsheng xiànshēn gémìng rénrén pèifú.* Dr. Sun Yat-sen dedicated himself to the revolution. Everyone admires him. [V-O]
xiàn yīnqin 獻殷勤	to offer attentive hospitality to a superior: *Yǒu xiē rén búkào běnshi kào xiàn yīnqin shēngguān.* Some people depend on offering attentive hospitality rather than their ability to get promotions.
xiànzèng 獻贈	a contribution (of gift or ideas): *Zhè shì wǒ duì guójia de xiànzèng.* This is my contribution to the country [CC/N]
xiànzhuō 獻拙	=*xiànchǒu* [V-O]
fèngxiàn 奉獻	to offer, to contribute (to church, superior) [CC/V]
gòngxiàn 貢獻	to contribute: *Qǐng nǐ gòngxiàn yìdiǎnr yìjiàn.* Please offer some suggestions. [CC/V]; contribution: *Tā zuòle hěn duō duì guójia yǒu gòngxiàn de shìqing.* He has done a lot of things which were beneficial (a contribution) to the country. [CC/N]

想

xiǎngbìshi 想必是　　probably it is that...: *Xiǎngbìshi tā bìng le.* Probably it is that he is sick.

xiǎngdào 想到　　to think of: *Xiǎngdedào, zuòdedào.* If one can think of it, one can do it. [VC]

xiǎng fázi 想法子 to figure out a way: *Wǒmen děi xiǎng fázi jiù ta.* We have to figure out a way to rescue him.

xiǎngjiā 想家　　to think of home, to be homesick [V-O]

xiǎngjiàn 想見　　to visualize: *Tā xīnkǔde qíngxing kéyi xiǎngjiàn.* His difficult situation may be visualized; *xiǎng jiàn,* want to see (somebody) [CC/V]

xiǎngkāi 想開　　to put something out of mind: *Ní xiǎngkāile jiù bùnánguò le.* If you have put that matter out of your mind, you won't feel bad anymore. [VC]

xiǎnglái 想來　　I suppose: *Xiǎnglái wǒ zhēn bùyīnggāi.* I suppose I shouldn't have done it; *xiang lai,* want to come

xiǎng lái xiǎng qù 想來想去　　to turn over and over in one's mind: *Tā xiǎng lái xiǎng qù yě xiǎngbuchū ge fázi lai.* He has thought it over and over, but still can't figure out a way.

xiǎngniàn 想念　　to long for, to miss: *Tā hěn xiǎngniàn tā gēge.* He misses his brother very much. [CC/V]

xiǎngqilai 想起來 to think of, to recollect: *Xiǎngqi nàjian shì lai jiù shāngxīn.* Whenever I think of that matter, I feel sad. [VC]

xiǎngsībìng 想思病　　lovesick

xiǎngsǐle 想死了　　to be dying for (something) [VC]

xiǎng tōng 想通 to think through, to realize (what the matter is) [VC]

xiǎngtou 想頭　　worth thinking about: *Nèizhong shì hái yǒu shénmo xiǎngtou ne?* Is that kind of business worth thinking about?

xiǎngxiàng 想像　　to imagine: *Tā nàzhǒng jiòngpòde qíngxing shì kéyi xiǎngxiàngde dào de.* His embarrassment may be imagined. [CC/V]; imagination, an idea: *Zhè shì yíge bùkěsīyìde xiǎngxiàng.* This is an unthinkable idea; *xiǎngxiànglì,* power of imagination

yì xiǎng tiān kāi 異想天開　　a sudden fanciful thought: *Tā shì yì xiǎng tiān kāi, yìdiǎnr dōu bùshíjì.* Those are only fanciful thoughts, not a bit practical.

xiàngbèi 向背   toward or away from/for or against: *Rénxīnde xiàngbèi*, the public attitude for or against (a regime) [CC/N]

xiàngdangr 向當兒   means of livelihood, way out: *Yìdiǎnr xiàngdangr dōu méiyou*. There is no way to make a living, no way out.

xiànglai 向來   hitherto: *Tā xiànglai shì zhè yang de*. He is like this all the time [Adv]

xiàngnèi 向內   introvert [VO]

xiàngqián 向前   to press forward: *xiàngqián zǒu*, to go forward [VO/Adv]

xiàngrìkui 向日葵   sunflower

xiàngshàn 向善   to seek the good [VO]

xiàngshàng 向上   to strive upwards: *Bú xiàngshàng jiù huì dàotuì de*. If one does not strive upwards, he will go backward. [VO]

xiàng tā 向他   to take his side (in an argument): *Nǐ kě bié lǎo xiàngzhe tā shuōhuà*. You shouldn't speak in his favor all the time. [V O]

xiàngwǎn 向晚   toward evening [VO/TW]

xiàngxīn cí 向心詞   endocentric words

xiàngxīnlì 向心力   centripetal force

xiàngxué 向學   to be inclined to study: *nǔlì xiàngxué*, to study hard [VO]

xiàngyáng 向陽   to face south or the sunny side [VO]

xiàngyú 向隅   facing a corner or dead end/to be left out: *yǐmiǎn xiàngyú*, (hurry to buy) so that you will not miss the great chance

fāngxiàng 方向   direction [CC/N]

nèixiàng 內向   introvert [SC/SV]

xīn xīn xiàng róng 欣欣向榮   to be prosperous, (of plants) grow luxuriantly

yíxiàng 一向   =*xiànglai* [Adv]

yìxiàng 意向   meaning or intention [CC/N]

xiàngfa 相法　the art of face reading in fortune-telling [SC/N]

xiàng fu jiao zi 相夫教子 to assist husband and bring up children.

xiānggān 相干　to have something to do with: *Zhè shì yú nǐ háo bùxiānggān.* This has nothing to do with you. [SC/V]

xiàng jī ér dòng 相機而動 to watch for the right moment for action

xiàngmao 相貌　looks, personal appearance (also 像貌) [CC/N]

xiàngmiàn 相面　to practice physiognomy, to consult a physiognomist [V-O]

xiàngmìng 相命　to tell fortune [V-O]

xiàng nǚxu 相女婿 to look at prospective son-in-law for approval

xiàngpiàn 相片　photograph (also 像片) [SC/N]

xiàngqin 相親　to look over prospective bride [V-O]

xiāng qīn xiāng ài 相親相愛 to love each other dearly

xiàngshēngr 相聲兒 act of two performers with a witty dialogue: *shuō xiàng-shēngrde*, one who does this kind of act [VO/N]

xiàngshi 相士　a fortune-teller [SC/N]

xiàngxiázi 相匣子 a camera (also *zhàoxiàngjī*)

guàixiàng 怪相　strange, disgusting looks [SC/N]

jí rén tiān xiàng 吉人天相　God protects good people

nán rén běi xiàng 南人北相 a southerner with the looks of a northerner (considered a feature of a good person)

xiōngxiàng 兇相　face indicating violence, ill luck, or violent accidental death [SC/N]

zhàoxiàng 照相　to take pictures, to have picture taken: *Tiānqi zhème hǎo, wǒmen chūqu zhàoxiàng qu.* The weather is so good, we're going out to take some pictures. *Wǒ jīntian dào zhàoxiàng-guǎn qù zhàoxiàng.* I am going to the photo studio to have my picture taken today.[V-O]

zhēnxiàng 真相　real situation, the truth: *Zhēnxiàng dà míng.* The truth is completely revealed. [SC/N]

像   *xiàng*
                                      to resemble, to seem to, to be like

xiàngmào 像貌   a person's looks (also 相貌): *xiàngmào fēi fán*, to have a distinguished appearance [CC/N]

xiàng mú xiàng yàng 像模像樣   to be with airs of importance

xiàngpiàn 像片   photographs (also 相片)[SC/N]

xiàng shā yǒu jiè shì 像煞有介事   to be with airs of importance: *Bié xiàng shā yǒu jiè shì de yàngzi. Nà búshì shénmo liǎobuqǐ de shìqing.* Don't put on airs of importance. It's not anything important.

xiàngr 像兒   general appearance; a threatening look: *Gěi tā yíge xiàngr qiáo.* Let him see what it is like.

xiàng shénmo 像甚麼   What does it look like/What kind of business is this? *Chuān zhèyangde qí zhuāng yì fú xiàng shénmo?* What is it to wear such strange clothes!

xiàngshengr 像生兒   assumed airs: *Nǐ yòngbuzháo zuò zhèxie xiàngshengr le.* You don't need to put on this act.

xiàngshi 像是   It looks like, it seems: *Tā xiàngshi méitīngjian.* It seems as if he didn't hear it. [Adv]

xiàngyàngr 像樣兒   to be presentable: *Nǐ jīntian kě děi chuānde xiàngyàngr diǎnr.* You must dress properly today. *Zhèyang zuò hái xiàngyàngr.* It is presentable to do this way. [VO/SV]

búdà xiàng 不大像   not likely: *Nèijian shì tīngzhe búdà xiàng. Tā zuòbuchūlai.* That matter does not sound likely. He can't do that.

búxiànghuà 不像話   does not resemble language/to go too far, beyond the limit: *Lián fùmǔ dōu bù guǎn. Zhēn tài búxiànghuà.* (He) doesn't even take care of his parents. It's really too preposterous.

búxiàng rén 不像人   not like a person (derogatory expression): *Nǐ kàn tā. Sānfēn búxiàng rén, qīfēn dào xiàng guǐ.* Look at him. He is more like a ghost than a human being.

hǎoxiàng...(shide) 好像...似的   it seems: *Tā hǎoxiàng bìngle shide.* It seems he is sick.

yíxiàng 遺像   a portrait of a deceased person: *Zǒnglǐ yíxiàng*, a portrait of the late Director General (Dr. Sun Yat-sen) [SC/N]

---

xiāochú 消除   to abolish, to do away with (obstacles); to remove (preju- dice, bad habits, etc.) [CC/V]

xiāodú 消毒   to sterilize, to disinfect [V-O]

xiāofángduì 消防隊   fire brigade

xiāofèi 消費   to consume [CC/V]; expenditure: *Wùjià gāo, xiāofèi gēnzhe zēngjiā*. Prices go up; expenditures increase. *xiāofèipǐn*, consumer goods.

xiāohào 消耗   to consume: *Dà qìchē xiāohào qìyóu tài duō*. Big cars consume too much gasoline. [CC/V]; consumption.

xiāohuà 消化   to digest [CC/V]; digestion: *xiāohuà bùliáng*, indigestion

xiāohuǒqì 消火器   fire extinguisher

xiāojí 消極   to be negative, pessimistic (opposite to *jījí*, positive, optimistic) [SC/SV]

xiāomiè 消滅   to exterminate, to destroy [CC/V]

xiāomó 消磨   to while away: *xiāomó suìyuè*, to while away the years [CC/V]

xiāoqiǎn 消遣   to relax: *Mángle yìnián le, gāi xiāoqiǎnxiaoqian la*. Having been busy all year, we ought to relax a little now. [CC/V]; relaxation, pastime

xiāoshì 消釋   to vanish, to be forgotten [CC/V]

xiāoshòu 消瘦   emaciated [CC/SV]

xiāowáng 消亡   to perish [CC/V]

xiāoxià 消夏   to take a summer vacation: *Nǐ jīnnian dào nǎr qù xiāoxià?* Where are you going for summer vacation this year? [V-O]

xiāoxián 消閒   to be idol, to have leisure time [CC/SV]

xiāoyán 消炎   to decrease inflammation [V-O]

xiāoyè 消夜   to have a night snack [V-O]; night snack

xiāozhǒng 消腫   to decrease swelling [V-O]

chībùxiāo 吃不消   cannot take it: *Gōngzuò tài kǔ, chībuxiāo*. The work is too hard, (I) can't take it. [VC]

xiàobǐng 笑柄   butt or target of laughter, a laughing-stock [SC/N]

xiào diào dà yá 笑掉大牙   to laugh one's teeth out/extremely laughable

xiàohāhā 笑哈哈   to roar with laughter

xiàohua 笑話   a joke, pleasantry: *Gěi wǒmen shuō ge xiàohua.* Tell us a joke. [SC/N]; to laugh at: *Wǒ chàngde bùhǎo, qǐng bié xiàohua.* My singing is not good. Please don't laugh at me.[SC/V]

xiào lǐ cáng dāo 笑裏藏刀   knife behind smile/smile of treachery

xiào mà yóu rén 笑罵由人   to let others say what they like

xiàomiànhǔ 笑面虎   tiger with a smiling face/a wicked person: *Tā shì ge xiàomiànhǔ. Nǐ kě děi xiǎoxīn diǎnr.* He is a wicked person. You really must be a little more careful.

xiàoróng kě jú 笑容可掬   a face beaming with smile: *Kàn tā xiàoróng kě jú, shízài kěài.* Look at him. Beaming with smile, he is really lovable.

xiàosǐrén 笑死人   to shame one to death; to die from laughing [VC]

xiàotou 笑頭   something to laugh at

xiàoxīxī 笑嘻嘻   to smile happily

hāhādàxiào 哈哈大笑   to roar with laughter

jīxiào 譏笑   to deride, to make sarcastic remarks at [CC/V]

kāi wánxiào 開玩笑   to make fun of: *Bié lǎo kāi tāde wánxiào.* Don't make fun of him all the time. *Zhège wánxiào kě kāi dà le.* You went too far in making fun of him this time.

kěxiào 可笑   to be funny [SV]

kuángxiào 狂笑   to howl with laughter [SC/V]

kǔxiào 苦笑   to give a wry smile [SC/V]

lěngxiào 冷笑   to give a cold smile [SC/V]

qǔxiào 取笑   to make a laughing-stock of (someone): *Qǐngqiú nǐ. Bié qǔxiào wo le, hǎo ma?* I beg you. Don't make a laughing-stock of me, O.K.? [VO/TV]

wéixiào 微笑   to give a smile [SC/V]; a smile

xiěběn 寫本	a draft manuscript	
xiěbudé 寫不得	cannot be written, should not be written [VC]	
xiěfǎ 寫法	style of handwriting, penmanship [SC/N]	
xiěgǎo 寫稿	to compose a draft [V-O]	
xiěmíng 寫明	to write plainly, to set forth clearly [VC]	
xiěshēng 寫生	to draw after a model [VO]	
xiěshípài 寫實派	realistic school (as contrasted with romantic school)	
xiěxialai 寫下來	to write it down [VC]	
xiě xìn 寫信	to write a letter [V O]	
xiěxíng 寫形	to make a portrait [VO]	
xiěyì 寫意	Impressionist outlines [VO]; to be pleased in spirit, relaxed, contented [SV]	
xiězhàng 寫賬	to make entry in bookkeeping [V-O]	
xiězhào 寫照	a portrait, a portrayal (of conditions)	
xiězhēn 寫真	to portray (a person, character) [VO]	
xiě zì 寫字	to write (characters) [V O]	
xiězìr 寫字兒	to make a contract in writing: *Wǒmen děi xiě ge zìr cái xíng*. It won't do until we make a contract in writing [V-O]	
bǐxiě 筆寫	to write with a brush [SC/V]	
chāoxiě 抄寫	to copy by hand [CC/V]	
miáoxiě 描寫	to describe [CC/V]; a description	
shǒuxiě 手寫	to write by hand [SC/V]	
shūxiě 書寫	to write [CC/V]	
sùxiě 速寫	to sketch [SC/V]; a sketch	

172

信

xìn bǐ zhí shū 信筆直書 to write freely without hesitation

xìn bù sàn yóu 信步散遊 to roam about wherever the feet take one

xìncóng 信從 to believe and obey (God, His teachings, etc.) [CC/V]

xìnde 信得 to be believable: *Tāde huà xìnde.* His words are believable.

xìnfèng 信奉 to believe in and worship: *Nǐ xìnfèng shénmo jiào?* What religion do you believe in? [CC/V]

xìnkào 信靠 to trust, to rely on (God) [CC/V]

xìn kǒu cí huáng 信口雌黃 to make thoughless criticisms or accusations

xìn kǒu hú shuō 信口胡說 to talk nonsense

xìn kǒu kāi hé 信口開河 to say whatever comes to one's mind, to make careless remarks

xìnniàn 信念 faith [CC/N]

xìnrèn 信任 to trust, to place confidence in: *xìnrènzhuàng*, credentials

xìn shǎng bì fá 信賞必罰 awards and punishments rigorously carried out: *Zhège zhèngfǔ shì xìn shǎng bì fá. Fànzuìde yíge yě táobuliǎo.* This government carries out its awards and punishments rigorously. No criminal can escape punishment.

xìntú 信徒 follower, believer: *Hóngwèibīng dōu shì Máo Zé Dōng de xìntú.* The red guards are all followers of Mao Tze-tung.[SC/N]

xìntuō 信託 to entrust [CC/V]

xìnxīn 信心 faith, confidence: *Tā duì nǐ yìdiǎnr xìnxīn yě méiyou.* He doesn't have any confidence in you. [SC/N]

xìnyǎng 信仰 to believe in and worship [CC/V]; faith, belief

xìnyòng 信用 a person's trustworthiness, credit: *bùshǒu xìnyòng*, does not keep one's word [CC/N]

qīngxìn 輕信 to believe in whatever one is told [SC/V]

xiāngxìn 相信 to believe: *Wǒ xiāngxìn nǐ duì.* I believe you are right.
to believe in: *Wǒ xiāngxìn nǐ.* I believe in you. [SC/V]

zìxìn xīn 自信心 self-confidence

xíngbutōng	行不通	cannot be carried out [VC]
xíng buxíng	行不行	Is it all right?
xíngchéng	行程	itinerary [SC/N]
xíngchuán	行船	to sail a boat [V-O]
xíngfáng	行房	to have sexual intercourse [V-O]
xínghǎo	行好	to do a good deed [V-O]
xínghuì	行賄	to commit bribery [V-O]
xínglè	行樂	to enjoy oneself: *jí shí xínglè*, make merry while possible [V-O]
xínglù	行路	to walk [V-O]
xíngqī	行期	date of departure [SC/N]
xíngrén	行人	pedestrians [SC/N]
xíng rénqing	行人情	to fulfill social obligations (to give gifts, etc.), to return visits
xíngshàn	行善	to do a good deed [V-O]
xíng shī zǒu ròu	行屍走肉	walking corpse (used figuratively)
xíngwéi	行為	behavior: *xíngwéi kēxué*, behavior science [CC/N]
xíngxiào	行孝	to practice filial piety [V-O]
xíngxiōng	行兇	to commit violence [V-O]
xíngzǒu	行走	to go about [CC/V]
bùxíng	步行	to go on foot [SC/V]
fēngxíng	風行	to be well received (books): *fēngxíng quánguó*, well received all over the country [SC/V]
hángxíng	航行	to travel by plane or boat [SC/V]
lìxíng	力行	to proceed with determination [SC/V]
lǚxíng	旅行	travel: *lǚxíngshè*, travel service [CC/V,N]

休

xiū
to rest, to retire, to stop

xiūguài	休怪	don't blame somebody for: *Xiūguài tā bù bāngmáng*. Don't blame him for not helping you.
xiūhuì	休會	to adjourn a meeting [V-O]
xiūjià	休假	to take leave, to have a holiday, vacation [V-O]
xiūjiào tā pǎo le	休叫他跑了	Don't let him run away.
xiūkān	休刊	to discontinue publication (of a magazine, etc.) [V-O]
xiūkè	休克	(medical) shock [Transliteration]
xiūlǎo	休老	to retire from old age [VO]
xiūpà	休怕	don't be afraid
xiūqī	休妻	to divorce wife [V-O]
xiūxi	休息	to rest: *Nǐ lèi le ba? Hǎohāor xiūxixiuxi*. You must be tired. Take a good rest. [CC/V]
xiūxiá	休暇	holiday, days of rest
xiūxiǎng	休想	don't expect that: *Xiūxiǎng tā huì huí xīn zhuǎn yì*. Don't expect that he will change his mind.
xiūxué	休學	to withdraw from school [V-O]
xiūyǎng	休養	to rest and nourish [CC/V]
xiūyǎng shēng xí	休養生息	to nourish the people
xiū yào zhèyang	休要這樣	Don't be like this.
xiūyè	休業	to close up business, to have a recess [V-O]
xiūzhàn	休戰	to cease fire, armistice [V-O]
bàxiū	罷休	to forget it, to let off: *Nèijian shì tā hái bùkěn bàxiū*. Concerning that matter, he still won't forget it. [CC/V]
bùmián bùxiū	不眠不休	to go without sleep and rest
tuìxiū	退休	to retire from office: *tuì ér bùxiū*, retired but not rest/ work after retirement [CC/V]

175

xǔ
to allow, to give consent 許

xǔ buxǔ 許不許	Permit it or not?	
xǔhūn 許婚	to pledge daughter's hand in marriage [V-O]	
xǔjià 許嫁	to pledge daughter in marriage [V-O]	
xǔkě 許可	to permit [CC/V]; permission	
xǔkězhèng 許可證	license	
xǔle rénjia 許了人家	to have been engaged to someone	
xǔnuò 許諾	a promise [CC/N]	
xǔpèi 許配	=xǔhūn [VO]	
xǔpìng 許聘	=xǔhūn [VO]	
xǔ shēn bào guó 許身報國	to dedicate oneself to country's cause	
xǔyuàn 許願	to give pledge before God [V-O]	
xǔzì 許字	=xǔhūn [VO]	
jiāxǔ 嘉許	to praise, to show appreciation (for an inferior's work) [CC/V]	
mòxǔ 默許	to give silent consent [SC/V]	
qíxǔ 期許	to aim at a goal: *qíxǔ xué chéng huí guó*, to expect someone to complete his studies and return to his native land [CC/V]	
xīnxǔ 心許	to give her heart to someone [SC/V]	
yǐ shēn xǔ guó 以身許國	to dedicate oneself to country's cause	
yìngxǔ 應許	to promise, to assent to [CC/V]	
yǔnxǔ 允許	to allow: *Bàba bùyǔnxǔ ni qù.* Father won't allow you to go. [CC/V]	
zànxǔ 讚許	to praise (by a superior): *Tā gōngzuò hěn nǔlì. Shàngsi duì tā dàjiā zànxǔ.* He works hard. His superior greatly praised him. [CC/V]	
zìxǔ 自許	to make promise to oneself to become somebody: *yǐ jiù guó jiù mín de dà rèn zìxǔ*, to make a promise to oneself to take the great responsibility to save the country and the people.	

選

xuǎnbá	選拔	to select someone for promotion or special assignment [CC/V]
xuǎnchū	選出	to select, to elect [VC]
xuǎndú	選讀	to take an elective course: *Wǒ zhège xuéqī xuǎndú Yīngwén.* This term I'm taking English as an elective.[CC/V]
xuǎngòu	選購	to purchase selectively [CC/V]
xuǎnjǔ	選舉	to elect [CC/V]; election: *xuǎnjǔ quán*, right to vote
xuǎnměi	選美	to elect beauty/beauty contest [V-O]
xuǎnpài	選派	to select and appoint, to select and send: *xuǎnpài liúxué-shēng*, to select and send students to study abroad [CC/V]
xuǎnshǒu	選手	champion, chosen members (of athletic team) [SC/N]
xuǎnxiū	選修	to take an elective course (=*xuǎndú*) [CC/V]
xuǎnyòng	選用	to select and appoint to post: *Xiànzàide zhèngfǔ duō xǐhuan xuǎnyòng qīngnián.* Governments now mostly prefer to select youth for appointments. [CC/V]
xuǎnzé	選擇	to pick out, to choose: *Mǎi dōngxi dāngran yào xuǎnzé hǎode.* When buying things, one naturally picks the good ones. [CC/V]: choice: *Zhè jiā gōngsī de huò tài shǎo, méi shénmo xuǎnzé.* This company doesn't have many things. There isn't any choice.
xuǎnzhǒng	選種	to select seeds [V-O]; selected breeds, select quality (of tea, etc.) [SC/N]
xuǎnzhòng	選中	to pick out someone by choice or examination, to succeed in such examinations [VC]
hòuxuǎnrén	候選人	candidate for election
jìngxuǎn	競選	to run for elective office [VO]
kǎoxuǎn	考選	to select by examinations: *Gōngwùyuán duōbàn shì kǎoxuǎn lái de.* Civil servants are mostly recruited by examination.[CC/V]
luòxuǎn	落選	to fail in election: *Jìngxuǎnde rén duō, luòxuǎnde rén yě duō.* Many ran for election, and many lost in the election. [VO]
tiāoxuǎn	挑選	to pick [CC/V]
tuīxuǎn	推選	to recommend or elect for post: *Dàjia tuīxuǎn Lǎo Zhāng zuò dàibiǎo.* All elected Old Chang to be the representative[CC/V]

xuébushànglai 學不上來 cannot imitate, cannot learn [VC]

xué ér bújuàn 學而不倦 to enjoy learning without getting tired

xué ér búyàn 學而不厭 to enjoy learning without getting bored

xuéfēn 學分 credit hours: *Zhège xuéqī nǐ xuǎnle jǐge xuéfēn de kè?* This term, how many credit hours are you taking? [SC/N]

xuéfǔ 學府 institution of higher learning: *zuìgāo xuéfǔ*, highest institution of learning [SC/N]

xué guāi le 學乖了 to learn how to behave

xué huài le 學壞了 to learn from bad examples: *Zhè háizi zuìjìn xué huài le.* This child has been spoiled by bad examples recently.

xuéhuì 學會 a learned society: *Yǎzhōu Xuéhuì,* Association for Asian Studies [SC/N]; to master, to learn well [VC]

xuékē 學科 branch of study, discipline of study [CC/N]

xué lǐmào 學禮貌 to learn good manners

xuéqī 學期 school term (semester, quarter, etc.) [SC/N]

xuéshé 學舌 to repeat gossip, to carry tales (=*xuézuǐ*) [V-O]

xuéwèn 學問 knowledge, scholarship: *yǒu xuéwèn,* to be learned [CC/N]

xué wú zhǐ jìng 學無止境 Learning has no end.

xuéxí 學習 to learn (a subject), to learn from models: *Wǒmen dōu yīngdāng xiàng Lǎo Lǐ xuéxí.* We all ought to learn from Old Li. [CC/V]

xuézhě 學者 a scholar

xuézuǐ 學嘴 to repeat gossip, to carry tales (=*xuéshé*) [V-O]

bùxué wúshù 不學無識 not learned and unskilled

bùxué yǒu shù 不學有術 not learned but skilled (know how to get favor from superior)

kēxué 科學 science, to be scientific [SV]

qínxué 勤學 to be studious: *Zhè háizi qínxuéde bùdeliǎo.* This child is awfully studious. [SC/SV]

yǎnbiàn	演變	to develop: *Jiānglai zěnmo yǎnbiàn, shéi yě bùgǎn shuō*. No one dares to say how it will develop in the future. [CC/V]; development, change
yǎnchàng	演唱	to give a singing performance [CC/V]
yǎnchū	演出	to give a performance [VC]; a performance: *Zhèchǎng yǎnchū hěn jiàozuò*. This performance is very well received.
yǎnhuà	演化	to evolve, to develop [CC/V]; evolution, development: *yǎnhuà lùn*, theory of evolution
yǎnjiǎng	演講	to give a lecture [V-O]; a lecture, also *jiǎngyǎn*
yǎnjìn	演進	to make progress [CC/V]
yǎnjù	演劇	to give a stage performance [V-O]
yǎnshuō	演說	to give a lecture, to address the public [V-O]; a lecture, address
yǎnsuàn	演算	to do exercise in mathematics [CC/V]
yǎnxí	演習	to hold a military drill, to rehearse: *shídàn yǎnxí*, to hold a military drill with live bullets [CC/V]; a military drill
yǎnxì	演戲	=*yǎnjù* [V-O]
yǎnyì	演義	a historical fiction: *Sānguó Zhì Yǎnyì*, <u>The Romance of the Three Kingdoms</u>
yǎnyìfǎ	演繹法	deductive method (opposite *guīnàfǎ*, inductive method)
yǎnyuán	演員	actor, performer [SC/N]
yǎnzòu	演奏	to give a recital [CC/V]; *yǎnzòuhuì*, a concert
bànyǎn	扮演	to play (a certain role) [CC/V]
biǎoyǎn	表演	to perform on stage [CC/V]
cāoyǎn	操演	to do military exercise [CC/V]
dàoyǎn	導演	to direct (movie, play, etc.) [VO]; director
gōngyǎn	公演	public performance [SC/N]
shàngyǎn	上演	to present a performance [V-O]

yàobude 要不得	to be extremely bad: *Zhè háizi zhēn yàobude.* This child is really very bad.	

yàoburán 要不然   if not, otherwise: *Jīntiān xiàyǔ le. Yàoburán wǒ jiù qù le.* It is raining today. If not, I would have gone.

yàodào 要道   main route: *jiāotōng yàodào,* important route for transportation [SC/N]

yàodiǎn 要點   important points [SC/N]

yàofàn 要飯   to beg for food: *yàofànde,* a beggar [V-O]

yàohài 要害   vital part of the body, vital area of defense: *guófáng yàohài*

yàohǎo 要好   to be friendly to each other: *Liǎngge rén hěn yàohǎo.* The two are very friendly to each other. [VO/SV]

yàohuǎng 要謊   to ask fantastic price for haggling: *Nèijia shēngyi kàobuzhù, yàohuǎng yàode tài dà.* That business is not dependable. They ask fantastic prices. [V-O]

yàojǐn 要緊   to be important [CC/SV]

yàoliǎn 要臉   to care for "face" [VO/SV]

yàolǐng 要領   main themes, points of discussion: *bùdé yàolǐng,* unlucid [CC/N]

yàomìng 要命   to be terrible: *Chǎode yàomìng.* The noise is terrible. [V-O/SV]

yàoqiáng 要強   to want to be successful, to be ambitious [VO/SV]

yāoqiú 要求   to demand [CC/V]; a demand

yàoren 要人   important person, V.I.P. [SC/N]; *yào rén,* to demand the return of a criminal or hostage [V O]

yāoxié 要脅   to coerce by threat of force or other pressure: *Nǐ zǒngshì zhèyang yāoxié rén. Zhēn yàomìng.* You coerce people (me) like this all the time. It kills me.

yào zài 要在   the important thing is that...: *Xué wàiguóhuà, yào zài duōduō liànxí.* To learn a foreign language, the important thing is that one get a lot of practice.

yàozhàng 要賬   to ask for repayment [V-O]

yàozuǐchī 要嘴吃   to ask for food like a glutton

180

yǎngbìng 養病   to recuperate [V-O]

yǎngchéng 養成   to form (good habits, etc.): *Xíguàn yǎngchéngle jiù bùhǎo gǎile.* When a habit has been formed, it will be hard to change. [VC]

yǎng háizi 養孩子 to give birth to, and to raise, children [V O]

yǎng hàn 養漢   (woman) to keep a lover [V-O]

yǎng hǔ yí huàn 養虎貽患   to raise a tiger cub and regret it later

yǎnghuo 養活   to feed (a family): *kào xīnshuǐ yǎnghuo jiā*, to depend on salary to feed the family [VC]

yǎngjiā 養家   to support a family [V-O]

yǎnglǎo 養老   to support the old/to live on pension: *yǎnglǎo jīn*, old age pension

yǎngliào 養料   nutrition, feed for animals [SC/N]

yǎnglù 養路   to maintain roads [VO]

yǎngqīn 養親   to support and serve parents [V-O]

yǎngshēn 養身   to nourish the body: *Tā yǎngshēn yǒu dào, zǒngshì nàmo jiànkāng.* He has a way to nourish his body and is always so healthy. [VO]

yǎngshén 養神   to refresh by keeping quiet for a little while [V-O]

yǎng xiǎo lǎopó 養小老婆   to keep a mistress

yǎngxīn 養心   to cultivate mental calmness [V-O]

yǎngxìng 養性   to cultivate mental poise [V-O]

yǎngyù 養育   to bring up (children): *Búwàng fùmǔ yǎngyù zhī ēn.* Don't forget parents' kindness in bringing up one from childhood. [CC/V]

yǎngzǐ 養子   foster son [SC/N]

yǎng zūn chǔ yōu 養尊處優 to live a comfortable, well-fed life

fúyǎng 扶養   to take care of (the aged, sick) [CC/V]

péiyǎng 培養   to train (personnel): *péiyǎng réncái*, to train personnel [CC/V]

yìnjiàn 印鑑	copy of seal, name chop for verification [CC/N]	
yìnmó 印模	metal dice used for marking (trademarks, etc.) [CC/N]	
yìnní 印泥	Chinese ink pad (containing cinnabar and oil) [SC/N]	
yìnr 印兒	a trace, a scratch: *Zhuōzishang yǒu hěn duō yìnr.* On the table there are many scratches.	
yìnsè 印色	=*yìnní* [SC/N]	
yìnshuā 印刷	to print: *yìnshuāpǐn*, printed materials [CC/V]	
yìnxiàng 印象	impressions or reactions: *Nǐ duì tā de yìnxiàng hǎo buhǎo?* Is your impression of him good? *Bié gěi rén huài yìnxiàng.* Don't give people bad impressions.	
yìnxiàngpài 印象派	impressionist	
yìnxìn 印信	official seal [CC/N]	
yìnxíng 印行	to publish: *Shāngwù Yìnshūguǎn yìnxíng*, published by Commercial Press [CC/V]	
yìnzhāng 印章	a seal, name chop [CC/N]	
yìngzhèng 印證	to corroborate: *hùxiāng yìnzhèng*, to corroborate each other [CC/V]	
chóngyìn 重印	to make reprints [SC/V]	
fùyìn 複印	to duplicate [SC/V]	
gàiyìn 蓋印	to stamp seal on paper [V-O]	
jiǎoyìn 腳印	footprint [SC/N]	
shuǐyìn 水印	watermark [SC/N]	
xīn xīn xiāng yìn 心心相印	hearts and feelings find perfect response (of two lovers)	
zhǐyìn 指印	fingerprint [SC/N]	

yìngbiàn 應變   to respond to changing situation [VO]

yìngcheng 應承   to promise [CC/V]

yìngchou 應酬   to socialize, to engage in social parties [CC/V]; social parties

yìng duì rú liú 應對如流 to respond fluently

yìngfu 應付   to deal with (situation, person, etc.): *Zhèzhǒng júmiàn zhēn nán yìngfu.* This kind of situation is really difficult to deal with. [CC/V]

yìngjí 應急   to meet an emergency: *Xiān gěi ni diǎnr qián yìng ge jí.* (I'll) give you a little money first to meet your urgent need [V-O]

yìngjiē bùxiá 應接不暇 too many (affairs, visitors) to attend to

yìngjǐngr 應景兒 to do something for a special occasion: *Jīnnian wǒmen yě mǎi-le ge shèngdàn shù yìngying jǐngr.* We bought a Christmas tree this year for the occasion. [V-O]

yìngkǎo 應考   to register or take part in an examination [V-O]

yìng shēng chóng 應聲蟲   a yes man

yìngshí 應時   fashionable, to be in season (dress, food) [VO/SV]

yìngshì 應世   to deal with business or social affairs, to know how to deal with people [VO]

yìngshì 應試   =*yìngkǎo* [V-O]

yìngxǔ 應許   to promise, to approve [CC/V]

yìngyòng 應用   to apply: *yìngyòng kēxué*, applied science

yìngyuán 應援   to make move to help an ally (in battle) [VO]

yìngyǔn 應允   to promise, to consent [CC/V]

yìngzhàn 應戰   to meet challenge to battle [V-O]

yìng zhāo nǚláng 應召女郎 call girl

fǎnyìng 反應   to react [SC/V]; reaction

yǒu qiú bì yìng 有求必應 requests always granted

yòngbuzháo 用不着   there is no need to: *Nǐ yòngbuzháo qù.* You don't have to go. *Jīntian nǐ yòngbuzháo zhèiběn shū ba?* You're not going to use this book to day, are you? [VC]

yòng chá 用茶   to drink tea (more elegant than *hē chá*) [V O]

yòngchǎng 用場   usefullness [SC/N]

yòngchu 用處   use, practical application [SC/N]

yòngdù 用度   habit of spending money [SC/N]

yòngfǎ 用法   instructions (included in appliances, etc.) [SC/N]

yòngfèi 用費   expenses, fees [SC/N]

yònggōng 用功   to work hard (esp. at studies) [V-O]; to be studious, dilligent [SV]

yòng gōngfu 用功夫   to practice hard, to spend time on practice, also *xià gōngfu: Duì xuéwèn tā zhēn kěn yòng gōngfu.* As for knowledge, he is really willing to spend time on it.

yòngjì 用計   to adopt strategy, to play trick [V-O]

yòngjìn 用盡   to exhaust (efforts, etc.): *Suīran wǒ yòngjìnle lìliang bāng tāde máng, kěshì tā háishi bùmǎnyì.* Although I did everything to help him, he is still not satisfied. [VC]

yònglì 用力   to apply effort, to try best at [V-O]

yòng qián 用錢   to spend money [V O]

yòngqian 用錢   commission [SC/N]

yòng qíng bùzhuān 用情不專   cannot concentrate one's love on one person

yòng rén 用人   to handle personnel: *Búhuì yòng rén, jiù zuòbuhǎo xíngzhèng gōngzuò.* If one doesn't know how to handle personnel, he can't do well in administrative work. [V O]

yòngxīn 用心   to be attentive, to pay attention: *yòngxīn zuòshì,* to work attentively [VO]

yòngyì 用意   intention: *Yòngyì hěn hǎo, kěshi jiéguǒ fǎn'ér bǎ péngyou gěi dézuì le.* His intentions were good, but the result was that he offended his friend instead. [VO/N]

búyòng 不用   don't have to, there is no need to: *Búyòng kèqi.* There is no need to be polite.

yóudàng 遊蕩	to loaf, to indulge in pleasure [CC/V]	

yóudàng 遊蕩　to loaf, to indulge in pleasure [CC/V]

yóuguàng 遊逛　to take a stroll, to visit (temples, fairs, etc.) [CC/V]

yóuhún 遊魂　a homeless spirit; (fig.) somebody with a departing spirit, a listless person [SC/N]

yóujiē 遊街　to hold a street demonstration, to parade a criminal on the street [V O]

yóukè 遊客　a tourist [SC/N]

yóulǎn 遊覽　to tour: *yóulǎn chē*, a tourist car or bus [CC/V]

yóuláng 遊廊　a covered corridor (in a Chinese garden) [SC/N]

yóulè 遊樂　to have fun: *yóulèchǎng*, amusement park [CC/V]

yóulì 遊歷　to travel, to visit (particularly foreign countries) [CC/V]

yóu shǒu hào xián 遊手好閒　to be lazy

yóutǐng 遊艇　yacht, pleasure boat for hire [SC/N]

yóuwàn 遊玩　to play [CC/V]

yóuxì 遊戲　to play [CC/V]; amusement, games

yóuxì rénjiān 遊戲人間　fairies descending to earth and worldly pleasures; (fig.) world of fun and frolic

yóuxíng 遊行　to hold a street demonstration [CC/V]; a demonstration: *àiguó yóuxíng*, patriotic demonstration

yóuxìng 遊興　interest in sightseeing and travel: *Yóuxìng dà fā.* Interest in sightseeing becomes very strong. [SC/N]

yóuxué 遊學　to study abroad [V-O]

yóuyìhuì 遊藝會　a talent show

yóuyuánhuì 遊園會　a fun party

yóuzōng 遊蹤　places one has traveled [SC/N]

jiāoyóu 交遊　to make friends with: *Tā xǐhuan gēn wàiguorén jiāoyóu.* He likes to make friends with foreigners. [CC/V]; social connections: *Jiāoyóu hěn guǎng.* Social connections are very extensive.

---

yǒu bǎn yǒu yǎn 有板有眼 to be methodical, to be orderly

yǒu biānr le 有邊兒了 to take shape, to be hopeful: *Nèijian shì yǐjing shuōde yǒu biānr le.* The discussion on that matter is taking shape.

yǒu búshi 有不是 to be in the wrong, if something is wrong: *Yǒu búshi zhǎo wǒ.* If anything goes wrong, come to me.

yǒude 有的 some: *Yǒude qù, yǒude búqù.* Some go, some don't. *yǒude rén*, some people; *yǒude shíhou*, sometimes

yǒude shi 有的是 to have plenty of: *Tā yǒude shi qián.* He has plenty of money

yǒu dú 有毒 to be poisonous: *Xiǎoxīn! Zhège dōngxi yǒu dú.* Be careful! This thing is poisonous. [V O]

yǒufèn 有分 to have proper share [V-O]

yǒuhéng 有恆 to have persistence, to be persistent [VO/SV]

yǒuhòu 有後 to have progeny after death, opposite *wúhòu* without progeny [V-O]

yǒujìn 有勁 to be strong, energetic [VO/SV]

yǒulǐ 有理 to have reason, to be reasonable, to be justifiable: *Gémìng yǒulǐ.* Revolution is justifiable. [VO/SV]

yǒuliǎn 有臉 to have honor (face): *yǒuliǎnde rén*, person with good social status [V-O]

yǒu ménr 有門兒 to have door/to know the ropes, to be on the right track [VO/SV]

yǒuqíng rén 有情人 person who has affection/lover

yǒuqùr 有趣兒 to be interesting [VO/SV]

yǒu xián jiē jí 有閒階級 leisure class

yǒuxīn 有心 to have the intention to: *yǒuxīn rén*, a good hearted person [V-O]

yǒu xīnxiōng 有心胸 to have ambition

yǒu xīnyǎnr 有心眼兒 to be calculating

yǒuzhǔnr 有準兒 to be sure: *Nǐ yǒuzhǔnr néng chénggōng ma?* Are you sure you can succeed? [V-O/SV]

yuē
to make an appointment, to restrain

yuēdìng 約定 to agree (on date, meeting): *Wǒmèn yuēdìng míngtian kāihuì.* We agree to hold the meeting tomorrow. [VC]

yuē dìng sú chéng 約定俗成 (of language) something conventional, customary: *Yǔyán shì yìzhǒng yuēdìng sú chéng de dōngxi.* Language is a kind of conventional thing.

yuē fǎ sān zhāng 約法三章 to have a simple agreement with the people by a new government

yuēhuì 約會 an appointment: *Nǐmen yǒu méiyou yuēhuì?* Do you have an appointment? [CC/N]

yuējì 約計 to reckon roughly: *Zhèci lǚxíng yuējì děi shítiān.* This trip, to reckon roughly, needs ten days. [SC/V]

yuējù 約據 written agreement [SC/N]

yuēluè 約略 roughly: *yuēluè zhège shíhou*, about this time; *yuēluè bànniánde shíjiān*, roughly half a year's time [CC/Adv]

yuēmo 約莫 =*yuēluè* [Adv]

yuēqǐng 約請 to invite: *yuēqǐng péngyou lái chīfàn*, to invite friends for dinner [CC/V]

yuēshù 約束 to restrain, to control [CC/V]; discipline: *Tāmen jiā de xiǎoháir, yìdiǎnr yuēshù dōu méiyou.* So far as the children of their family are concerned, there is no discipline at all.

yuētóng 約同 to do together with: *Wǒmen yuētóng Lǎo Zhāng yíkuàir qù wánr.* We will get Old Chang to go with us (for the fun). [CC/V]

héyuē 合約 peace treaty [SC/N]

hūnyuē 婚約 marriage agreement [SC/N]

jiùyuē 舊約 the Old Testament [SC/N]

lìyuē 立約 to make an agreement [V-O]

méngyuē 盟約 treaty of alliance [SC/N]

qìyuē 契約 deeds, commercial agreement [CC/N]

tiáoyuē 條約 treaty: *bùpíngděng tiáoyuē*, unequal treaties [CC/N]

xīnyuē 新約 the New Testament [SC/N]

yuèchū 越出   to exceed: *yuèchū fànwéi*, to exceed the limits [VC]

yuèděng 越等   to overstep one's proper rank [V-O]

yuè duō yuè hǎo 越多越好 the more the better

yuèfā 越發   more and more: *Tā zhǎngde yuèfa hǎokàn le.* She grows prettier and prettier. [Adv]

yuèfèn 越分   to over step propriety [V-O/Adj]

yuèguǐ 越軌   to be out of bounds: *yuèguǐ xíngwéi*, rude behavior [V-O]

yuèguò 越過   to surpass, to cross over, to cross

yuèjí 越級   to go over the head of immediate supervisor [V-O]

yuèjiè 越界   to cross the border (=*yuèjìng*) [V-O]

yuèjìng 越境   to cross the border (=*yuèjiè*) [V-O]

yuè lái yuè máng 越來越忙 to get busier and busier

yuèlǐ 越禮   to overstep propriety, indecorous [V-O]

yuèqī 越期   to pass the time limit: *Jiè shū yuèqī yào fá qián de.* When borrowed books are overdue, there will be a fine. [V-O]

yuèquán 越權   to exceed one's power [V-O]

yuèyě sàipǎo 越野賽跑 crosscountry race

yuèyù 越獄   to escape from prison [V-O]

chāoyuè 超越   to stand above: *Tāde chéngjī chāoyuè rènhé rén.* His achievement stands above all others'. [CC/V]

yuèzhòng 越重   to exceed the weight limit, from *yuèguò zhòngliang* [V-O]

yuè zǒu yuè kuài 越走越快 the more one walks, the faster one gets

yuè zǔ dài páo 越組代庖   kitchen assistant taking the place of the chef/to do what is not in one's department

在

zàicháo 在朝   (of politicians) to be in power: *zàicháo dǎng*, party in power [VO]

zàiháng 在行   to be an expert in some field: *Tā duì guǎnjiā zhēn zàiháng.* She is an expert in housekeeping. [VO/SV]

zàihu 在乎   to attach importance to: *Tā shuō wǒ shénmo wǒ yě búzàihu.* I don't care what he says about me.

zài nǐ shēnshang 在你身上   to be on your body/to depend on you: *Zhèjian shì néngbuneng chénggōng wánquán zài nǐ shēnshang le.* It depends completely on you whether this matter will succeed or not.

zàishì 在世   to be alive: *Wǒ fùmǔ dōu hái zàishì.* My parents are both alive. [VO]

zài suǒ bùmiǎn 在所不免   to be unavoidable (one of those things)

zàitáo 在逃   to be at large [VO]

zàiwài 在外   to be away from home; to be excluded: *Xiǎozhàng zàiwài.* Tips are not included.

zàiwàng 在望   to be within sight, within reach [VO]

zài wǒ kàn 在我看   in my opinion: *Zài wǒ kàn, yídìng bùxíng.* In my opinion, it is definitely unsatisfactory.

zàixiān 在先   to be first, formerly [VO]

zàixīn 在心   to be attentive: *Zhèjian shì nǐ kě děi zàixīn zuò a.* You must pay special attention to this matter. [VO]

zàixué 在學   to attend school [VO]

zàiyě 在野   (of politicians) to be in opposition: *zàiyě dǎng*, opposition party [VO]

zàiyì 在意   to be careful, to be attentive, to mind [VO]

zàizhí 在職   to be in active service [VO]

búzàiyì 不在意   to be unconcerned: *Nǐ shuōle bàntiān, tā yìdiǎnr yě búzàiyì.* Although you talked for a long time, he didn't pay any attention to it.

móu shì zài rén, chéng shì zài tiān 謀事在人,成事在天   Plan as one may, success depends on luck.

zào
to build, to produce, to make 造

zàobào 造報	to compile report on funds expended [V-O]	

zàofǎn 造反　to revolt, to rebel: *Zàofǎn wúzuì*. To rebel is not a crime; (of children) to be noisy: *Háizi zàofǎnle*. The children are too noisy. [V-O]

zàofǎng 造訪　to pay a visit to [CC/V]

zàofú rénqún 造福人群 to benefit the masses

zàohuà 造化　fortune, blessings: *Nǐde zàohuà kě bùxiǎo*. Your blessings are many.

zàojiù 造就　to help somebody to succeed in life: *zàojiù réncái*, to help train personnel [CC/V]; accomplishments

zàojù 造句　to make sentences [V-O]

zàojù 造具　to compile (reports, tables, etc.) [CC/V]

zàolín 造林　to afforest [V-O]

zàoniè 造孽　to do evil, to do something detestable [V-O]

zàoxiàng 造像　to make a statue [V-O]; a statue, a portrait

zàoyì 造詣　to visit with, to call on [CC/V]; scholastic attainments: *Wáng Xiānsheng zài shùxué fāngmiàn de zàoyì hěn gāo*. Mr. Wang's attainments in mathematics are very high.

zàozuì 造罪　to sin (against gods) [V-O]

chéngzào 承造　to enter into a contract to build [CC/V]

chuàngzào 創造　to create [CC/V]

gǎizào 改造　to reform, to reshape, to remodel [CC/V]

jiànzào 建造　to construct [CC/V]

niēzào 捏造　to fabricate, to invent (stories, alibi) [CC/V]

rénzào sī 人造絲 artificial silk

wěizào 偽造　to falsify, to forge [SC/V]

xiūzào 修造　to repair [CC/V]

zhìzào 製造　to manufacture [CC/V]

zēngbīng	增兵	to reinforce, to send more troops [V O]
zēngchǎn	增產	to increase production [V-O]
zēngdà	增大	to enlarge, to swell [VC]
zēngduō	增多	to become more [VC]
zēngfáng	增防	to increase the defense: *Díren zài nǎr zēngfáng?* Where is the enemy increasing its defense? [V-O]
zēngguāng	增光	to add honor, luster: *Nǐde qiányán gěi wǒde shū zēngguāng bùshǎo.* Your foreword adds much luster to my book.[V-O]
zēnghuī	增輝	to add luster, brightness of the presence of a person [VO]
zēngjiā	增加	to increase, to add to: *zēngjiā fùdān*, to increase burden; *rénkǒu zēngjiā*, population increases [CC/V]
zēngjià	增價	to increase the price, to appreciate in value [V-O]
zēngjiǎn	增減	increase and decrease, fluctuation [CC/N]
zēngjìn	增進	to develop (skills, technical knowledge, etc.), to cultivate (friendship), to improve (relations, mutual understanding, etc.) [CC/V]
zēngjù	增劇	to increase in severity: *bìngqíng zēngjù.* The illness becomes more severe. [VO]
zēngqiáng	增強	to reinforce, to become stronger [VC]
zēngshān	增刪	to edit, to emendate: *Biānjí yǒu zēngshān quán.* The editor has the right to emendate. [CC/V]
zēngsǔn	增損	increase or decrease, fluctuation [CC/N]
zēngtiān	增添	=*zēngjiā* [CC/V]
zēngyì	增益	to add something to the original stock [VO]
zēngyuán	增援	to reinforce [V-O]
zēngzhǎng	增長	to grow, to increase: *zēngzhǎng zhīshi*, to increase knowledge [CC/V]
zēngzhí	增值	to increase in value: *tǔdì zēngzhí shuì*, land increment tax [V-O]

zhǎn
to open up, to extend, to show

展

zhǎnbài 展拜　to kowtow [SC/V]

zhǎnchì 展翅　to open wings [V-O]

zhǎnhuǎn 展緩　to postpone [CC/V]

zhǎnjì 展技　to show one's skill [V-O]

zhǎn juàn yǒu yì 展卷有益　It is beneficial to read (open a book)

zhǎnkāi 展開　to open up [VC]

zhǎnlǎn 展覽　to exhibit, exhibition [CC/V, N]

zhǎnméi 展眉　to look pleasant [V-O]

zhǎnmù 展墓　to visit a grave [V-O]

zhǎnqī 展期　to extend the time limit, to postpone: *Zhǎnlǎn zhǎnqìle.*
The exhibition has been extended. [V-O]

zhǎnsuò 展縮　flexibility [CC/N]

zhǎnwàng 展望　to look into the future; prospect, hope

zhǎnxiàn 展限　to extend time limit [VO]

zhǎnyàng 展樣　stately: *yòu zhǎnyàng yòu dàfang*, both stately and digni-
fied [SC/Adj]

zhǎnzhuǎn 展轉　to proceed amidst setbacks or by circuitous route; to
wander aimlessly or restlessly [CC/V]

dà zhǎn hóng tú 大展鴻圖　to put one's talents to use

dà zhǎn shēn shǒu 大展身手　to show one's capabilities

fāzhǎn 發展　to develop: *fāzhǎnzhōng guójiā*, developing countries [CC/V];
development: *Zhè shi yìzhǒng xīnde fāzhǎn.* This is a new
development.

jìnzhǎn 進展　to make progress: *Méi shénmo jìnzhǎn.* There has not been any
progress. [CC/V]

kāizhǎn 開展　to be open-minded [CC/SV]; to develop [V]

站

zhànbān 站班	to stand on duty, to line up: *Mǎi dōngxi děi zhànbān. Shòubuliǎo.* One has to stand in line when buying things. It is unbearable. [V-O]
zhànbuzhù 站不住	cannot hold position: *Zhèyang zuòxiaqu shì zhànbuzhù de.* If this continues, (we) can't hold our position. [VC]
zhàndezhù jiǎo 站得住脚	to be able to stand on one's feet/to be tenable, convincing
zhàngǎng 站崗	to stand guard at a post: *Jīntian wǎnshang lún shéi zhàngǎng?* Whose turn is it to stand guard tonight? [V-O]
zhànkāi 站開	to stand aside, to move on: *Qìchē lái le. Qǐng zhànkāi diǎnr.* A car is coming. Please stand aside. [VC]
zhànlóng 站籠	(of criminal) to put in a cage and shown in public [VO]
zhàntái 站臺	railway platform [SC/N]
zhànwěn 站穩	to stand firmly: *Zhànwěn, xiǎoxīn shuāixialai.* Stand firmly. Be careful, you may fall. [VC]
zhànzhǎng 站長	stationmaster [SC/N]
zhànzhù 站住	to stand still; "Stop!" [VC]
búpà màn jiù pà zhàn 不怕慢就怕站	Don't be afraid of being slow, but fear standing still. *Búpà màn jiù pà zhàn. Měitiān duōshǎo zuò yìdiǎnr, zǒng yǒu zuòwán de shíhou.* Don't be afraid of being slow. If you do a little every day, one day you will finish.
chēzhàn 車站	railway or bus station [SC/N]
gōngyìngzhàn 供應站	supply station [SC/N]
jiāyóuzhàn 加油站	filling station [SC/N]
qǐzhàn 起站	start station [SC/N]
zhōngzhàn 終站	last station [SC/N]

---

zhāngběn 張本   a copy as model, a ground plan or outline for future reference

zhāngdà 張大   to open wide: *zhāngdà zuǐ*, to open mouth wider [RC]

zhāngdà qí cí 張大其詞 to exaggerate: *Shuōhuà bié zhāngdà qí cí*. When talking don't exaggerate.

zhāng dēng jié cǎi 張燈結彩   to hang up lanterns and silk festoons

zhānghuáng shí cuò 張皇失措   to be nervous, to lose mental control

zhāngkāi 張開   to open up or wide: *zhāngkāi yǎnjing*, to open eyes wide [VC]

zhāngkuáng 張狂   to be unruly, insolent [CC/SV]

zhāngkǒu 張口   to open mouth: *qián lái shēn shǒu, fàn lái zhāngkǒu*. When money comes, just extend your hands; when food comes, just open your mouth/to lead a very easy life. [V-O]

zhāng kǒu jié shé 張口結舌   tongue-tied

zhāngluo 張羅   to try to get (money, etc.) [CC/V]

zhāngshè 張設   to set up (tables, decorations, etc.) for occasions [CC/V]

zhāngtiē 張貼   to post (bills): *Bùzhǔn zhāngtiē*, Post no bills [CC/V]

zhāngwàng 張望   to look about or watch for (signs of enemy, etc.) [CC/V]

zhāngyáng 張揚 to make widely known: *Zhèjian shì qǐng bié zhāngyángchuqu*. Please keep this matter to yourself. [CC/V]

zhāng yá wǔ zǎo 張牙舞爪   to show one's fangs and claws/ready to fight

zhāngzuǐ 張嘴   to open mouth, to speak up: *bùhǎoyìsi zhāngzuǐ*, to feel embarrassed to speak up [V-O]

kāizhāng 開張   to open (shop): *dà kāizhāng*, grand opening [CC/V]

kuāzhāng 誇張   to boast [CC/V]

pūzhāng 鋪張   to embellish for showing off [CC/V]

xiāozhāng 囂張   to be unruly [CC/SV]

zhǔzhāng 主張   to advocate: *Tā zhǔzhāng nán nǚ píngděng*. He advocates that men and women should be equal. [CC/V]

找

zhǎo
to look for, to invite, to get the balance of change

---

zhǎobìng 找病　to invite trouble [V-O]

zhǎochǎng 找場　to try to save one's face [V-O]

zhǎochár 找碴兒　to pick quarrel: *Bié lǎoshi zhǎo wǒde chár.* Don't pick quarrels with me all the time. [V-O]

zhǎo chūlù 找出路　to look for a way out or for a job with a future

zhǎocuòr 找錯兒　to find fault [VO]

zhǎofèngzi 找縫子　to look for a crack/to look for an opening for attack, to look for a pretext [VO]

zhǎoluòr 找落兒　to look for a steady job [V-O]

zhǎomà 找罵　to ask for scolding: *Hǎohāo zuò, miǎnde zhǎomà.* Be careful with your work, or you will be asking for a scolding. [VO]

zhǎo máfan 找麻煩　to ask for unnecessary trouble: *Nǐ lǐ tā jiù shì zì zhǎo máfan.* Your bothering with him is to ask for unnecessary trouble for yourself.

zhǎo máobìng 找毛病　to find fault: *Tā zhuān xǐhuan zhǎo rénde máobìng.* He particularly enjoys finding fault with people.

zhǎo ménlù 找門路　to look for approach to an important person.

zhǎo miànzi 找面子　to try to save face [V O]

zhǎo qián 找錢　to give change: *Nǐ gěi wǒ zhǎo qián.* You give me change. *Wǒ zhǎogei nǐ qián.* I give you change [V O]

zhǎo shìr 找事兒　to look for job; to look for trouble [V O]

zhǎosǐ 找死　to look for death (contemptuous remark): *Nǐ lái zhǎosǐ.* This is your end (I warn you). [VO]

zhǎo tìshēn 找替身　to look for a substitute

zhǎotou 找頭　change due at a purchase

zhǎoxún 找尋　to search for, to look for [CC/V]

dōng zhǎo xī zhǎo 東找西找　to look for in all directions

yǒu shì zhǎo wǒ 有事找我　If anything happens look for me (I shall be responsible).

195

zhuó (zhāo, zháo, zhe)
to send, to put on, to put one's hand on

著（着）

zhāohuāng 著慌　to become nervous, tense: *línshí zhāohuāng*, to become nervous at the last moment. [V-O]

zháohuǒ 著火　to catch fire [V-O]

zhāojí 著急　to become anxious, agitated: *wèile háizide shì zhāojí*, to become agitated on account of children [V-O]

zhuólì 著力　to put forth effort (to do things): *Zhuólì zuò hái bùyídìng zuòde hǎo, nǎr gǎn tōulǎn ne?* Even when one puts forth an effort, he may not do it well. How can he loaf on it? [V-O]

zhuólìng 著令　to order [CC/V]

zhuóluò 著落　whereabouts: *Zhuóluò bùmíng.* Whereabouts are not known; settlement: *Nèijian shì, hái yìdiǎnr zhuóluò dōu méiyou ne.* So far as that matter is concerned, there has not been any settlement. [CC/N]

zhuómáng 著忙　to be in a hurry: *Zhèyixia tā kě zhuóle máng le.* At once he was in a hurry. [V-O]

zhuó rén qù bàn 著人去辦　to send someone to do it: *Nèijian shì kuài zhuó rén qù bàn ba.* Send someone to do that right away, won't you?

zhuósè 著色　to apply color: *Nǐde huàr zhuósè le meiyou?* Have you applied color on your painting? [V-O]

zhuóshí 著實　really, in earnest: *Zhèizhāng huà zhuóshí huàde búcuò.* This picture is really well done. [Adv]

zhuóshǒu 著手　to begin to (write, build, etc.): *Wǒ nèiběn shū hái méi zhuóshǒu xiě ne.* I haven't started writing that book of mine yet. [VO]

zhuóyì 著意　to give attention to (do something) [VO]

cāizháole 猜著了　to have guessed correctly [VC]

dà chu zhuóyǎn, xiǎo chu zhuóshǒu 大處著眼，小處著手　to set one's eyes on big things, to lay one's hands on small things.

dǎzháo 打著　to succeed in hitting, to light (a match, lighter) [VC]

huǒ zháole 火著了　the fire begins to burn

qízhe lǘ xún lǘ 騎著驢尋驢　to find a donkey by riding one/before locating a new job, hold on to the present one.

shuìzháo 睡著　to fall asleep [VC]

196

zhàobàn 照辦　to do accordingly: *Nǐ fēnfu-xiàlai, wǒmen yídìng zhàobàn.* You tell us, and we will act accordingly. [CC/V]

zhàocháng 照常　as usual [VO/Adv]

zhàofu 照拂　to look after another's welfare: *Wǒde xiǎohái'r qǐng ni duōduō zhàofu.* Please take care of my children as much as you can. [CC/V]

zhàogu 照顧　to look after another's welfare, to attend to (patient, child, etc.) [CC/V]

zhàoguǎn 照管　to look after (house, children, etc.) [CC/V]

zhàohuì 照會　official communication, diplomatic note

zhàojìngzi 照鏡子　to look into the mirror [V-O]

zhàojiù 照舊　to be as before: *zhàojiù yǒuxiào,* to be valid as usual [VO/Adv]

zhàokàn 照看　=zhàogu [CC/V]

zhàolì 照例　according to precedence, regulations, etc.: *zhàolì miǎnfèi,* fees exempted according to regulations [VO/Adv]

zhàoliào 照料　=zhàofu [CC/V]

zhàomiàn'r 照面兒　to meet face to face: *Wǒ gēn tā méizhào ge miàn'r jiù zǒu le.* I left without seeing him face to face. [V-O]

zhàopiàn 照片　a photograph [SC/N]

zhàoshè 照射　to project light upon, to illuminate [CC/V]

zhàoxiàng 照相　to photograph [V-O]; a photograph: *zhàoxiàngjī,* camera

zhàoyàngr 照樣兒　to follow the pattern [V-O]; in the same manner [Adv]

zhàoyào 照耀　to illuminate, to shine in glory [CC/V]

zhàoyāojìng 照妖鏡　a mirror which reveals disguise of monster or demon

zhàoying 照應　to look after; to fit with (prophecy, original) [CC/V]

zhàozhǔn 照准　to give approval to request from inferior: *shēnqǐng zhàozhǔn,* request approved [SC/V]

guānzhào 關照　to look after [CC/V]

争

---

zhēngbà 争霸   to compete for hegemony among states [V-O]

zhēngbiàn 争辩   to argue: *gēn tā zhēngbiànle bàntiān*, argued with him for a long time [CC/V]

zhēngchǎo 争吵   to squabble, to quarrel [CC/V]

zhēngchí 争持   to wrangle, to contend: *zhēngchí búràng*, to contend without yielding [CC/V]

zhēngduó 争夺   to fight for possession (of land, power, woman, etc.) [CC/V]

zhēngdòu 争鬥   to fight [CC/V]

zhēng fēng chī cù 争風吃醋   fight for love, to quarrel for jealousy

zhēnggōng 争功   to fight for recognition of merit [V-O]

zhēngguāng 争光   to vie for honor: *tì guójiā zhēngguāng*, to win honor for the country [V-O]

zhēnglùn 争論   to argue [CC/V]; argument

zhēngmíng 争名   to fight for fame [V-O]

zhēngqì 争氣   to fight for emotional reasons, to be honor conscious: *Zhè háizi zhēn buzhēngqì.* This child is really disappointing; *zhēng kǒu qì*, to win some honor [V-O]

zhēngqiáng 争強   to compete for supremacy [VO]

zhēngqǔ 争取   to strive for, to fight for: *zhēngqǔ zuìhòu shènglì*, to fight for final victory; *zhēngqǔ péngyou*, to win friends [CC/V]

zhēng quán duó lì 争權奪利   to struggle for power and money

zhēng xiān kǒng hòu 争先恐後   in a mad rush to be first

zhēng xiánqì 争閒氣   to fight for vain or trivial reasons

zhēngzhí 争執   =zhēngchí [CC/V]

zhēngzuǐ 争嘴   to bicker, to squabble [V-O]

dòuzhēng 鬥争   to struggle [CC/V]; a struggle: *jiējí dòuzhēng*, class struggle (PRC)

jìngzhēng 競争   to compete, to contest [CC/V]; a competition, a contest

zhěngbiān	整編	to reorganize, to regroup (military) [CC/V]
zhěngdùn	整頓	to put to order, to restore to good shape: *zhěngdùn xué-fēng*, to restore good order in the school [CC/V]
zhěngfēng	整風	to rectify atmosphere (of schools, party, etc.), to restore morale [VO]
zhěnggèr	整個兒	whole piece [SC/N]; completely: *zhěnggèr kuǎle*, completely collapsed [Adv]
zhěngjié	整潔	to be clean and neat [CC/SV]
zhěnglǐ	整理	to put to order, to tidy up, to revise, to sort out (material for manuscript): *bǎ cáiliao zhěnglǐ-yixia xiě pian wénzhāng*. To sort out the material for writing an article. [CC/V]
zhěngqí	整齊	to be tidy, orderly, to be complete [CC/SV]; *zhěngzhengqiqi*, reduplication of *zhěngqí*

zhěnqí huà yī 整齊劃一 to be adjusted to uniformity (weights and measures)

zhěngrì(jia) 整日價 the whole day [SC/TW]

zhěng rì zhěng yè 整日整夜 whole day and night

zhěngróng	整容	to dress up, especially to shave [V-O]
zhěngshù	整數	a whole number, integral [SC/N]
zhěngsù	整肅	to purge [CC/V]

zhěng tā yixia 整他一下 to discipline him

zhěngtǐ	整體	the whole [SC/N]
zhěngtiān	整天	the whole day: *zhěngtiān wánr, yìdiǎnr shì yě búzuò*, to play all day, don't do any work [SC/TW]

zhěng yuànzi 整院子 to straighten out the yard [VO]; the whole courtyard [SC/N]

zhěngzhēng	整整	exactly: *zhěngzhēng shíkuài qián*, exactly ten dollars [Adv]
zhěngzhì	整治	to put to order, to teach a lesson, to punish: *zhěngzhì-zhengzhi ta*, to teach him a lesson [CC/V]

zhīchǐ 知恥   to have a sense of shame or of honor: *bùzhīchǐ*, to be shameless [VO]

zhī fǎ fàn fǎ 知法犯法   to flout the law deliberately

zhīgēnr 知根兒   to know the root/to be an expert [VO]

zhī guò gǎi guò 知過改過   to realize one's mistake and correct it

zhījǐ 知己   a bosom friend [VO/N]

zhī jǐ zhī běi 知己知彼   to know one's own and enemy's strength

zhījué 知覺   to perceive; perception [CC/V]

zhīmíng 知名   to be well-known [VO/SV]

zhī mìng zhī nián 知命之年   the year when one knows the decrees of Heaven/ fifty years of age

zhīqùr 知趣兒   to be tactful, to have a sense of the situation (know what is right for the situation): *Nèige rén bùzhīqùr*. That person is insensible. [VO/SV]

zhī rén zhī miàn bùzhī xīn 知人知面不知心 to know a man's exterior but not his heart

zhī rén zhī míng 知人之明   capacity to judge a person's qualities

zhīshi 知識   knowledge: *zhīshi fènzǐ*, intellectuals [CC/N]

zhīxīn huà 知心話   heart to heart talk: *Tā shuōde dōu shi zhīxīn huà*. What he said are all heartfelt words.

zhīyīn 知音   a good understanding friend [VO/N]

zhīyǒu 知友   a bosom friend [SC/N]

zhī yù zhī ēn 知遇之恩   gratitude for a superior's recognition and encouragement

zhīzú 知足   to be contented: *Zhī zú cháng lè*. One who is contented is always happy. [VO/SV]

wú suǒ bùzhī 無所不知   to know everything

yì wú suǒ zhī 一無所知   to know nothing

yì zhī bàn jiě 一知半解   to have superficial knowledge

zhǐbù 止步   don't go further: *Qǐng zhǐbù*. Please don't go any further (used by a departing guest when a host is accompanying him to the door.) *yóu rén zhǐbù*, visitors stop here/no admittance (sign in park) [V-O]

zhǐ tòng 止痛   to relieve pain: *shénmo yào zhǐ tòng zuì yǒuxiào?* What drug relieves pain most effectively? [V O]

zhǐtòngjì 止痛劑   pain reliever: *Asīpǐlíng shì zuì pǔtōngde zhǐtòngjì.* Aspirin is the most common pain reliever.

zhǐ xuě 止血   to stop bleeding [VO]

zhǐzhù 止住   stopped: *Xuě zhǐzhùle ma?* Has the bleeding been stopped? *Zhǐzhùle.* Yes, it has. [VC]

jiézhǐ 截止   to expire: *bàomíng hòutiān jiézhǐ.* Registration expires day after tomorrow. [CC/V]

jìnzhǐ 禁止   to forbid: *jìnzhǐ chōuyān*, no smoking [CC/V]

liú ge bùzhǐ 流個不止 to flow without stopping

shì kě ér zhǐ 適可而止 not to overdo it: *Fán shì shì kě ér zhǐ, búyào zuòde tài guòfèn le.* For anything, play it just right. Don't overdo it too much.

wàng méi zhǐ kě 望梅止渴 to stop the thirst by looking at the plums/wishful thinking

xīn rú zhǐ shuǐ 心如止水 mind as tranquil as still water/to refuse to be affected: *Tā xīn rú zhǐ shuǐ, bùguǎn nǐ zěnmo tiǎodòu yě búhuì dǎdòng ta de.* Her mind is so tranquil that you simply can't arouse her no matter how hard you try.

xué wú zhǐ jìng 學無止境 There is no end to learning.

zhōngzhǐ 中止   to stop halfway [SC/V]

zǔzhǐ 阻止   to obstruct: *zǔzhǐ qiánjìn*, to obstruct the advance [CC/V] zhǐbiāo 指標 an index sign; (mathematics) characteristic [SC/N]

zhǐchì 指斥 to censure, blame [CC/V]

zhǐdào 指導 to guide, to advise: zhǐdào jiàoshòu, major professor (adviser) [CC/V]

zhǐdiǎn 指點 to point out (mistakes, pitfalls), to advise [CC/V]

zhǐdìng 指定 to assign (date, person, etc.): Zhǔrèn zhǐdìng shéi jiù shì shéi. The person will be whoever the chairman assigns.[CC/V]

zhǐhuà 指畫 finger painting [SC/N]; to gesticulate with fingers [CC/V]

zhǐhuī 指揮 to direct (a choir, a battle, etc.), to conduct (a performance), to command (army) [CC/V]

zhǐjiào 指教 to instruct, to advise, to offer suggestions for revision (used courteously for opinion): Qǐng duōduō zhǐjiào. Please offer suggestions for improvement. [CC/V]

zhǐ jī mà gǒu 指鷄罵狗 to point to the chicken while scolding the dog/ to scold one by ostensibly pointing to the other

zhǐmíng 指名 to mention names (in accusations): zhǐmíng mà, to mention names in scolding [V-O]

zhǐnán 指南 a guide book [VO/N]

zhǐnánzhēn 指南針 a compass

zhǐ sāng mà huái 指桑罵槐 to point to the mulberry tree while scolding the locust tree/to scold one by ostensibly pointing to the other

zhǐshì 指示 to advise (inferior), to instruct [CC/V]

zhǐ shǒu huà jiǎo 指手畫脚 to gesticulate wildly

zhǐwàng 指望 to hope: zhǐwàng chénggōng, to look forward to success [CC/V]; hope: yǒu meiyou diǎnr zhǐwàngr? Is there any hope?

zhǐyǐn 指引 to guide: zhǐyǐn nǐ zǒushang dà lù, to guide you to get on the highway [CC/V]; guidance

zhǐzhé 指摘 to point out (fault) [CC/V]

shí shǒu suǒ zhǐ 十手所指 that which ten hands point to/target of public accusation

治

zhìān 治安   public security: *Zhège dìfangde zhìān hǎo buhao?* Is the public security here good? [CC/N]

zhìběn 治本   to effect basic reform, to give basic cure in medicine [V-O]

zhìbiāo 治標   to alleviate symptoms of disease or social ills without thorough cure [V-O]

zhìbìng 治病   to treat a patient [V-O]

zhìchǎn 治產   to manage property: *Tā zhèjǐnián zhìle bùshǎo chǎn.* These few years he has acquired quite a bit of property. [V-O]

zhìguó 治國   to rule a country [V-O]

zhìjiā 治家   to run a family [V-O]

zhìjīng 治經   to study classics [V-O]

zhìjūn 治軍   to train and command military forces [V-O]

zhìlǐ 治理   to rule, manage, put in order [CC/V]

zhìliáo 治療   to cure [CC/V]; a therapy: *jīngshen zhìliáo*, psychotherapy

zhìsāng 治喪   to manage, set up a funeral [V-O]

zhìshù 治術   statecraft, the art of government [SC/N]

zhì wénxué 治文學   to do research on literature

zhìxia 治下   under the jurisdiction: *zài shěng zhèngfǔde zhìxia*, under the jurisdiction of the provincial government

zhìxué 治學   to study: *zhuānxīn zhìxué*, to concentrate on studies [VO]

zhìzhuāng 治裝   to buy clothing and other things for a journey: *zhìzhuāng fèi*, allowance for purchasing clothing, etc. for foreign assignment [V-O]

zhìzuì 治罪   to punish: *zhì tāde zuì*, to punish him [V-O]

chǔzhì 處治   to dispose: *Tāde qǐngqiú yīngdāng rúhé chǔzhì?* How should his request be dealt with? to deal punishment to: *chǔzhì bùliáng shàonian*, to deal punishment to juvenile delinquents [CC/V]

tǒngzhì 統治   to rule (a country) [CC/V]

zìzhì 自治   self-governing, self-government; *dìfang zìzhì*, local autonomy [SC/N] *zhìcái* 制裁 to impose sanction on (aggressor), to bring under control: *zhìcái qīnlüè zhě*, to impose sanction on aggressors [CC/V]; sanction: *fǎlü zhìcái*, legal sanction

zhìdí 制敵 to subdue the enemy [VO]

zhìdìng 制定 to set up (rules, rites, etc.) [CC/V]

zhìfú 制伏 to subdue: *Tā lì dà rú niú, hěn bùróngyi zhìfú.* He is strong like a cow, not easy to subdue. [CC/V]

zhìlǐ 制禮 to set up rites and ceremonies [V-O]

zhìshèng 制勝 to overcome, to come out victorious [VO]

zhìxiàn 制憲 to write, establish constitution [V-O]

zhìyù 制慾 to restrain the passions [VO]

zhìzhǐ 制止 to stop (riot, strike, etc.): *Wúlǐde bàgōng yídìng yào zhìzhǐ.* Unreasonable strikes must be stopped. [CC/V]

zhìzuò 制作 creation (of art, music, etc.) [CC/N]

dǐzhì 抵制 to boycott: *dǐzhì yánghuò*, to boycott foreign goods [CC/V]

guǎnzhì 管制 to control: *guǎnzhì jiāotōng*, to control traffic [CC/V]; control: *jiāotōng guǎnzhì*, traffic control

jiézhì 節制 to control: *jiézhì shēngyù*, to practice birth control [CC/V]

jìnzhì 禁制 to forbid, to prohibit [CC/V]

xiànzhì 限制 to limit: *xiànzhì xíngdòng*, to limit activities [CC/V]; limits, restrictions: *Xuéxiàode xiànzhì tài duō.* The school has too many restrictions.

zhuānzhì 專制 to be tyrannical [SC/SV]

zìzhì 自制 self-restraint: *zìzhì nénglì*, ability to control oneself [SC/V]

助

zhùcí 助詞　(grammer) an auxiliary, grammatical particles [SC/N]

zhùchǎnshì 助產士　a midwife

zhùdòngcí 助動詞　(grammer) auxiliary verb

zhùjiào 助教　an assistant at college [SC/N]

zhùlǐ 助理　to assist [CC/V]; an assistant: *Tā shì wǒde zhùlǐ.* He is my assistant·

zhùlì 助力　help, a helping hand: *Zuótian wǒ mángjíle. Nǐ gěi wǒ de zhùlì zuì dà.* Yesterday I was extremely busy. The help you gave me was the biggest. [SC/N]

zhùmáng 助忙　to help (someone because he is busy): *Jīntian Zhāngjia bàn xǐshì. Línjū dōu lái zhùmáng.* The Chang family has a wedding today. All the neighbors came to help. [V-O]

zhùrén 助人　to help others: *Zhùrén wéi kuàilè zhī běn.* To help others is the source of happiness. [VO]

zhùshì 助勢　to give oral or moral support [V-O]

zhùshǒu 助手　an assistant [SC/N]

zhùwēi 助威　to give oral or moral support [V-O]

zhùxuéjīn 助學金　scholarship

bá miáo zhù zhǎng 拔苗助長　to help a plant grow by pulling/wrong approach to do anything

bāngzhù 幫助　to help [CC/V]

bǔzhù 補助　to subsidize [CC/V]; subsidy

nèizhù 內助　inside help/wife [SC/N]

tiān zhù zì zhù 天助自助　Heaven helps those who help themselves

xiāngzhù 相助　to help each other [SC/V]

zīzhù 資助　to help with money: *zīzhù tā chūguó,* to help him financially to go abroad

zìzhùcān 自助餐　self-help meal/buffet or cafeteria style meal

---

zhùbuxià 住不下   cannot accommodate: *Wūzi tài xiǎo, zhùbuxià zhème duō rén.* The room is too small to accommodate so many people. [VC]

zhùchù 住處   place where one lives [SC/N]

zhùhù 住戶   inhabitant, house [SC/N]

zhùjiā 住家   to stay at home, same as *zhùzai jiāli;* to live: *Nǐ zài nǎr zhùjiā?* Where do you live? [V-O]

zhùkǒu 住口   stop mouth/shut up! [V-O]

zhùrén 住人   to accommodate people: *Zhège dìfang néng zhùrén ma?* Is this place suitable for people to live in? [V-O]

zhùshǒu 住手   stop hand/stop! [V-O]

zhùsuǒ 住所   place where one lives (=*zhùchù*) [SC/N]

zhùxia 住下   to lodge: *Tiān wǎn le. Wǒmen zhùxia zài shuō.* It is getting late. Let's lodge here and then talk about it. [VC]

zhùxiào 住校   to live in a dormitory: *Xuésheng yǒude zhùjiā, yǒude zhùxiào.* Some of the students stay home, some stay in the dormitory. [V-O]

zhùzái 住宅   residence, house [SC/N]

zhùzhǐ 住址   address (location of residence) [SC/N]

zhùzuǐ 住嘴   Shut up! (=*zhùkǒu*) [V-O]

jūzhù 居住   to live: *Nǐ zài nǎr jūzhù?* Where do you live? [CC/V]

kàobuzhù 靠不住   to be unreliable: *Tāde huà kàobuzhù.* His words are not reliable. [VC]

liúzhù 留住   to ask guest to stay longer: *Tā jīntian yídìng yào zǒu. Wǒ zěnmo yě liúbuzhù.* He insists on leaving today. No matter what, I cannot get him to stay longer. [VC]

rěnzhù 忍住   to bear: *Zhèzhǒng wěiqū, nǐ yàoshi rěndezhù jiù bié gàosong ta.* Concerning the grievance, if you can bear it, don't tell him. [VC]

zhūazhu 抓住   to hold fast: *Yú tài huá, wǒ jiǎnzhí zhuābuzhù.* The fish is too slippery; I simply cannot hold it.

抓

zhuā dàtóu 抓大頭 a game of picking lines leading to covered numbers (for pooling money), in which the *dàtóu* pays more than others; to make a fool of someone: *Bié zhuā wǒde dàtóu.* Don't make a fool of me.

zhuā gōngfu 抓功夫 to steal time for idling

zhuāhuì 抓會 a club in which subscribers pay a certain amount monthly, the sum going to the person who shakes the best dice. [V-O/N]

zhuā jiēr mài kuài 抓尖兒賣快 to pay avid attention to someone to curry favor

zhuājiūr 抓鬮兒 to draw lots [V-O]

zhuākōng 抓空 to fail in an attempt [V-O]

zhuāpò liǎn 抓破臉 to scratch the face so that it bleeds,(figuratively) don't care about the matter of face: *Zhuāpòle liǎn, shénmo dōu búzàihu.* Without considering face, nothing matters.

zhuā rén 抓人 to arrest people: *Jǐngchá jìnlai zhuāle bùshǎode rén.* The police arrested many people recently. [V O]

zhuā shēngchǎn 抓生產 to catch up with production (PRC)

zhuāyǎng 抓癢 to scratch an itchy spot [V-O]

zhuā yào 抓藥 to fill a prescription (particularly in a Chinese herb shop) [V O]

zhuozhour 抓周兒 to test a child on his first birthday by placing different things around him. The item he grabs will indicate his future. [V-O]

zhuāzhu jīhui 抓住機會 to grab the opportunity

zhuǎnbiàn 轉變   to change: *zhuǎnbiàn fāngxiàng*, to change direction [CC/V]; a change: *Méiyou shénmo zhuǎnbiàn*. There is no change.

zhuǎndòng 轉動   to revolve (machine), to turn about (body) [SC/V]

zhuǎnhuán 轉圜   to go around, to save a situation by going about or speaking to someone: *Zhèjian shì jiǎnzhí méiyou zhuǎnhuánde yúdì*. About this matter, there is simply no way to do anything about it.

zhuǎnjī 轉機 a change for the better: *Tāde bìng yǒu diǎnr zhuǎnjī le*. His condition (physical) shows some improvement.

zhuǎnjià 轉嫁 to remarry [SC/V]

zhuǎnlù 轉錄   to reprint [SC/V]

zhuǎnmài 轉賣   to resell to a third party [SC/V]

zhuǎnniànjiān 轉念間   in a short while, before you know it [Adv]

zhuǎnràng 轉讓   to sell out, to transfer [SC/V]

zhuǎnshēng 轉生   to be born in next incarnation (as dog, donkey, another human being, etc.) [SC/V]

zhuǎnshǒu 轉手   to change hands, to pass on to another [V-O]; in a moment: *Tā zhuǎnshǒu jiù biànguà le*. He changes his mind so quickly. [Adv]

zhuǎnshùnjiān 轉瞬間   in the twinkling of an eye, quickly [Adv]

zhuǎntuō 轉託   to request through a third person [SC/V]

zhuǎnwān(r) 轉彎兒 to turn a corner, to make a turn, to drive around: *zhuǎnle yíge dà wānr*, to make a big round [V-O]

zhuǎnwānzi 轉彎子   to beat about the bush: *Bié zhuǎnwānzi mà rén*. Don't make oblique remarks. [V-O]

zhuǎnxiàng 轉向   to change directions [V-O]

zhuǎnxué 轉學   to transfer to another school: *zhuǎnxué-shēng*, transfer students (from *zhuǎnxuéde xuésheng*)

zhuǎnyǎn 轉眼 in the twinkling of an eye: *Tā zhuǎnyǎn jiù bújiàn le*. In the twinkling of an eye; he is nowhere. [VO/Adv]

zhuǎnyí 轉移 to change, to shift: *zhuǎnyí zhèndì*, to shift battlefield [SC/V]

重

zhòngdà 重大 to be important, to be serious: *Zérèn zhòngdà.* The responsibility is great. [CC/SV]

zhòngdì 重地 place of strategic importance: *Jūnshì zhòngdì, yóu rén zhǐ bù.* Place of military importance, please don't enter. [SC/N]

zhòngdiǎn 重點 important point: *Shuōhuà yào zhuādezhù zhòngdiǎn.* To speak, one must be able to grasp the important points. [SC/N]

zhòngfàn 重犯 key criminal, a person convicted of grave crime [SC/N]

zhòng gōngyè 重工業 heavy industry

zhònglì 重力 gravitation [SC/N]

zhònglì 重利 to place value on money [VO/SV]; big profit [SC/N]

zhòngliàng 重量 weight, substance: *Zhèpiān dōngxi yǒu zhòngliàng.* This article has real substance. [SC/N]

zhòngmíng 重名 great reputation [SC/N]; to place value on reputation [VO]

zhòngshēnzi 重身子 to be pregnant: *Tā xiànzài zhòngshēnzi chūbude mén.* She is now pregnant, cannot go out. [SC/SV]

zhòngshì 重視 to value (friendship, money, etc.) [SC/SV]

zhòngtīng 重聽 to be hard of hearing [SC/SV]

zhòngtóu xì 重頭戲 an opera that is difficult to perform: *Nà shì yìchū zhòngtóu xì.* That is an opera difficult to perform.

zhòngxiào 重孝 deep mourning for parents [SC/N]

zhòngxīn 重心 center for gravity [SC/N]

zhòngyā 重壓 heavy pressure [SC/N]

zhòngyào 重要 to be important [CC/SV]

zhòngyīn 重音 stress (of words) [SC/N]

zhòngzhèn 重鎮 important military base [SC/N]

zhòngzuì 重罪 a grave crime [SC/N]

zhēnzhòng 珍重 to take good care of one's health [CC/V]

zìzhòng 自重 to have self-respect [SC/V]

---

zhuāngbāo 裝包　to pack [V-O]

zhuāngbìng 裝病　to malinger [V-O]

zhuāngdìng 裝訂　to bind a book [CC/V]

zhuānghuang 裝潢　to furnish and decorate [CC/V]; furniture and decorations, handsome book-binding: *Zhèběn shūde zhuānghuang hěn bucuò.* The binding of this book is really good.

zhuānghuàngzi 裝幌子　to put up a false front, to put up a show to deceive [V-O]

zhuāngjiǎ 裝甲　to armor: *zhuāngjiǎ bùduì*, armored unit [VO]

zhuāngjiǎ 裝假　to pretend: *Tā jiù xǐhuan zhuāngjiǎ. Shéi zhīdao tā xīnli xiǎngde shi shénmo.* He enjoys to pretend. Who knows what is in his mind. [V-O]

zhuānglǎo 裝老　to pretend to be old [V-O]

zhuāng ménmiàn 裝門面　to put up a front

zhuāngpèi 裝配　to provide with accessories, to decorate [CC/V]

zhuāngqiāng 裝腔　to affect certain airs: *zhuāngqiāng zuòshì*, to assume airs of importance [V-O]

zhuāngshǎ 裝傻　to pretend to be stupid: *Tā xīnli míngbai biǎomiànr zhuāngshǎ.* He knows it but pretends to be ignorant. [V-O]

zhuāngshi 裝飾　to decorate [CC/V]; *zhuāngshipǐn*, jewelry and ornaments

zhuāngshù 裝束　attire [CC/N]

zhuāngsuàn 裝蒜　to assume airs, to put up a false show: *Tā shi shuǐxiān bùkāihuā, zhuāngsuàn.* He is like an unblooming narcissus, pretending to be garlic/He is just putting up a false show. [V-O]

zhuāngxiāng 裝箱　to pack the box (for shipping) [V-O]

zhuāngxiū 裝修　to repair and install [CC/V]

zhuāngyùn 裝運　to transport, to ship [CC/V]

zhuāngzài 裝載　to load [CC/V]

zhuāngzhì 裝置　to arrange, to set up, to install: *zhuāngzhì yíge diànhuà*, to install a telephone [CC/V]

追
to chase, to reminisce, to act retroactively

zhuībǔ	追捕	to search and arrest (thief, deserter, etc.) [CC/V]
zhuīdào	追悼	to grieve for the dead: *zhuīdàohuì*, memorial service for the dead [CC/V]
zhuīdaoshǒu	追到手	to succeed in chasing (girl friend): *Nǚ péngyou yì zhuīdaoshǒu, tā jiù búyào le.* As soon as he wins a girl's heart, he will give her up.
zhuīgǎn	追趕	to chase after: *Zéi pǎole, kwàidianr zhuīgǎn.* The thief ran away. Chase after him quickly. [CC/V]
zhuīhuán jiù zhài	追還舊債	to demand payment on old debt
zhuīhuí	追回	to recover (debt, lost property) [VC]
zhuīhuǐ	追悔	to regret [CC/V]
zhuījiā yùsuàn	追加預算	to pass addition to budget
zhuījiù	追究	to pursue investigation of origin, cause, sources of event, etc. [CC/V]
zhuīná	追拿	to pursue and apprehend: *zhuīná táo fàn*, to pursue and apprehend a criminal at large [CC/V]
zhuīniàn	追念	to remember with fond regret [CC/V]
zhuīqiú	追求	to seek after (truth, progress, girl friend) [CC/V]
zhuīrèn	追認	to approve, admit retroactively [CC/V]
zhuīshang	追上	to catch up in chasing: *Tā pǎode zhēn kuài, zúrán néng zhuīshang nèitiáo gǒu.* He runs really fast, he can even catch up with that dog. [VC]
zhuīsuí	追隨	to follow (a leader, master): *Tā zhuīsuí lǐngxiù hǎoduō nián le.* He has followed the leader for many years. [CC/V]
zhuīwèn	追問	to cross-examine, to examine with thoroughness [CC/V]
zhuīxiǎng	追想	to think back (upon old days, etc.) [CC/V]
zhuīyì	追憶	to think back (past events) [CC/V]
zhuīzāng	追贓	to recover thief's booty [V-O]
zhuīzōng	追蹤	to follow in the steps of those who have gone before [V-O]

211

zǒubǎn 走板　to be out of tune: *Tā chàng zǒubǎnle.* He is out of tune. [V-O]

zǒubukāi 走不開　to be unable to tear oneself away, to be too narrow to allow easy passage: *Hútong tài zhǎi, qìchē zǒubukāi.* The alley is too narrow for the car to go through. [VC]

zǒudòng 走動　to be able to walk: *Tā lǎode zǒubudòng le.* He is too old to walk. [VC]; to have social intercourse with friends: *Tā cháng dào Zhāngjia zǒudòng.* He has social intercourse with the Changs; to take a stroll [CC/V]

zǒugǒu 走狗　a running dog/a lacky [SC/N]

zǒuhóng 走紅　to have good luck, to be more popular [VO/SV]

zǒuhuǒ 走火　to have a short circuit, to fire accidentally [V-O]

zǒu jiānghu 走江湖　to go from place to place to stage show for a living (acrobats, magicians, singers, etc.)

zǒulòu 走漏　to leak out: *zǒulòu fēngshēng,* leak a secret [CC/V]

zǒu mǎ kàn huā 走馬看花　to view the flowers on horseback/to go over things quickly

zǒu nèixiàn 走內線　to bring influence to bear on someone through his close relatives

zǒushuǐ 走水　to catch fire [V-O]

zǒusī 走私　to smuggle: *zǒusī huò,* smuggled goods [V-O]

zǒu xiédàor 走斜道兒　to approach through devious means; to patronize brothels

zǒuyàngr 走樣兒　to be out of shape, to fail to conform to the norm [V-O]

zǒuyùn 走運　to have luck: *Tā zhè jǐnián zǒu hǎoyùn.* He has had good luck in recent years; *zǒu bèiyùn,* to have bad luck [V-O]

zǒuzhe qiáo 走着瞧　Let's see what will happen later: *Nǐ xiànzai xiān bié déyì. Wǒmen zǒuzhe qiáo.* Don't you be so happy now. Let's see what will happen to you later.

zǒuzīpài 走資派　capitalist routers (PRC)

bānzǒu 搬走　to move away [VC]

zuòchuáng 坐牀   (of newly weds) to be seated on the edge of the bed in the bridal room after the wedding ceremony [V-O]; inaugural ceremony of the Lamas in Tibet

zuòdà 坐大   to allow someone to wax strong (without doing something to prevent it) [CC/V]

zuò dì fēn zāng 坐地分贓 to divide the booty on the spot

zuò dìwōr 坐地窩兒   at the beginning: *Tā zuò dìwōr jiù búhuì.* He doesn't know how in the first place; right there and then: *Zuò dìwōr jiù bàntuō le.* It was done right away. [Adv]

zuòfǎ 坐法   to be punished for crime [V-O]

zuògōng 坐功   (Taoism) the practice of sitting in silence to meditate [SC/N]

zuò hóng yǐzi 坐紅椅子 to sit on a red chair/to be the last of a roster of successful candidates (alludes to the practice of making a red check mark at the end of the roster.)

zuòjìng 坐靜   to sit quietly for meditation [V-O]

zuò jǐng guān tiān 坐井觀天   to see the sky by sitting in a well/to take a narrow view of things

zuòkè 坐客   a passenger on boat, etc. [SC/N]

zuò lì bùān 坐立不安 to feel uneasy, restless whether sitting or standing

zuò lǐng bǎndèng 坐冷板凳 to sit on a cold stool/to be given the cold shoulder

zuò shī liáng jī 坐失良機 to let a golden opportunity slip by

zuò chī shān kōng 坐吃山空 to remain at home and eat away a whole future

zuòtáng 坐堂   to sit as a judge or magistrate [V-O]

zuòxí 坐席   to take seat at a banquet [V-O]

zuòyè 坐夜   to sit up all night, to keep vigil in the night [V-O]

zuòzhèn 坐鎮   to garrison (a city, area, etc.) [CC/V]

zuòzhuāng 坐莊   to be the banker in games of chance [V-O]

---

zuòbà 作罷　to dismiss as not worth further discussion or action: *Zhèjian shì jìran dàjia dōu méiyou xìngqu jiù zuòbà.* Since nobody is interested in this matter, no further discussion is needed. [VO]

zuòbàn(r) 作伴兒　to serve as companion, to keep company: *Shéi gěi nǐ zuòbànr?* Who keeps you company? [V-O]

zuòbǎo 作保　to be guarantor: *Wǒ gěi nǐ zuòbǎo.* I will be your guarantor. [V-O]

zuòbì 作弊　to practice irregularities (fraud), to cheat (in examinations, etc.): *Zuòbìde rén chízǎo huì bèi rén fāxiàn de.* Those who cheat will be discovered sooner or later. [V-O]

zuòbié 作別　to bid goodbye [V-O]

zuòdǎi 作歹　to do evil [V-O]

zuòduì 作對　to set against, to be opposed to: *Tā gēn wǒ zuòduì.* He is opposed to me. [V-O]

zuòfǎ 作法　method of making, doing things, course of action [SC/N]

zuòfēng 作風　way of doing things, manner in which one does things [SC/N]

zuòguài 作怪　to cause trouble, to play tricks, to act in a strange way: *Tā jìnlai bùzhīdao zài zuò shénmo guài.* Nobody knows what tricks he is playing lately. [V-O]

zuòhuó(r) 作活兒　to do work: *Nǐ zhèjǐtiān zuò xie shénmo huór?* What kind of work have you been doing these few days? [V-O]

zuòkè 作客　to be a guest at a friend's; to travel in a foreign country [V-O]

zuòmèng 作夢　to dream, to attempt something unpractical: *Nǐ jiǎnzhí shì zuòmèng mo!* You are simply dreaming/You are attempting the impossible. [V-O]

zuònán 作難　to find oneself in a predicament, to be put on the spot [V-O]

zuòshēng 作聲　to break silence, to begin to speak: *Nǐ wèi shénmo búzuòshēng ne?* Why don't you say something? [V-O]

zuòzhǔ 作主　to make decision: *Nǐmen jiā shéi zuòzhǔ?* Who makes the decisions in your family? [V-O]

dàngzuò 當作　to treat as: *bǎ ta dàngzuò hǎorén kàndài,* to treat him as a good person *zuòcài* 做菜   to cook (dishes) [V O]

zuòde 做得   can be done: *Nà jian shì zuòde.* That matter can be done.

zuòdōng 做東   to be host, to pay the bill: *Jīntian wǒ zuòdōng.* Today I am the host. [V-O]

zuò è'rén 做惡人   to act the part of a villain

zuòguān 做官   to be in an official position [V O]

zuòguǐr 做鬼兒   to play tricks, to practice irregularities [V-O]

zuò hǎorén 做好人   to act the part of a sympathizer

zuò hǎoshì 做好事   to do good deeds

zuòjiǎo 做脚   to serve to pass secret messages [V-O]

zuòkuò 做闊   to show off one's riches [V-O]

zuò liǎn(r) 做臉兒   to do something for the sake of appearance [V-O]

zuòlòng 做弄   to manipulate for selfish ends, to take someone as a sucker: *zuòlòng rén* [CC/V]

zuòqīn 做親   to make marriage arrangements for one's child [V-O]

zuò rénqíng 做人情   to do someone a favor

zuò shēngrì 做生日   to hold a birthday party

zuòshòu 做壽   to give a birthday in honor of an elder [V-O]

zuò shǒujiǎo 做手脚 to resort to irregular practices, to make secret arrangements

zuòtou 做頭   expected results: *Zhèjian shì méi shénmo zuòtou.* You cannot expect any results from doing this.

zuòxiàn 做綫   to serve to pass secret messages (=*zuòjiǎo*) [V-O]

zuòxiǎo 做小   to be someone's concubine [V-O]

zuòyǎn 做眼   to gather information: *zuòyǎn jiǔdiàn*, undercover taverns [V-O]

zuò zéi xīn xū 做賊心虛   to have a guilty conscience

Chinese Characters for the Examples

Examples under the entries are in romanized versions. Chinese characters are given below according to order of appearance. Entries are underlined.

Page   *EXAMPLES IN CHINESE CHARACTERS*

1   多謝您的愛顧. 愛國心　要是一個人愛護他的名譽,他
絕不會作出這種見不得人的事的. 愛美的觀念
愛人如己　你怎麼會愛上她?

2   請你給他安插一個職位. 等他安定一下再說吧.
住在這兒很安定. 安分守己　安家費　他安然渡過
難關. 他日子過得很安閒. 電話已經安裝好了.
他這樣對你顯然是不安好心.

3   這個辦不到. 這件事由我辦理. 他很會辦事.
這個學校是甚麼時候創辦的?　沒辦法作.
只要你說出來我一定照辦.

4   這事由我包辦. 抖摟包袱底兒　包管沒錯兒. 包管來回兒
包工制　包工活　這句話包含的意思很多. 一個月的包金
是多少?　那本小說真是包羅萬象.

5   保管人　保護國　保護色　那個保險公司不保險.
人權的保障　保證人　保證書　請好好兒保重身體.
保準兒沒事. 難保他不會生氣.

6   新聞報導　報父母養育之恩　這部車子報廢了. 立志
報國　無以報命　報喜不報憂

7   主動　原告　這次起義被難的烈士很多. 怎麼你沒
被請? 你說這話不怕被人聽見? 賊被抓住了.

8   我們得時時防備敵人的襲擊. 在敵人地區我們
必須時時戒備.

9　我比不上他。　比方說　舉個比方　比較好　比較語言學
拿…作比例　比例尺　比賽講故事　講演比賽
比照看這張畫兒畫　你把他比作甚麼?

10　別老是編派人好嗎?　編造謠言

11　變動很大。這孩子變好了。千變萬化　變態心理
變天了.別忘了帶傘。　變通辦理　變相賣淫
她已經變了心.你就別再死心眼兒了。

12　寫文章你得參考很多書.給你作個參考.從昨天起我參與
了他們的討論。

13　查經班　查明真相　隨信寄給你像片三張.請查收.
請查照辦理.你要是有不認識的字就查字典。

14　察明責任　細察來意

15　不動產

16　他就會唱高調兒.別指望他作出甚麼來。　留聲機
唱個唱兒　今天晚上城裡唱戲.

17　人人稱便　稱道不絕　這件衣裳很稱身。

18　不計成敗　成本太高的生意不好作.我這樣作還不是
想成全他那一片孝心。　他成心氣他媽媽.

19　請乘便把他帶回去。　乘機脫逃　你現在沒事,還不
乘空兒把那封信寫完?　乘興多畫幾張吧.

20　時局很吃緊.這件事很吃勁.你得吃勁拉.
大吃一驚　這種紙不太吃水。他現在很吃香.
這件事很吃重.

21　持法森嚴　持久戰　持論公正　持平之論
老成持重　跟他還是保持點兒距離好些。

22　出版一本書　要是出個岔兒誰負責?學音樂,出路
不太好.這件事由我出面接洽.買汽車,誰出錢?
他是做買賣出身.你好好兒作,總有出頭的一天.
這孩子真沒出息。

23　除非你去不行. 斬草除根　政府應當替老百姓除害.
除了你以外沒有別人會. 除了你以外還有別人去,
他常常逃學, 所以被學校除名了. 被除數　星期日除外.
廢除不平等條約　破除迷信

24　我跟他處不來. 這件事真不好處理. 他不會待人處世, 所以
常常得罪人. 處世之道　處極刑　他們兩個相處得很好.

25　傳達命令　傳家之寶　傳教士　傳染病　傳聞敵人佔領
王莊. 傳信兒

26　現在請王博士致答詞. 不答應　你亂花錢, 爸爸不
答應. 問答題

28　請替我帶個好兒給你父母. 說話帶口音　別把小孩兒帶
壞了.

29　你當面對他講. 當權派　當頭棒喝　當眾宣佈
他當真不會.

30　好幾家銀行倒閉了. 倒頭紙　走倒運

31　喝倒彩　叫個倒好兒　他原來欠我很多錢. 後來我倒
欠他. 他是倒數第一. 因果倒置

32　到處是水. 今天動身的話, 甚麼時候可以到達?
這到底是怎麼回事? 抗戰到底　我到過紐約.
他的畫兒可畫得到家兒了. 八月一號到期. 你借的
書到期了嗎? 那些錢甚麼時候才能到手? 到頭來
全丟了. 想到這件事就頭疼. 我的帽子找到了.
他作事很週到, 從來不得罪人.

33　點頭朋友　打點行李

34　下定義　說不定他會來. 我們說定了明天一塊兒走.

35　這孩子動不動就哭. 我的腳動手麻了. 動用公款
動員民眾　五四運動

36　漢語讀本　讀書人　讀者文摘

37　度量大　過度小心

38　發表意見　發動機　你發瘋了. 發生誤會　發咒
紅得發紫

39 反串老生　反動派　反對派　反覆解釋　反覆無常
引起反感　他非常反共。　反臉不認人　他反正不會反正。

40 飛行員

41 改編軍隊　把那些不好的習慣改變過來。　改過自新
改嘴　改日再談　改天　改正錯誤

42 大功告成　告病假

43 國民革命　裁員　她先生被革了職。

44 給了三天假　給臉不要臉　被人打了　請你把這張
畫兒交給他。　給人打了

45 講臺跟前　你跟前有沒有小孩兒？　跟手兒去做
栽跟頭　翻跟頭　他跟尾兒就出來了。　跟着就來了

46 共產黨　國際共管　共計多少錢？　你跟他共過事
嗎？　公私共營　這些東西為我們所共有。

47 懷念　這件事跟那件事沒有甚麼關連。　牽涉
關涉別人私事　關託您替我說說情。　他跟她
有沒有關係沒關係。　他很關心你。　關心國事
關於這件事,我一點兒都不知道。　照應　有事,請關
照一聲,請你多多關照。　注意

48 各人有各人的觀點。　你們進去,我在外邊兒觀風。
觀光客　觀光事業　新觀念　觀看　欣賞　採觀
望態度　觀望不前　有碍觀瞻　袖手旁觀

49 我管保他不來。　這件事我可管不了。　管家的　管教小
孩兒　管教他給你說好話。　這兒誰管事？　管事的
約束　管賬的　節制

50 害了兩天病　害人不淺　你害死我了。　利益　害處
厲害得很　病得很厲害　壓迫

51 合乎道理　定合同

52 花不起這麼多錢　沒甚麼花項。東西都漲了。花銷太
大。　看得我眼花。

53 化除成見　化合物　化妝品　風化區　叫花子
歐化句子　這都是你的造化。

219

55　歡呼萬歲　這個小孩歡虎兒似的。大家歡聚一堂。
　歡送會　我歡喜她。　歡欣鼓舞　歡宴賓客　受歡迎
　他那本書很受歡迎。

56　夠還本

57　回頭見見　回敬一杯

58　我們在王家會齊, 然後出發。　會同管理　會心的微笑

59　活動一官半職　他活該挨打. 誰叫他那麼壞呢。
　幹活兒　連戲都不能看, 還有甚麼活頭兒。　活頁文選
　他在政治方面很活躍。

60　中央集權　集體領導　集體農場　集體安全　共產集團
　集團結婚　集郵家　集中注意　集中營

61　我記得他是誰。　作個記號兒就不會忘了。　記名投票
　記取教訓　那時我才記事。　我的記性兒太壞。　記憶力
　記住別忘了。

62　食品加工　小費加一　加意招呼

63　這個人很有見地。　請別見怪。　活見鬼　瞭解
　他的病見輕了。　請你不要見外。　他見聞很廣。

64　你講交情不講?　講究穿　他這樣作一定有甚麼講究。
　講求外表

66　這就叫做自討苦吃。　我們把孔子叫做至聖先師。

65　交代差事　交代他不要多嘴。　辦交代　很難跟他打交道。
　交換教授　交際花兒　文化交流　情誼　新舊交替
　證券交易所　交戰國

67　跟誰結仇?　結存一千塊錢　動賓結構

68　解除婚約　解放黑奴　先把他解決了。解散議會

69　進口貨　進取心　進退兩難　進行工作

70　一舉一動　舉世聞名　舉手贊成　舉止大方　一舉得子

71　未開化國家　開口大笑　他父母很開通。別拿我開胃。
　開消很大。　別拿我開心。

72　看不出來他是誰　茶房!看酒!　要不是看你的面子, 我才不會
　替他辦那件事呢。　你怎麼會看上她?　他甚麼都看

220

透了，一點兒也不在乎。這件事你看着辦吧。

73 我們得抗拒敵人的侵畧。司令要你去，你可不能抗命不去。把這包東西抗起來吧。你應當提出抗議才對。抗日戰爭我們抗了八年的戰才把日本打敗了。你是誰？怎麼敢跟他分庭抗禮呢？

74 我明年要到中國去考古。考古學 他的衣裳真考究。他真考究穿。把原因考究出來就知道是怎麼回事了。這件事你得好好兒的考慮考慮。考求病源 臺大的入學考試，你考上了沒有？ 時代考驗青年。他缺點太多是經不起考驗的。

75 克當重任 克服困難 克復失地 克難運動 克難成果 克難房屋 老王克勤克儉，日子過得一天比一天好。克私為公 克享天年 克制情感 你柔能克剛 說幾句好話 不就完了嗎？

76 他一向寬洪大量 才不會跟那些小人一般見識呢。寬容政策 看在他父親的面上，把他寬恕了吧。要寬慰父母，就得好好兒念書。你好好兒地念書才能讓父母感到寬慰。寬限一個月 他總是很寬心。

77 請別把我拉扯進去。他把樹拉倒了。這件事我看還是拉倒吧。跟他拉不上關係 你拉攏他作甚麼？你替他們兩個拉攏拉攏。拉拉雜雜地說了半天。

78 你這句話來得厲害。來回票 來歷不明 來人啊。來人了啊。 他的來頭不小。這種遊戲還有甚麼來頭呢。我們早就不來往了。你跟他有來往嗎？來信收到了。你很久沒給我來信了。他的來意不善。 他說他姓甚麼來着？

79 我們離別以後沒通過信。他那種人離不了女人。說話別離格兒。他們老早離婚了。你得小心小人離間我們。小孩兒離不開父母。這件事作得有點兒離譜了。一家人因為戰爭都離散了。他們不願意分離。

80 他不理睬我。他常常不理會人。張太太真會理家。他的理解力很高。主任病了。誰代理他的職務？

221

那個不良少年昨天被警察好好兒修理了一次。

81　一連串兒的不幸事件　連環圖　我連接看了三個病人。
我連累你了。　連連點頭　你跟他連絡一下。　連絡處
他看見上司來，就連忙過去打招呼。　連年旱災　連篇錯字
一連氣兒跑了三里路。連續下了三天雨。

82　聯合國大會　我們聯合起來誰也不怕。我們聯名
申請。　為了這件事的成功，你應當跟他聯系聯系（繫）。
公私聯營

83　春秋列國　列舉人名罪狀　請把這件事列入議程。
你把要買的東西開列一個單子吧。請解釋下列各名詞。

84　這個問題太複雜，小孩子恐怕不能領會。明天我再來
領教。　你的好意我領情就是了。　領養一個小孩兒。

85　他的計畫不幸流產了。　流動財產　萬世流芳　他被
流放到新疆去了。　他的中國話說得很流利。　流連忘返
真情流露　流亡海外　流線型火車

86　論交情你不應該反對他。　博士論文　不論你怎麼
樣　總統言論

87　落成典禮　落地窗　落地式電視　把敵人打得落花
流水。　落後國家　那是落實毛主席指示的重要措施。
打落水狗　思想落伍

88　買他的好　買好了就走。買賣好嗎？你把他買通了就
沒問題了。

89　賣國賊　唱歌兒的賣臉不賣身。　賣弄文墨

90　他對那件事滿不在乎。他們兩個的事鬧得滿城風雨。
他近來滿面春風得意得很。我滿以為他會當選，沒想
到會輸得這麼慘。今天戲園子一定滿座。他的精神
總是很飽滿。　結果圓滿。

91　迷迷瞪瞪的樣子　迷迷糊糊　迷魂湯　他竟然
會迷戀一個妓女。我因為迷了路，怎麼也找不着他的
家。　迷你裙　迷人精　破除迷信　迷醉新思想

92　他真無能，甚麼事都拿不起來。拿不住人別想當主管。

222

這種皮鞋不拿滑。 他拿甚麼臭架子：誰不知道地是誰. 拿毛
打架   他對足球很拿手。

93 他常常念叨着你。 念念叨叨 他老是在那兒念念叨叨。
他總是念念有辭, 不知道說些甚麼。 為了一個女人,他
不知道轉了多少念頭。 這棵樹是為了紀念我母親
種的。 結婚紀念 大哥留念. 他很想念他母親。

94 怕不也還要三四十天的工夫。 怕的是明天下雪不能開車。
不做虧心事, 不怕鬼叫門。 這個小孩兒怕人。 這張畫兒
真怕人。 女孩兒多半兒怕臊。 這個人怕事的不得了,你
最好別找他。 他恐怕不會來了。

95 我只能替人家跑跑龍套而已。

96 一路平安 男女平等 地方上很平定。 一件很平凡的事
那個人可不平凡。 我們平分這些東西。 這個地方很平
靜。 平均一個人賺多少錢？ 近來一切平平 沒有甚麼可說
的。 平時我不睡午覺。 道路平坦。

97 破除迷信 破費！破費！今天讓您破費了。 破壞名譽
破壞家庭 撿破爛兒過活 感情破裂 他破天荒
第一次來。

98 經濟起飛。他是做生意起家的。 為了省錢起見,
他做事真起勁兒。 他近來起居很正常。 說起話來
沒有完。 說起來,話長。 他的病有點起色。 誰
起的頭兒？

99 強暴少女 他錯了還要強辯。 他一直強調他反對
的理由. 中國現在可強區起來了。 敵人的態度很
強硬。 一個強有力的國家   你要是不願意,請別勉
強。 我實在做不了,你一定要我做,我只好勉強試試.

100 切齒之恨 切合事實 切切記住 切身問題
切身之痛 切切實實 切切實實地做事 他的話
一點兒都不切實際。 他對我的事情一向很關切。
他很關切我。 他們倆的關係很密切。 請你密切
注意,他的行動。 他的態度很親切。 這件事很迫
切。

223

101　親愛的母親　親近小人　親口答應　王大年先生親啓
中美親善　親身經驗　親生子女　親生父母　親自出
馬　親她(他)的嘴　跟她親了個嘴　他們是親兄
弟,當然應該相親相愛。

102　請病假　請事假　今天我請客。我請你的客。你要是
不向上司請示,做錯了事誰負責? 請託人做一件事
請問你貴姓? 請問吧。聘請家教(家庭教師)
申請工作

103　我是沒事絕不求人的。　那真是一件求之不得的事。

104　我們取道香港到中國去。取得學位　我們都要取法
岳飛愛國的精神。我們家的事由太太取決。他專門
駡人取樂兒。他取名大強。大強是他爸爸給他取
的名兒。我們這樣決定不過是取其便而已。喜歡投機
取巧的人常常會失望。別取笑他。這個人真是一無可取。

105　沒有個去處　不知去處　去不得　去核兒紅棗兒　不知去向

106　那兩個人一吵起來誰也不讓過兒。要是你不讓點兒價,我
就不買。客人都坐好了,怎麼還不讓酒? 汽車來了,請讓開。
讓讓就是了。來不來在他。把房產權讓與李四。他年紀
小,你就讓着他點兒。

107　羅美歐熱愛朱麗葉。他的情緒很熱烈。熱門兒人物
熱熱鬧鬧　熱鬧熱鬧　人家辦生日,咱們去湊個熱鬧
兒吧。這種天氣能把人熱死。這個人辦事很熱心。他
熱心公益。這個人熱心腸,誰的忙他不幫? 他對賭博很
熱中。他熱中名利。

108　爸爸在生你的氣。還不快去認個不是。　他認錯了人了。
我認得這個字(人)。我輸多少錢也認了。王同志不這
樣認為。　識字

109　政府官員都要有能容納大眾意見的雅量。無地容身

110　蛐蜒　他們說得入港。他已經入了美國籍了。他看武俠
小說看得入扣兒。國語入門兒　他下棋下得入迷了,甚麼
事都不管了。

224

111 張家的三個女孩子,長得一個賽過一個。 今天我們比賽寫字。
112 商量商量 商商量量的 討論 這件事我們得商同王先生一塊兒去辦。 斟酌
113 今天我上了個大當。 上趕著叫老伯 把螺絲上緊 她今天光給我上勁. 坐飛機比較上算。 看不上眼
114 你太太甚麼時候生產? 吃生活 生死關頭 生死之交 做生意 生長得漂亮 生殖器
115 這個學校設備不錯。 我們得設法省錢。 設騙局 設立學校 為人設想 設座華國飯店
116 處置失當 房子失火了。 失禮 失言 飛機失事了。 情場失意
117 他要是稍微識相點兒也不會讓人家笑話他。 為識者所笑 才能 老王的上司很賞識他的工作。 學問
118 這把刀子使不得。 買書使不了這麼多錢。 昨兒買的那件大衣使得嗎? 他會使喚人。 使勁兒念書 上次他沒有完成使命。 她喜歡使性子是因為父母把她慣壞了。 外國人不會使用筷子。
119 抓周 試驗管 試用期間我不敢請假。 試驗紙
120 收場太令人難受了。 今年的收成特別好。 收復失地 收條兒 收攬民心 收買人心 收容難民 不可收拾 好好收拾收拾那個壞蛋。 收音機
121 受寵若驚 受氣包兒 天熱喝杯冰茶很受用。 受洋罪
122 人太多,我數不過來。 好學生裏頭怎麼樣也數不上他。 成天價數落他,你有沒有個完呢? 你數數數兒不就知道他給你多少了嗎? 他是美國數一數二的科學家。 朋友裏頭數著他最有錢了。
123 他這種作風真說不過去。 彼此說不來 這張畫兒說不上傑作。 說穿了一錢不值。 說長道短 說天道地 說三道四 說好話 我本來不想告訴他。可是我說溜了嘴了。 說起來話長 說起話來沒有完。 說書的 我是說著玩兒的。 說大話

124 他是我的死對頭。你這個死鬼。他死皮賴臉求了一天。
他被打得死去活來。看你那個死相！死硬派

125 送親太太

126 算不了一回事。小心被人家算計。不去算了。算命的
算起來還是這個好。你組織旅學團別忘了把我算上。
你說的話算數兒不算數兒？回頭我跟你算賬。
他就會打如意算盤。計算機

127 他們兩個很談得來。談鋒甚健 他昨天的談話真有
意思。談吐很風雅。

128 逃避責任 逃避現實 這次讓你逃掉了。逃亡在外
我從來沒逃過學

129 討飯的 讓他討個便宜。討人嫌

130 我很久沒提過筆了。提出意見 書上提到你沒有？
提防敵人進攻 提高警覺 這個節目是福特公司提
供的。提起來她的女兒就掉淚。這個人沒甚麼大
提頭兒。

131 調不動 整天工作，週末到鄉下去玩兒玩兒，調劑調
劑生活。玩弄 調味品 調整公教人員待遇

132 降落傘 我有點兒心跳。

133 這個小孩兒不聽話。聽取意見 聽信兒

134 停車場 不停的動

135 政治學通論 請通扁虫一下。你常跟家裏人通信嗎？
這樣實在說不通

136 同情心

137 偷空兒看朋友

138 推卸責任

139 託你的福。託福託福。把這件事就託付給你了。
託故不去 他是牛託生的。拜託你一件事。拜託拜託！
委託行

140 這個學校的一切都很完備。工作完畢。完成任務

我們的廚房甚麼時候完工? 一切都完了! 婚姻很完滿.

141 玩弄人　他是說着玩兒的. 你不要認真. 別玩兒花樣.
老老實實地做最好. 開玩笑

142 往常他不喝酒.　往東走　往後走兩步　我們常常往還.
我們沒有往來.　往日我有很多朋友. 往事還提它做甚
麼?　他往往兒把人記錯了. 這條路上來來往往的車子
真多.

143 名譽　人望　為人　名聲　心願

144 政府委派誰去談判? 委屈你了. 你的委屈我知道. 委任
官(職)　委實不錯　委託你替我做一件事　他話說得
很委婉, 要不然怎麼吃得消. 委員會

145 溫存話兒　溫度計　氣候溫和　脾氣溫和　厚道
溫習功課　善良　人間溫暖　柔和　孝順　文雅

146 他要我向你問安. 問答題　你把我問倒了. 他要我問
候你. 這件事一定得問明是誰搞的. 你的書甚麼時候
問世?　問訊處

147 他今天受洗禮了. 他被洗腦了. 他洗手不幹了. 他已
經洗心革面不再做壞事了.

148 甚麼時候吃你的喜酒?　這個人喜怒無常, 不是哭就
是笑.　他升官的事你給他道過喜了沒有?

149 他當着那麼多人開我的玩笑. 真叫我下不了台. 請你
給民主下個定義.　不管做甚麼事都得下功夫。
這些都是下酒的好菜.　我難過得都下淚了. 我們的
州長甚麼時候下台(臺)?

150 出了事千萬別改變現場. 吃現成兒飯　說現成兒話
毛病現出來了. 你有多少現款?　誰是現任市長?
這個人真現實啊。 國際現勢　老王的妻子跑了又死
了兒子. 那才真是現世報了. 現報　你請回去吧. 別
再現眼了. 到現在為止我還沒看見他呢. 維持現狀

151　他就會向上司獻媚。中山先生獻身革命人人佩服。有些人不靠本事靠獻殷勤升官。這是我對國家的獻贈。請你貢獻一點兒意見。他做了很多對國家有貢獻的事情。

152　想必是他病了。想得到,做得到。我們得想法子救他。他辛苦的情形可以想見。你想開了就不難過了。想來我真不應該。他想來想去也想不出個法子來。他很想念他哥哥。想起那件事來就傷心。那種事還有甚麼想頭呢? 他那種窘迫的情形是可以想像得到的。這是一個不可思議的想像。他是異想天開,一點兒都不實際。

153　人心向背　一點向當兒都沒有。他向來是這樣的。向前走　不向上就會倒退的。你可別老向著他說話。努力向學　以免向隅

154　這事與你毫不相干。說相聲兒的　照相(像)機　天氣這麼好,我們出去照相(像)去。我今天到照相館去照相。真相大明

155　像貌非凡　別像煞有介事的樣子。那不是甚麼了不起的事情。給他一個像兒瞧。穿這樣的奇裝異服像甚麼? 你用不著作這些像生兒了。他像是沒聽見。你今天可得穿得像樣兒點兒。這樣作還像樣兒。那件事聽著不大像。他作不出來。連父母都不管。真太不像話。你看他。三分不像人,七分倒像鬼。他好像病了似的。總理遺像

156　物價高,消費跟著增加。消費品　大汽車消耗汽油太多。消化不良　積極　消磨歲月　忙了一年了,該消遣消遣了啊。你今年到那兒去消夏? 工作太苦,吃不消。

157　給我們說個笑話。我唱得不好,請別笑話。他是個笑面虎。你可得小心點兒。看他笑容可掬,實在可愛。別老開他的玩笑。這個玩笑可開大了。請求你,別取笑我了,好嗎?

158　我們得寫個字兒才行。

159　他的話信得。　你信奉甚麼教？　信任狀　這個政府是信賞必罰。犯罪的一個也逃不了。　紅衛兵都是毛澤東的信徒。　他對你一點信心也沒有。　不守信用　我相信你對。我相信你。

160　及時行樂　行為科學　風行全國　旅行社

161　休怪他不幫忙。　你累了吧？好好兒休息休息。　休想他會回心轉意。　那件事他還不肯罷休。　退而不休

162　期許學成回國　爸爸不允許你去。　他工作很努力。上司對他大加讚許。　以救國救民的大任自許。

163　我這個學期選讀英文。　選舉權　選派留學生　現在的政府都喜歡選用青年。　買東西當然要選擇好的。這家公司的貨太少，沒甚麼選擇。　公務員多半是考選來的。竟選的人多，落選的人也多。　大家推選老張作代表。

164　這個學期你選了幾個學分的課？　最高學府　這孩子最近學壞了。　亞洲學會　我們都應當向老李學習。這孩子勤學得不得。

165　將來怎麼演變，誰也不敢說。　這場演出很叫座。　進化論實彈演習　三國志演義　歸納法　演奏會

166　這孩子真要不得。　今天下雨了。要不然我就去了。　交通要道要飯的　國防要害　兩個人很要好。　那家生意靠不住，要謊要的太大。　不得要領　吵得要命。　你總是這樣要脅人。學外國話，要在多多練習。

167　習慣養成了就不好改了。　靠薪水養活家　養老金　他養身有道總是那麼健康。　不忘父母養育之恩。　培養人材

168　桌子上有很多印兒。　印刷品　你對他的印象好不好？別給人壞印象。　商務印書館印行　互相印證

169　這種局面真難應付。　先給你點錢應個急。　今年我們也買了個聖誕樹應應景兒。　應用科學

170　你用不着去。　今天你用不着這本書吧？　下功夫　對學問他真肯用功夫。　雖我用盡了力量幫他的忙，可是他還是不滿意。　不會用人就作不好行政工作。　用心做事用意很好，可是結果反而把朋友給得罪了。　不用客氣。

171　遊覽車　遊樂場　愛國遊行　遊興大發　他喜歡跟外國人

229

交遊. 交遊很廣

172 那件事已經說得有邊兒了. 有不是找我. 有的去, 有的不去.
有的人 有的時候 他有的是錢. 小心! 這個東西有毒.
無後 革命有理. 有臉的人 有心人 你有準兒能成功嗎?

173 我們約定明天開會. 語言是一種約定俗成的東西. 你們
有沒有約會? 這次旅行約計得十天. 約略這個時候
約莫半年的時間 約請朋友來吃飯 他們家的小孩兒,
一點兒約束都沒有. 我們約同老張一塊兒去玩兒. 不平等
條約

174 越出範圍 她長得越發好看了. 越軌行為 借書越期要
罰錢的. 他的成績超越任何人. 越過重量

175 在朝黨 她對管家真在行. 他說我甚麼 我也不在乎. 這件
事能不能成功完全在你身上了. 我父母都還在世. 小張在外.
在我看, 一定不行. 這件事你可得在心作啊. 在野黨. 你說了
半天, 他一點兒也不在意.

176 造反無罪 孩子造反了. 你的造化可不小. 造就人材
王先生在數學方面的造詣很高.

177 敵人在那兒增防? 你的前言給我的書增光不少. 增加負
擔 人口增加 病情增劇 編輯有增刪權 增長知識
土地增值稅

178 展覽展期了. 又展樣又大方 發展中國家 這是一種新的發展.
沒甚麼進展.

179 買東西得站班. 受不了. 這樣作下去是站不住的. 今天晚上
輪誰站崗? 汽車來了. 請站開點兒. 站穩, 小心摔下
來. 不怕慢 就怕站. 每天多少作一點兒, 總有作完的時
候.

180 張大嘴 說話別張大其詞. 張開眼睛 錢來伸手, 飯
來張口. 不准張貼 這件事請別張揚出去. 不好意思,
張嘴 大開張 他主張男女平等.

181 別老是找我的碴兒. 好好作, 免得找罵. 你理他就
是自找麻煩. 他事喜歡找人的毛病. 你給我找錢,
我找給你錢. 你來找死.

182 臨時着慌 為了孩子的事着急 着力作還不一定作得
好, 那兒敢偷懶呢? 着落不明. 那件事還一點着落

都没有呢。這一下他可着了忙了。那件事快着人去辦吧。
你的畫兒着色了沒有？這張畫着實畫得不錯。我那本書
還沒着手寫呢。

183　你吩咐下來，我們一定照辦。我的小孩兒請你多多照
照舊有效　照例免費　我跟他沒照個面兒就走了。照相
（像）機　申請照准

184　跟他爭辯了半天　爭持不讓　替國家爭光　這孩子真不爭氣。
爭口氣　爭取最後勝利　爭取朋友　階級鬥爭

185　整頓學風　整個垮了　把材料整理一下寫篇文章。
整天玩兒，一點兒事也不做　整整十塊錢　整治整治

186　不知恥　那個人不知趣兒。知識份子　他說的都是知
心話。　知足常樂

187　請止步　遊人止步　甚麼藥止痛最有效？阿司匹靈是最
普通的止痛劑。血止住了嗎？止住了。報名後天截止。
禁止抽煙　凡事適可而止，不要作得太過分了。她心如止
水，不管你怎麼挑逗也不會打動她的。阻止前進

188　指導教授　主任指定誰就是誰。請多多指教。指名罵
指望成功　有沒有點指望？　指引你走上大路

189　這個地方的治安好不好？他這幾年治了不少產。精神
治療　在省政府的治下　專心治學　治裝費　治他的罪
他的請求應當如何處治？　處治不良少年　地方自治

190　制裁侵略者　法律制裁　他力大如牛，很不容易制伏。
無理的罷工一定要制止。抵制洋貨　管制交通　交通
管制　節制生育　限制行動　學校的限制太多。自制
能力

191　他是我的助理。昨天我忙極了。你給我的助力最大。
今天張家辦喜事，鄰居都來助忙。助人為快樂之本。
資助他出國

192　屋子太小，住不下這麼多人。住在家裏　你在那兒住家？
這個地方能住人嗎？天晚了。我們住下再說。學生
有的住家，有的住校。　你在那兒居住？他的話靠不
住。他今天一定要走。我怎麼也留不住。這種委屈，你

要是忍得住就別告訴他。魚太滑，我簡直抓不住。

193　別抓我的大頭。抓破了臉，甚麼都不在乎。警察近來抓了不少的人。

194　轉變方向　沒有甚麼轉變　這件事簡直沒有轉圜的餘地。他的病有點兒轉機了。他轉手就變卦了。轉了一個大彎兒　別轉彎子罵人。轉學生（轉學的學生）他轉眼就不見了。轉移陣地

195　責任重大　軍事重地，遊人止步。說話要抓得住重點。這篇東西有重量。她現在重身子出不得門。那是一齣的重頭戲。

196　這本書的裝潢很不錯。裝甲部隊　他就喜歡裝假，誰知道他心裏想的是甚麼。裝腔做勢　他心裏明白表面兒裝傻。裝飾品　他是水仙不開花，裝蒜。裝置一個電話

197　追悼會　女朋友一追到手，他就不要了。賊跑了，快點兒追趕。追拿逃犯　他跑得真快，居然能追上那條狗。他追隨領袖好多年了。

198　他唱走板了。胡同太窄，汽車走不開。他老得走不動了。他常到張家走動。走漏風聲　走私貨　他這幾年走好運。走背運　你現在先別得意。我們走着瞧。

199　他坐地窩兒就不會。坐地窩就辦妥了

200　這件事情既然大家都沒有興趣就作罷。誰給你作伴兒？我給你作保。作弊的人遲早會被人發現的。他跟我作對。他近來不知道在作甚麼怪？你這幾天作些甚麼活兒？你簡直是作夢嚜！你為甚麼不作聲呢？你們家誰作主？把他當作好人看待

201　那件事做得。今天我做東。做弄人　這件事沒甚麼做頭。做眼酒店

232

Conversion from Regular to Simplified Characters

7 笔

〔車〕车
〔夾〕夹
〔貝〕贝
〔見〕见
〔壯〕壮
〔妝〕妆

8 笔

【一】

〔長〕长
〔亞〕亚
〔軋〕轧
〔東〕东
〔兩〕两
〔協〕协
〔來〕来
〔戔〕戋

【丨】

〔門〕门
〔岡〕冈

【丿】

〔侖〕仑
〔兒〕儿

【㇕】

〔狀〕状
〔糾〕纠

9 笔

【一】

〔剋〕克
〔軌〕轨
〔庫〕厍
〔頁〕页
〔郟〕郏
〔剄〕刭
〔勁〕劲

【丨】

〔貞〕贞
〔則〕则
〔閂〕闩
〔迴〕回

【丿】

〔俠〕侠
〔係〕系
〔鳧〕凫
〔帥〕帅
〔後〕后
〔釓〕钆
〔釔〕钇
〔負〕负
〔風〕风

【丶】

〔訂〕订
〔計〕计

〔訃〕讣
〔軍〕军
〔衹〕只

【㇕】

〔陣〕阵
〔韋〕韦
〔陝〕陕
〔陘〕陉
〔飛〕飞
〔紆〕纡
〔紅〕红
〔紂〕纣
〔紈〕纨
〔級〕级
〔約〕约
〔紇〕纥
〔紀〕纪
〔紉〕纫

10 笔

【一】

〔馬〕马
〔挾〕挟
〔貢〕贡
〔華〕华
〔莢〕荚
〔莖〕茎
〔莧〕苋
〔莊〕庄

〔軒〕轩
〔連〕连
〔軔〕轫
〔劃〕划

【丨】

〔鬥〕斗
〔時〕时
〔畢〕毕
〔財〕财
〔覎〕觃
〔閃〕闪
〔唄〕呗
〔員〕员
〔豈〕岂
〔峽〕峡
〔峴〕岘
〔剛〕刚
〔剮〕剐

【丿】

〔氣〕气
〔郵〕邮
〔倀〕伥
〔倆〕俩
〔條〕条
〔們〕们
〔個〕个
〔倫〕伦
〔隻〕只
〔島〕岛

〔烏〕乌
〔師〕师
〔徑〕径
〔釘〕钉
〔針〕针
〔釗〕钊
〔釕〕钋
〔釘〕钉
〔殺〕杀
〔倉〕仓
〔脅〕胁
〔狹〕狭
〔狽〕狈
〔芻〕刍

【丶】

〔訐〕讦
〔訌〕讧
〔討〕讨
〔訕〕讪
〔訖〕讫
〔訓〕训
〔這〕这
〔訊〕讯
〔記〕记
〔凍〕冻
〔畝〕亩
〔庫〕库
〔浹〕浃
〔涇〕泾

【㇕】

〔書〕书
〔陸〕陆
〔陳〕陈
〔孫〕孙
〔陰〕阴
〔務〕务
〔紜〕纭
〔純〕纯
〔紕〕纰
〔紗〕纱
〔納〕纳
〔紝〕纴
〔紛〕纷
〔紙〕纸
〔紋〕纹
〔紡〕纺
〔紖〕纼
〔紐〕纽
〔紓〕纾

11 笔

【一】

〔責〕责
〔現〕现
〔匭〕匦
〔規〕规
〔殼〕壳
〔埡〕垭
〔掗〕挜

〔捨〕舍	〔喎〕㖞	〔訝〕讶	〔組〕组	〔蒔〕莳	〔單〕单
〔捫〕扪	〔帳〕帐	〔訥〕讷	〔紳〕绅	〔棖〕枨	〔喲〕哟
〔摳〕抠	〔崬〕崬	〔許〕许	〔紬〕䌷	〔棟〕栋	〔買〕买
〔堝〕埚	〔崍〕崃	〔訛〕讹	〔細〕细	〔棧〕栈	〔剴〕剀
〔頂〕顶	〔崗〕岗	〔訴〕诉	〔終〕终	〔楓〕枫	〔凱〕凯
〔掄〕抡	〔圇〕囵	〔詗〕诇	〔絆〕绊	〔軲〕轱	〔幀〕帧
〔執〕执	〔過〕过	〔訟〕讼	〔紼〕绋	〔軻〕轲	〔嵐〕岚
〔捲〕卷	【丿】	〔設〕设	〔絀〕绌	〔軸〕轴	〔幃〕帏
〔掃〕扫	〔氫〕氢	〔訪〕访	〔紹〕绍	〔軼〕轶	〔圍〕围
〔堊〕垩	〔動〕动	〔訣〕诀	〔紿〕绐	〔軤〕轷	【丿】
〔萊〕莱	〔偵〕侦	〔產〕产	〔貫〕贯	〔軫〕轸	〔無〕无
〔萵〕莴	〔側〕侧	〔牽〕牵	〔鄉〕乡	〔軺〕轺	〔氬〕氩
〔乾〕干	〔貨〕货	〔烴〕烃		〔畫〕画	〔喬〕乔
〔梘〕枧	〔進〕进	〔淶〕涞	**12笔**	〔腎〕肾	〔筆〕笔
〔軛〕轭	〔梟〕枭	〔淺〕浅	【一】	〔棗〕枣	〔備〕备
〔斬〕斩	〔鳥〕鸟	〔渦〕涡	〔貳〕贰	〔硨〕砗	〔貸〕贷
〔軟〕软	〔偉〕伟	〔淪〕沦	〔頇〕顸	〔硤〕硖	〔順〕顺
〔專〕专	〔徠〕徕	〔悵〕怅	〔堯〕尧	〔硯〕砚	〔傖〕伧
〔區〕区	〔術〕术	〔鄆〕郓	〔揀〕拣	〔殘〕残	〔傯〕偬
〔堅〕坚	〔從〕从	〔啓〕启	〔馭〕驭	〔雲〕云	〔傢〕家
〔帶〕带	〔釷〕钍	〔視〕视	〔項〕项	【丨】	〔鄔〕邬
〔厠〕厕	〔釬〕钎	【乛】	〔賁〕贲	〔覘〕觇	〔衆〕众
〔硃〕朱	〔釧〕钏	〔將〕将	〔場〕场	〔睏〕困	〔復〕复
〔麥〕麦	〔釤〕钐	〔晝〕昼	〔揚〕扬	〔貼〕贴	〔須〕须
〔頃〕顷	〔釣〕钓	〔張〕张	〔塊〕块	〔貺〕贶	〔鈃〕钘
【丨】	〔釩〕钒	〔階〕阶	〔達〕达	〔貯〕贮	〔鈣〕钙
〔鹵〕卤	〔釹〕钕	〔陽〕阳	〔報〕报	〔貽〕贻	〔鈈〕钚
〔處〕处	〔釵〕钗	〔隊〕队	〔揮〕挥	〔閏〕闰	〔鈦〕钛
〔敗〕败	〔貪〕贪	〔婭〕娅	〔壺〕壶	〔開〕开	〔鈥〕钬
〔販〕贩	〔覓〕觅	〔媧〕娲	〔惡〕恶	〔閑〕闲	〔鈍〕钝
〔貶〕贬	〔飥〕饦	〔婦〕妇	〔葉〕叶	〔間〕间	〔鈔〕钞
〔啞〕哑	〔貧〕贫	〔習〕习	〔萬〕万	〔閔〕闵	〔鈉〕钠
〔閉〕闭	〔脛〕胫	〔參〕参	〔葷〕荤	〔悶〕闷	〔鈴〕铃
〔問〕问	〔魚〕鱼	〔紺〕绀	〔喪〕丧	〔貴〕贵	〔欽〕钦
〔婁〕娄	【丶】	〔紲〕绁	〔葦〕苇	〔鄖〕郧	〔鈞〕钧
〔唡〕唡	〔詎〕讵	〔絰〕绖	〔葒〕荭	〔勛〕勋	〔鈎〕钩
〔國〕国					〔鈧〕钪

〔鈁〕钫	〔痙〕痉	〔幾〕几	〔楓〕枫	〔鳴〕鸣	〔鉚〕铆
〔鈇〕钬	〔勞〕劳		〔軾〕轼	〔嗆〕呛	〔鈰〕铈
〔鈄〕钭	〔滇〕滇	**13笔**	〔輕〕轻	〔圓〕圆	〔鉉〕铉
〔鈕〕钮	〔測〕测	【一】	〔輅〕辂	〔骯〕肮	〔鉈〕铊
〔鈀〕钯	〔湯〕汤		〔較〕较		〔鉍〕铋
〔傘〕伞	〔淵〕渊	〔項〕项	〔竪〕竖	【丿】	〔鈮〕铌
〔爺〕爷	〔渢〕沨	〔琿〕珲	〔賈〕贾		〔鈹〕铍
〔創〕创	〔渾〕浑	〔瑋〕玮	〔匯〕汇	〔筧〕笕	〔僉〕佥
〔鈍〕钝	〔惬〕惬	〔頑〕顽	〔電〕电	〔節〕节	〔會〕会
〔飪〕饪	〔惻〕恻	〔載〕载	〔頓〕顿	〔與〕与	〔亂〕乱
〔飫〕饫	〔惲〕恽	〔馱〕驮	〔盞〕盏	〔債〕债	〔愛〕爱
〔飭〕饬	〔惱〕恼	〔馴〕驯		〔僅〕仅	〔飾〕饰
〔飯〕饭	〔運〕运	〔馳〕驰	【丨】	〔傳〕传	〔飽〕饱
〔飲〕饮	〔補〕补	〔塒〕埘		〔傴〕伛	〔飼〕饲
〔爲〕为	〔禍〕祸	〔塤〕埙	〔歲〕岁	〔傾〕倾	〔飿〕饳
〔脹〕胀		〔損〕损	〔虜〕虏	〔僂〕偻	〔飴〕饴
〔腖〕胨	【一】	〔遠〕远	〔業〕业	〔賃〕赁	〔頒〕颁
〔腡〕脶	〔尋〕寻	〔塏〕垲	〔當〕当	〔傷〕伤	〔頌〕颂
〔勝〕胜	〔費〕费	〔勢〕势	〔睞〕睐	〔傭〕佣	〔腸〕肠
〔猶〕犹	〔違〕违	〔搶〕抢	〔賊〕贼	〔裊〕袅	〔腫〕肿
〔貿〕贸	〔韌〕韧	〔搗〕捣	〔賄〕贿	〔頎〕颀	〔腦〕脑
〔鄒〕邹	〔隕〕陨	〔塢〕坞	〔賂〕赂	〔鈺〕钰	〔魛〕鱽
	〔賀〕贺	〔壺〕壶	〔賅〕赅	〔鉦〕钲	〔像〕象
【、】	〔發〕发	〔聖〕圣	〔嗎〕吗	〔鉗〕钳	〔獁〕犸
〔詁〕诂	〔綁〕绑	〔蓋〕盖	〔嘩〕哗	〔鈷〕钴	〔鳩〕鸠
〔詞〕词	〔絨〕绒	〔蓮〕莲	〔嗊〕唝	〔鉢〕钵	〔獅〕狮
〔評〕评	〔結〕结	〔蒔〕莳	〔暘〕旸	〔鉅〕钜	〔猻〕狲
〔詛〕诅	〔絝〕绔	〔蓽〕荜	〔閘〕闸	〔鈳〕钶	
〔詗〕诇	〔經〕经	〔夢〕梦	〔黽〕黾	〔鈸〕钹	【、】
〔詐〕诈	〔絎〕绗	〔蒼〕苍	〔暈〕晕	〔鉞〕钺	〔誆〕诓
〔訴〕诉	〔給〕给	〔幹〕干	〔號〕号	〔鉬〕钼	〔誄〕诔
〔診〕诊	〔絢〕绚	〔蓀〕荪	〔園〕园	〔鉭〕钽	〔試〕试
〔詆〕诋	〔絳〕绛	〔蔭〕荫	〔蛺〕蛱	〔鉀〕钾	〔詿〕诖
〔詞〕词	〔絡〕络	〔蒓〕莼	〔蜆〕蚬	〔鈾〕铀	〔詩〕诗
〔詘〕诎	〔絞〕绞	〔楨〕桢	〔農〕农	〔鈿〕钿	〔詰〕诘
〔詔〕诏	〔統〕统	〔楊〕杨	〔嗩〕唢	〔鉑〕铂	〔誇〕夸
〔詒〕诒	〔絕〕绝	〔嗇〕啬	〔嗶〕哔	〔鈴〕铃	〔詼〕诙
〔馮〕冯	〔絲〕丝			〔鉛〕铅	

〔誠〕诚　〔愴〕怆　〔撾〕挝　【丨】　〔製〕制　〔餞〕饯
〔誅〕诛　〔惻〕恻　〔墊〕垫　〔對〕对　〔種〕种　〔餌〕饵
〔話〕话　〔窩〕窝　〔壽〕寿　〔幣〕币　〔稱〕称　〔蝕〕蚀
〔誕〕诞　〔禎〕祯　〔摺〕折　〔彆〕别　〔箋〕笺　〔餉〕饷
〔詬〕诟　〔褘〕袆　〔摻〕掺　〔嘗〕尝　〔僥〕侥　〔餄〕饸
〔詮〕诠　【一】　〔摜〕掼　〔嘖〕啧　〔債〕债　〔餎〕饹
〔詭〕诡　〔肅〕肃　〔勩〕勚　〔曄〕晔　〔僕〕仆　〔餃〕饺
〔詢〕询　〔裝〕装　〔蔞〕蒌　〔夥〕伙　〔僑〕侨　〔餏〕饻
〔詣〕诣　〔遜〕逊　〔蔦〕茑　〔賑〕赈　〔僞〕伪　〔餅〕饼
〔諍〕诤　〔際〕际　〔蓯〕苁　〔賒〕赊　〔銜〕衔　〔領〕领
〔該〕该　〔媽〕妈　〔蔔〕卜　〔嘆〕叹　〔鉶〕铏　〔鳳〕凤
〔詳〕详　〔預〕预　〔蔣〕蒋　〔暢〕畅　〔銬〕铐　〔颱〕台
〔詫〕诧　〔疊〕迭　〔薌〕芗　〔嘜〕唛　〔銠〕铑　〔獄〕狱
〔詡〕诩　〔綆〕绠　〔構〕构　〔閨〕闺　〔鉺〕铒　【丶】
〔裏〕里　〔經〕经　〔樺〕桦　〔聞〕闻　〔銪〕铕　〔誡〕诫
〔準〕准　〔綃〕绡　〔橙〕桤　〔閩〕闽　〔鋁〕铝　〔誑〕诳
〔頑〕顽　〔絹〕绢　〔覡〕觋　〔閭〕闾　〔銅〕铜　〔語〕语
〔資〕资　〔綉〕绣　〔槍〕枪　〔閥〕阀　〔銦〕铟　〔誚〕诮
〔脛〕胫　〔綏〕绥　〔輒〕辄　〔閤〕合　〔銖〕铢　〔誤〕误
〔義〕义　〔綈〕绨　〔輔〕辅　〔閣〕阁　〔銑〕铣　〔誥〕诰
〔煉〕炼　〔彙〕汇　〔輕〕轻　〔閫〕阃　〔銩〕铥　〔誘〕诱
〔煩〕烦　　　　　〔塹〕堑　〔閡〕阂　〔銓〕铨　〔誨〕诲
〔煬〕炀　**14笔**　〔匱〕匮　〔嘔〕呕　〔鉿〕铪　〔誑〕诳
〔塋〕茔　【一】　〔監〕监　〔蝸〕蜗　〔銚〕铫　〔説〕说
〔熒〕荧　　　　　〔緊〕紧　〔團〕团　〔銘〕铭　〔認〕认
〔煒〕炜　〔瑪〕玛　〔厲〕厉　〔嘍〕喽　〔鉻〕铬　〔誦〕诵
〔遞〕递　〔璉〕琏　〔厭〕厌　〔鄲〕郸　〔錚〕铮　〔誒〕诶
〔溝〕沟　〔瑣〕琐　〔碩〕硕　〔鳴〕鸣　〔銫〕铯　〔廣〕广
〔漣〕涟　〔瑲〕玱　〔碭〕砀　〔幘〕帻　〔鉸〕铰　〔麽〕么
〔滅〕灭　〔駁〕驳　〔碸〕砜　〔嶄〕崭　〔銥〕铱　〔廎〕庼
〔湞〕浈　〔摶〕抟　〔奩〕奁　〔嶇〕岖　〔銃〕铳　〔瘧〕疟
〔滌〕涤　〔摳〕抠　〔爾〕尔　〔罰〕罚　〔銨〕铵　〔瘍〕疡
〔漁〕浉　〔趙〕赵　〔奪〕夺　〔嶁〕嵝　〔銀〕银　〔瘋〕疯
〔塗〕涂　〔趕〕赶　〔殞〕殒　〔幗〕帼　〔銣〕铷　〔塵〕尘
〔滄〕沧　〔摟〕搂　〔鳶〕鸢　〔圖〕图　　　　　〔颯〕飒
〔愷〕恺　〔摑〕掴　〔巰〕巯　【丿】　　　　　〔適〕适
〔愾〕忾　〔臺〕台　　　　　　　　　　　　　〔齊〕齐

〔養〕养
〔鄰〕邻
〔鄭〕郑
〔燁〕烨
〔熗〕炝
〔榮〕荣
〔熒〕荧
〔犖〕荦
〔滎〕荥
〔漬〕渍
〔漢〕汉
〔滿〕满
〔漸〕渐
〔漚〕沤
〔滯〕滞
〔滷〕卤
〔漊〕溇
〔漁〕渔
〔滸〕浒
〔漣〕涟
〔滬〕沪
〔漲〕涨
〔滲〕渗
〔慚〕惭
〔慪〕怄
〔慳〕悭
〔慟〕恸
〔慘〕惨
〔慣〕惯
〔寬〕宽
〔賓〕宾
〔窪〕洼
〔寧〕宁
〔寢〕寝
〔實〕实
〔皸〕皲
〔複〕复

【乛】
〔劃〕划
〔盡〕尽
〔屢〕屡
〔獎〕奖
〔墮〕堕
〔隨〕随
〔骳〕骹
〔墜〕坠
〔嫗〕妪
〔頗〕颇
〔態〕态
〔鄧〕邓
〔緒〕绪
〔綾〕绫
〔綺〕绮
〔綫〕线
〔緋〕绯
〔綽〕绰
〔緄〕绲
〔綱〕纲
〔網〕网
〔維〕维
〔綿〕绵
〔綸〕纶
〔綳〕绷
〔綢〕绸
〔綹〕绺
〔綣〕绻
〔綜〕综
〔綻〕绽
〔綰〕绾
〔綠〕绿
〔綴〕缀
〔緇〕缁

15笔

【一】
〔鬧〕闹
〔璡〕琎
〔靚〕靓
〔輦〕辇
〔髮〕发
〔撓〕挠
〔墳〕坟
〔撻〕挞
〔駔〕驵
〔駛〕驶
〔駟〕驷
〔駙〕驸
〔駒〕驹
〔駐〕驻
〔駝〕驼
〔駘〕骀
〔撲〕扑
〔頡〕颉
〔撣〕掸
〔賣〕卖
〔撫〕抚
〔撟〕挢
〔撳〕揿
〔熱〕热
〔鞏〕巩
〔摯〕挚
〔撈〕捞
〔穀〕谷
〔慤〕悫
〔撏〕挦
〔撥〕拨
〔蕘〕荛
〔蕆〕蒇

〔蕓〕芸
〔邁〕迈
〔蕢〕蒉
〔蕒〕荬
〔蕪〕芜
〔蕎〕荞
〔蕕〕莸
〔蕩〕荡
〔蕁〕荨
〔樁〕桩
〔樞〕枢
〔標〕标
〔樓〕楼
〔樅〕枞
〔麩〕麸
〔賫〕赍
〔樣〕样
〔橢〕椭
〔輛〕辆
〔輥〕辊
〔輞〕辋
〔槧〕椠
〔暫〕暂
〔輪〕轮
〔輟〕辍
〔輜〕辎
〔甌〕瓯
〔歐〕欧
〔毆〕殴
〔賢〕贤
〔遷〕迁
〔鳾〕䴓
〔憂〕忧
〔碼〕码
〔磑〕硙
〔確〕确
〔賚〕赉

〔遼〕辽
〔殤〕殇
〔鴉〕鸦

【丨】
〔輩〕辈
〔劌〕刿
〔齒〕齿
〔劇〕剧
〔膚〕肤
〔慮〕虑
〔鄲〕郸
〔輝〕辉
〔賞〕赏
〔賦〕赋
〔賵〕赗
〔賬〕账
〔賭〕赌
〔賤〕贱
〔賜〕赐
〔賙〕赒
〔賠〕赔
〔賧〕赕
〔嘵〕哓
〔噴〕喷
〔噠〕哒
〔噁〕恶
〔閬〕阆
〔閫〕阃
〔閱〕阅
〔閬〕阆
〔數〕数
〔踐〕践
〔遺〕遗
〔蝦〕虾
〔嘸〕呒
〔嘮〕唠
〔噚〕㖊

〔嘰〕叽
〔嶢〕峣
〔罷〕罢
〔嶠〕峤
〔嶔〕嵚
〔幟〕帜
〔嶗〕崂

【丿】
〔頦〕颏
〔篋〕箧
〔範〕范
〔價〕价
〔儂〕侬
〔儉〕俭
〔儈〕侩
〔億〕亿
〔儀〕仪
〔皚〕皑
〔樂〕乐
〔質〕质
〔徵〕征
〔衝〕冲
〔慫〕怂
〔徹〕彻
〔衛〕卫
〔盤〕盘
〔鋪〕铺
〔鋏〕铗
〔鋱〕铽
〔銷〕销
〔鋥〕锃
〔鋰〕锂
〔鋇〕钡
〔鋤〕锄
〔鋯〕锆
〔鋨〕锇
〔銹〕锈

〔銼〕锉	〔諛〕谀	〔憒〕愦	〔緼〕缊	〔薩〕萨	〔閼〕阏
〔鋒〕锋	〔誰〕谁	〔憚〕惮	〔緦〕缌	〔蕷〕蓣	〔閹〕阉
〔鋅〕锌	〔論〕论	〔憮〕怃	〔緞〕缎	〔橈〕桡	〔閭〕闾
〔銳〕锐	〔諗〕谂	〔憐〕怜	〔緱〕缑	〔樹〕树	〔閱〕阅
〔銻〕锑	〔調〕调	〔寫〕写	〔縋〕缒	〔樸〕朴	〔閣〕阁
〔銀〕银	〔諂〕谄	〔審〕审	〔緩〕缓	〔橋〕桥	〔閡〕阂
〔鋟〕锓	〔諒〕谅	〔窮〕穷	〔締〕缔	〔機〕机	〔曇〕昙
〔鋼〕钢	〔諄〕谆	〔褳〕裢	〔編〕编	〔輳〕辏	〔噸〕吨
〔錒〕锕	〔誶〕谇	〔褲〕裤	〔緡〕缗	〔輻〕辐	〔鴞〕鸮
〔頜〕颌	〔談〕谈	〔鴆〕鸩	〔緯〕纬	〔輯〕辑	〔噦〕哕
〔劍〕剑	〔誼〕谊	**【乛】**	〔緣〕缘	〔輸〕输	〔踴〕踊
〔劊〕刽	〔廟〕庙	〔遲〕迟		〔賴〕赖	〔螞〕蚂
〔鄶〕郐	〔廠〕厂	〔層〕层	**16笔**	〔頭〕头	〔螄〕蛳
〔餑〕饽	〔廡〕庑	〔彈〕弹	**【一】**	〔醖〕酝	〔噹〕当
〔餓〕饿	〔瘞〕瘗	〔選〕选	〔璣〕玑	〔醜〕丑	〔罵〕骂
〔餘〕余	〔瘡〕疮	〔槳〕桨	〔墻〕墙	〔勵〕励	〔噥〕哝
〔餒〕馁	〔賡〕赓	〔漿〕浆	〔駱〕骆	〔磧〕碛	〔戰〕战
〔膞〕膞	〔慶〕庆	〔險〕险	〔駭〕骇	〔磚〕砖	〔噲〕哙
〔膕〕腘	〔廢〕废	〔嬈〕娆	〔駢〕骈	〔磣〕碜	〔鴦〕鸯
〔膠〕胶	〔敵〕敌	〔嫻〕娴	〔擓〕㧟	〔歷〕历	〔噯〕嗳
〔鴇〕鸨	〔頦〕颏	〔駕〕驾	〔擄〕掳	〔曆〕历	〔嘯〕啸
〔魷〕鱿	〔導〕导	〔嬋〕婵	〔擋〕挡	〔奮〕奋	〔還〕还
〔魯〕鲁	〔瑩〕莹	〔嫵〕妩	〔擇〕择	〔頰〕颊	〔嶧〕峄
〔魴〕鲂	〔潔〕洁	〔嬌〕娇	〔頳〕赪	〔殨〕㱮	〔嶼〕屿
〔穎〕颖	〔澆〕浇	〔嫿〕妫	〔撿〕捡	〔殫〕殚	**【丿】**
〔颳〕刮	〔澾〕达	〔嬡〕媛	〔擔〕担	〔頸〕颈	〔積〕积
〔劉〕刘	〔潤〕润	〔駑〕驽	〔壇〕坛	**【丨】**	〔頹〕颓
〔皺〕皱	〔澗〕涧	〔翬〕翚	〔擁〕拥	〔頻〕频	〔穆〕穆
【、】	〔潰〕溃	〔毿〕毵	〔據〕据	〔盧〕卢	〔篤〕笃
〔請〕请	〔潿〕涠	〔緙〕缂	〔薔〕蔷	〔曉〕晓	〔築〕筑
〔諸〕诸	〔潯〕浔	〔緗〕缃	〔薑〕姜	〔瞞〕瞒	〔篳〕筚
〔諏〕诹	〔潙〕沩	〔練〕练	〔薈〕荟	〔縣〕县	〔篩〕筛
〔諾〕诺	〔澇〕涝	〔緘〕缄	〔薊〕蓟	〔瞘〕眍	〔舉〕举
〔諑〕诼	〔潑〕泼	〔緬〕缅	〔薦〕荐	〔瞜〕䁖	〔興〕兴
〔誹〕诽	〔憤〕愤	〔緹〕缇	〔蕭〕萧	〔贈〕赠	〔嶨〕峃
〔課〕课	〔憫〕悯	〔緲〕缈	〔頤〕颐	〔鴨〕鸭	〔學〕学
〔諉〕诿		〔緝〕缉	〔鴣〕鸪		

〔儔〕俦　〔餜〕餜　〔諼〕谖　〔憶〕忆　〔駿〕骏　〔臨〕临

〔懺〕忏　〔餛〕馄　〔諷〕讽　〔憲〕宪　〔趨〕趋　〔磽〕硗

〔儕〕侪　〔餡〕馅　〔諳〕谙　〔窺〕窥　〔擱〕搁　〔壓〕压

〔儐〕傧　〔館〕馆　〔諮〕谘　〔竄〕窜　〔擬〕拟　〔礄〕硚

〔儘〕尽　〔頷〕颔　〔諦〕谛　〔窩〕窝　〔擴〕扩　〔磯〕矶

〔鴕〕鸵　〔鴿〕鸽　〔謎〕谜　〔褸〕褛　〔壙〕圹　〔鴯〕鸸

〔艙〕舱　〔膩〕腻　〔諢〕诨　〔禪〕禅　〔擠〕挤　〔邇〕迩

〔錶〕表　〔鷗〕鸥　〔諞〕谝　【一】　〔蟄〕蛰　〔尷〕尴

〔鍺〕锗　〔鮁〕鲅　〔諱〕讳　〔隱〕隐　〔縶〕絷　〔鴷〕䴕

〔錯〕错　〔鮃〕鲆　〔憑〕凭　〔嬙〕嫱　〔擲〕掷　〔殮〕殓

〔鍩〕锘　〔鮎〕鲇　〔鄺〕邝　〔嬡〕嫒　〔擯〕摈　【丨】

〔錨〕锚　〔鮓〕鲊　〔瘻〕瘘　〔縉〕缙　〔擰〕拧　〔齔〕龀

〔錛〕锛　〔穌〕稣　〔瘮〕瘆　〔縝〕缜　〔轂〕毂　〔戲〕戏

〔錸〕铼　〔鮒〕鲋　〔親〕亲　〔縛〕缚　〔聲〕声　〔虧〕亏

〔錢〕钱　〔鮍〕鲏　〔辦〕办　〔縟〕缛　〔藉〕借　〔斃〕毙

〔鍀〕锝　〔鮊〕鲌　〔龍〕龙　〔緻〕致　〔聰〕聪　〔瞭〕了

〔錁〕锞　〔鮐〕鲐　〔劑〕剂　〔縧〕绦　〔聯〕联　〔顆〕颗

〔錕〕锟　〔鴝〕鸲　〔燒〕烧　〔縫〕缝　〔艱〕艰　〔購〕购

〔鍆〕钔　〔獲〕获　〔燜〕焖　〔縐〕绉　〔藍〕蓝　〔賻〕赙

〔錫〕锡　〔穎〕颖　〔熾〕炽　〔縭〕缡　〔舊〕旧　〔嬰〕婴

〔錮〕锢　〔獨〕独　〔螢〕萤　〔縑〕缣　〔薺〕荠　〔賺〕赚

〔鋼〕钢　〔獫〕猃　〔營〕营　〔縊〕缢　〔薹〕薹　〔嚇〕吓

〔鍋〕锅　〔獪〕狯　〔縈〕萦　　　　　〔韓〕韩　〔闌〕阑

〔錘〕锤　〔鴛〕鸳　〔燈〕灯　**17笔**　〔隸〕隶　〔闃〕阒

〔錐〕锥　　　　　〔濛〕蒙　【一】　〔檉〕柽　〔闆〕板

〔錦〕锦　【、】　〔燙〕烫　〔樓〕楼　〔檣〕樯　〔闊〕阔

〔鍬〕锹　〔謀〕谋　〔澠〕渑　〔環〕环　〔檟〕槚　〔闈〕闱

〔錇〕锫　〔諶〕谌　〔濃〕浓　〔贅〕赘　〔檔〕档　〔闋〕阕

〔錠〕锭　〔諜〕谍　〔澤〕泽　〔璦〕瑷　〔櫛〕栉　〔曖〕暧

〔鍵〕键　〔謊〕谎　〔濁〕浊　〔靚〕靓　〔檢〕检　〔蹕〕跸

〔錄〕录　〔諫〕谏　〔澮〕浍　〔黿〕鼋　〔檜〕桧　〔蹌〕跄

〔鋸〕锯　〔諧〕谐　〔澱〕淀　〔幫〕帮　〔麯〕曲　〔蟎〕螨

〔錳〕锰　〔謔〕谑　〔澦〕滪　〔騁〕骋　〔轅〕辕　〔螻〕蝼

〔錙〕锱　〔謁〕谒　〔懞〕蒙　〔駸〕骎　〔轄〕辖　〔蟈〕蝈

〔覦〕觎　〔謂〕谓　〔懌〕怿　　　　　〔輾〕辗　〔雖〕虽

〔墾〕垦　〔諤〕谔　　　　　　　　　〔擊〕击　〔嚀〕咛

〔餞〕饯　〔諭〕谕

〔覬〕觊
〔嶺〕岭
〔嶸〕嵘
〔點〕点
【丿】
〔矯〕矫
〔鴰〕鸹
〔簀〕箦
〔簍〕篓
〔輿〕舆
〔歟〕欤
〔鵂〕鸺
〔龜〕龟
〔優〕优
〔償〕偿
〔儲〕储
〔魈〕魈
〔鵃〕鸼
〔禦〕御
〔聳〕耸
〔鵮〕鹐
〔鍥〕锲
〔鍇〕锴
〔鍘〕铡
〔錫〕锡
〔鍶〕锶
〔鍔〕锷
〔鍤〕锸
〔鍾〕钟
〔鍛〕锻
〔鎪〕锼
〔鍬〕锹
〔鍰〕锾
〔鍍〕镀
〔鎂〕镁

〔鎡〕镃
〔鎇〕镅
〔懇〕恳
〔餷〕馇
〔餳〕饧
〔餶〕馉
〔餿〕馊
〔斂〕敛
〔鴿〕鸽
〔膿〕脓
〔臉〕脸
〔膾〕脍
〔膽〕胆
〔謄〕誊
〔鮭〕鲑
〔鮚〕鲒
〔鮪〕鲔
〔鮦〕鲖
〔鮫〕鲛
〔鮮〕鲜
〔颶〕飓
〔獷〕犷
〔獰〕狞
【丶】
〔講〕讲
〔謨〕谟
〔謖〕谡
〔謝〕谢
〔謠〕谣
〔謅〕诌
〔謗〕谤
〔謚〕谥
〔謙〕谦
〔謐〕谧
〔褻〕亵
〔氈〕毡

〔應〕应
〔癘〕疠
〔療〕疗
〔癇〕痫
〔癉〕瘅
〔癆〕痨
〔鵁〕鹪
〔齋〕斋
〔鮺〕鲝
〔鮝〕鲞
〔糞〕粪
〔糝〕糁
〔燦〕灿
〔燭〕烛
〔燴〕烩
〔鴻〕鸿
〔濤〕涛
〔濫〕滥
〔濕〕湿
〔濟〕济
〔濱〕滨
〔濘〕泞
〔澀〕涩
〔濰〕潍
〔憶〕忆
〔賽〕赛
〔襇〕裥
〔禕〕祎
〔襖〕袄
〔禮〕礼
【一】
〔屨〕屦
〔彌〕弥
〔嬪〕嫔

〔績〕绩
〔縹〕缥
〔縷〕缕
〔縵〕缦
〔縲〕缧
〔總〕总
〔縱〕纵
〔縴〕纤
〔縮〕缩
〔繆〕缪
〔繅〕缫
〔嚮〕向

18笔

【一】
〔耮〕耢
〔鬩〕阋
〔瓊〕琼
〔撻〕挞
〔鬆〕松
〔翹〕翘
〔擷〕撷
〔擾〕扰
〔騏〕骐
〔騎〕骑
〔騍〕骒
〔騅〕骓
〔攄〕摅
〔擻〕擞
〔鼕〕冬
〔擺〕摆
〔贅〕赘
〔燾〕焘
〔聶〕聂
〔聵〕聩
〔職〕职

〔藝〕艺
〔覲〕觐
〔鞦〕秋
〔藪〕薮
〔蠆〕虿
〔繭〕茧
〔藥〕药
〔藭〕芎
〔贖〕赎
〔蘊〕蕴
〔檯〕台
〔櫃〕柜
〔檻〕槛
〔檳〕槟
〔檸〕柠
〔鵓〕鹁
〔轉〕转
〔轆〕辘
〔覆〕复
〔醫〕医
〔礎〕础
〔殯〕殡
〔霧〕雾
【丨】
〔豐〕丰
〔覷〕觑
〔懟〕怼
〔叢〕丛
〔矇〕蒙
〔題〕题
〔韙〕韪
〔瞼〕睑
〔闖〕闯
〔闔〕阖
〔闐〕阗

〔闓〕闿
〔闕〕阙
〔顒〕颙
〔曠〕旷
〔蹣〕蹒
〔嚙〕啮
〔壘〕垒
〔蟯〕蛲
〔蟲〕虫
〔蟬〕蝉
〔蟣〕虮
〔鵑〕鹃
〔嚕〕噜
〔顓〕颛
【丿】
〔鵠〕鹄
〔鵝〕鹅
〔穫〕获
〔穡〕穑
〔穢〕秽
〔簡〕简
〔簣〕篑
〔簞〕箪
〔雙〕双
〔軀〕躯
〔邊〕边
〔歸〕归
〔鏵〕铧
〔鎮〕镇
〔鏈〕链
〔鎘〕镉
〔鎖〕锁
〔鎧〕铠
〔鐫〕镌
〔鎳〕镍
〔鎢〕钨

〔鍛〕锻	〔糧〕粮	〔騷〕骚	〔願〕愿	〔鏞〕镛	〔癟〕瘪
〔錚〕铮	〔燼〕烬	〔壢〕坜	〔鶘〕鹕	〔鏡〕镜	〔癢〕痒
〔鎦〕馏	〔鵜〕鹈	〔壚〕垆	〔璽〕玺	〔鏟〕铲	〔龐〕庞
〔鎬〕镐	〔瀆〕渎	〔壞〕坏	〔豶〕豮	〔鏑〕镝	〔壟〕垄
〔鎊〕镑	〔懣〕懑	〔攏〕拢	【丨】	〔鏃〕镞	〔鶊〕鹒
〔鎰〕镒	〔濾〕滤	〔蘀〕萚	〔贈〕赠	〔鏇〕旋	〔類〕类
〔鎵〕镓	〔鯊〕鲨	〔難〕难	〔闞〕阚	〔鏘〕锵	〔爍〕烁
〔鎘〕镉	〔濺〕溅	〔鵲〕鹊	〔關〕关	〔辭〕辞	〔瀟〕潇
〔鵒〕鹆	〔瀏〕浏	〔藶〕苈	〔嚦〕呖	〔饉〕馑	〔瀨〕濑
〔饃〕馍	〔濼〕泺	〔蘋〕苹	〔疇〕畴	〔饅〕馒	〔瀝〕沥
〔餺〕馎	〔瀉〕泻	〔蘆〕芦	〔蹺〕跷	〔鵬〕鹏	〔瀕〕濒
〔餼〕饩	〔瀋〕沈	〔鶓〕鹋	〔蟶〕蛏	〔臘〕腊	〔瀘〕泸
〔餾〕馏	〔竄〕窜	〔藺〕蔺	〔蠅〕蝇	〔鯖〕鲭	〔瀧〕泷
〔饊〕馓	〔竅〕窍	〔躉〕趸	〔蟻〕蚁	〔鯪〕鲮	〔懶〕懒
〔臍〕脐	〔額〕额	〔蘄〕蕲	〔嚴〕严	〔鯫〕鲰	〔懷〕怀
〔鯁〕鲠	〔禰〕祢	〔勸〕劝	〔獸〕兽	〔鯡〕鲱	〔寵〕宠
〔鯉〕鲤	〔襠〕裆	〔蘇〕苏	〔嚨〕咙	〔鯤〕鲲	〔襪〕袜
〔鯀〕鲧	〔襝〕裣	〔藹〕蔼	〔羆〕罴	〔鯧〕鲳	〔襤〕褴
〔鯇〕鲩	〔禱〕祷	〔蘢〕茏	〔羅〕罗	〔鯢〕鲵	【乛】
〔鯽〕鲫	【乛】	〔顛〕颠	【丿】	〔鯰〕鲶	〔韜〕韬
〔颸〕飔	〔醬〕酱	〔櫝〕椟	〔氌〕氇	〔鯛〕鲷	〔騭〕骘
〔颺〕飏	〔韞〕韫	〔櫟〕栎	〔犢〕犊	〔鯨〕鲸	〔騖〕骛
〔觴〕觞	〔隴〕陇	〔櫓〕橹	〔贊〕赞	〔鯔〕鲻	〔顙〕颡
〔獵〕猎	〔嬸〕婶	〔櫧〕槠	〔穩〕稳	〔獺〕獭	〔繮〕缰
〔雛〕雏	〔繞〕绕	〔櫞〕橼	〔簽〕签	〔鶿〕鹚	〔繩〕绳
〔臏〕膑	〔繚〕缭	〔轎〕轿	〔簾〕帘	〔颼〕飕	〔繾〕缱
【丶】	〔織〕织	〔鏨〕錾	〔簫〕箫	【丶】	〔繰〕缲
〔謹〕谨	〔繕〕缮	〔轍〕辙	〔牘〕牍	〔譚〕谭	〔繹〕绎
〔謳〕讴	〔繒〕缯	〔轔〕辚	〔懲〕惩	〔譖〕谮	〔繯〕缳
〔謾〕谩	〔斷〕断	〔繫〕系	〔鐯〕䦂	〔譙〕谯	〔繳〕缴
〔謫〕谪	**19笔**	〔鵮〕鹐	〔鏗〕铿	〔識〕识	〔繪〕绘
〔謭〕谫	【一】	〔麗〕丽	〔鏢〕镖	〔譜〕谱	**20笔**
〔謬〕谬	〔鵡〕鹉	〔厴〕厣	〔鏜〕镗	〔證〕证	【一】
〔癤〕疖	〔鶄〕鹢	〔礪〕砺	〔鏤〕镂	〔譎〕谲	〔瓏〕珑
〔雜〕杂	〔鬍〕胡	〔礙〕碍	〔鏝〕镘	〔譏〕讥	〔驁〕骜
〔離〕离	〔騙〕骗	〔礦〕矿	〔鏰〕镚	〔鶉〕鹑	〔驊〕骅
〔顏〕颜		〔贗〕赝		〔廬〕庐	〔驛〕驿

〔驑〕骝
〔驊〕骅
〔騙〕骗
〔攖〕撄
〔攔〕拦
〔攙〕搀
〔聹〕聍
〔顢〕颟
〔驀〕蓦
〔蘭〕兰
〔蘞〕蔹
〔蘚〕藓
〔鶘〕鹕
〔飄〕飘
〔櫪〕枥
〔櫨〕栌
〔櫸〕榉
〔礬〕矾
〔麵〕面
〔櫬〕榇
〔櫳〕栊
〔礫〕砾

【丨】
〔鹹〕咸
〔齚〕龃
〔齟〕龃
〔齣〕出
〔齙〕龅
〔齠〕龆
〔獻〕献
〔黨〕党
〔懸〕悬
〔鶪〕䴗
〔罌〕罂
〔贍〕赡

〔闥〕闼
〔闡〕阐
〔鶡〕鹖
〔曨〕昽
〔蠣〕蛎
〔蠐〕蛴
〔蠑〕蝾
〔嚶〕嘤
〔鶚〕鹗
〔髏〕髅
〔鶻〕鹘

【丿】
〔犧〕牺
〔鶩〕鹜
〔籌〕筹
〔籃〕篮
〔譽〕誉
〔覺〕觉
〔譽〕誊
〔嶬〕蒇
〔艦〕舰
〔饒〕铙
〔鐯〕镶
〔鏌〕镆
〔鐦〕锎
〔鐧〕锏
〔鐓〕镦
〔鐘〕钟
〔鐠〕镨
〔鐥〕错
〔鐒〕铹
〔鐋〕铴
〔鐙〕镫
〔鏺〕钹

〔釋〕释
〔饒〕饶
〔饊〕馓
〔饋〕馈
〔饌〕馔
〔饑〕饥
〔臚〕胪
〔朧〕胧
〔騰〕腾
〔鰣〕鲥
〔鰈〕鲽
〔鰂〕鲗
〔鰓〕鳃
〔鰐〕鳄
〔鰍〕鳅
〔鰒〕鳆
〔鰉〕鳇
〔鰌〕鳎
〔鯿〕鳊
〔獼〕猕
〔觸〕触

【丶】
〔護〕护
〔譴〕谴
〔譯〕译
〔譫〕谵
〔議〕议
〔癥〕症
〔辮〕辫
〔龑〕龑
〔競〕竞
〔贏〕赢
〔糲〕粝
〔糰〕团
〔鷀〕鹚

〔爐〕炉
〔瀾〕澜
〔瀲〕潋
〔瀰〕弥
〔懺〕忏
〔寶〕宝
〔騫〕骞
〔竇〕窦
〔襬〕摆

【乛】
〔鶺〕鹛
〔鷙〕鸷
〔纊〕纩
〔繽〕缤
〔繼〕继
〔饗〕飨
〔響〕响

21笔

【一】
〔糲〕耰
〔瓔〕璎
〔鼇〕鳌
〔攝〕摄
〔騾〕骡
〔驅〕驱
〔驃〕骠
〔驄〕骢
〔驂〕骖
〔攛〕撺
〔擻〕掳
〔鞽〕鞒
〔韉〕鞯
〔歡〕欢
〔權〕权
〔櫻〕樱
〔欄〕栏

〔轟〕轰
〔覽〕览
〔酈〕郦
〔飆〕飙
〔殲〕歼

【丨】
〔齜〕龇
〔齦〕龈
〔齩〕龀
〔黶〕黡
〔囁〕嗫
〔囈〕呓
〔闢〕辟
〔囀〕啭
〔顥〕颢
〔躊〕踌
〔躋〕跻
〔躑〕踯
〔躍〕跃
〔纍〕累
〔蠟〕蜡
〔囂〕嚣
〔巋〕岿
〔髒〕脏

【丿】
〔儺〕傩
〔儷〕俪
〔儼〕俨
〔鷗〕鸥
〔鐵〕铁
〔鑊〕镬
〔鐳〕镭
〔鐺〕铛
〔鐸〕铎
〔鐶〕镯

〔鐮〕镰
〔鐿〕镱
〔鶺〕鹡
〔鷂〕鹞
〔雞〕鸡
〔鴿〕鸽
〔臟〕脏
〔鰧〕䲢
〔鰭〕鳍
〔鰱〕鲢
〔鰥〕鳏
〔鰨〕鳎
〔鰩〕鳐
〔鰟〕鳑
〔鰜〕鳒

【丶】
〔癲〕癫
〔癱〕瘫
〔癮〕瘾
〔斕〕斓
〔辯〕辩
〔礱〕砻
〔鶼〕鹣
〔爛〕烂
〔鶯〕莺
〔灄〕滠
〔灃〕沣
〔灘〕滩
〔懾〕慑
〔懼〕惧
〔竈〕灶
〔顧〕顾
〔襯〕衬
〔鶴〕鹤

【乛】
〔屬〕属

〔纈〕缬
〔續〕续
〔纏〕缠

22笔

【一】
〔鬚〕须
〔驍〕骁
〔驕〕骄
〔攤〕摊
〔覿〕觌
〔攢〕攒
〔鷙〕鸷
〔聽〕听
〔蘿〕萝
〔驚〕惊
〔轢〕轹
〔鷗〕鸥
〔鑒〕鉴
〔邐〕逦
〔鷺〕鹭
〔霽〕霁

【丨】
〔齬〕龉
〔齪〕龊
〔鼇〕鳌
〔贖〕赎
〔躚〕跹
〔躓〕踬
〔蠨〕蟏
〔囌〕苏
〔囉〕罗
〔囁〕嗫
〔轡〕辔
〔巔〕巅
〔邏〕逻
〔體〕体

【丿】
〔罎〕坛
〔籜〕箨
〔籟〕籁
〔籙〕箓
〔籠〕笼
〔鼈〕鳖
〔儻〕傥
〔艫〕舻
〔鑄〕铸
〔鑌〕镔
〔鑔〕镲
〔龕〕龛
〔糴〕籴
〔鰳〕鳓
〔鰹〕鲣
〔鰾〕鳔
〔鱈〕鳕
〔鰻〕鳗
〔鱅〕鳙
〔鰠〕鳋
〔玀〕猡

【丶】
〔讀〕读
〔讅〕谉
〔孌〕娈
〔彎〕弯
〔孿〕孪
〔變〕变
〔顫〕颤
〔鷓〕鹧
〔癭〕瘿
〔癬〕癣
〔聾〕聋
〔龔〕龚
〔襲〕袭

〔灘〕滩
〔灑〕洒
〔竊〕窃

【㇆】
〔鷯〕鹩
〔巒〕峦

23笔

【一】
〔瓚〕瓒
〔驛〕驿
〔驗〕验
〔攪〕搅
〔欏〕椤
〔轤〕轳
〔靨〕靥
〔魘〕魇
〔饜〕餍
〔鷦〕鹪
〔韃〕鞑
〔顳〕颞

【丨】
〔曬〕晒
〔鷳〕鹇
〔顯〕显
〔蠱〕蛊
〔髖〕髋
〔髕〕髌

【丿】
〔籤〕签
〔讎〕雠
〔鷲〕鹫
〔黴〕霉
〔鑠〕铄
〔鑕〕锧
〔鑪〕镥
〔鑣〕镳

〔鑭〕镧
〔臢〕臜
〔鱖〕鳜
〔鱔〕鳝
〔鱗〕鳞
〔鱒〕鳟
〔鱘〕鲟

【丶】
〔讌〕讌
〔欒〕栾
〔攣〕挛
〔戀〕恋
〔鷟〕鷟
〔癰〕痈
〔齏〕齑
〔讋〕詟

【㇆】
〔鷸〕鹬
〔纓〕缨
〔纖〕纤
〔纔〕才
〔鷥〕鸶

24笔

【一】
〔鬢〕鬓
〔攬〕揽
〔驟〕骤
〔壩〕坝
〔韆〕千
〔觀〕观
〔鹽〕盐
〔釀〕酿
〔靉〕叆
〔靈〕灵
〔靄〕霭

〔蠶〕蚕

【丨】
〔艷〕艳
〔顰〕颦
〔齲〕龋
〔齷〕龌
〔鹼〕硷
〔臟〕脏
〔鸒〕鹭
〔囑〕嘱
〔羈〕羁

【丿】
〔籩〕笾
〔籬〕篱
〔籪〕簖
〔黌〕黉
〔鱟〕鲎
〔鱭〕鲚
〔鱠〕鲙
〔鱣〕鳣

【丶】
〔讕〕谰
〔讖〕谶
〔讒〕谗
〔讓〕让
〔鸇〕鹯
〔鷹〕鹰
〔癱〕瘫
〔癲〕癫
〔贛〕赣
〔灝〕灏

【㇆】
〔鸊〕䴙

25笔

【一】
〔韉〕鞯

〔欖〕榄
〔灤〕滦

【丨】
〔顱〕颅
〔躡〕蹑
〔躦〕躜
〔鼉〕鼍

【丿】
〔籮〕箩
〔鑭〕锏
〔鑰〕钥
〔鑲〕镶
〔饞〕馋
〔鱨〕鲿
〔鱭〕鲚

【丶】
〔蠻〕蛮
〔臠〕脔
〔廳〕厅
〔灣〕湾

【㇆】
〔糶〕粜
〔纘〕缵

26笔

【一】
〔驥〕骥
〔驢〕驴
〔趲〕趱
〔顴〕颧
〔黶〕黡
〔釃〕酾
〔釅〕酽

【丨】
〔矚〕瞩
〔躪〕躏

〔躓〕踬	【一】	〔鑼〕锣	【㇕】	〔钁〕镢	〔鸝〕鹂
【丿】	〔鬮〕阄	〔鑽〕钻	〔纜〕缆	〔钁〕镢	〔鑲〕镶
〔釁〕衅	〔驤〕骧	〔鱸〕鲈		〔戇〕戆	〔鱷〕鳄
〔鑷〕镊	〔顴〕颧		**28笔**		〔鸞〕鸾
〔鑹〕镩	【丨】	【丶】	〔鸛〕鹳	**29笔**	
【丶】	〔鸕〕鸬	〔讞〕谳	〔欞〕棂	〔驪〕骊	**32笔**
〔灤〕滦	〔黷〕黩	〔讜〕谠	〔鑿〕凿	〔鬱〕郁	
	【丿】	〔鑾〕銮	〔鸚〕鹦		〔籲〕吁
27笔		〔灩〕滟		**30笔**	

APPENDIX III

Initials and Finals in Various Phonetic Symbols

A. Initials in Pinyin[*]

Place \ Manner	Unaspirated Stops	Aspirated Stops	Nasals	Fricatives	Voiced Continuants
Labials	b	p	m	f	
Dentals	d	t	n		l
Dental sibilants	z	c		s	
Retroflexes	zh	ch		sh	r
Palatals	j	q		x	
Gutturals	g	k		h	

Pinyin and Other Phonetic Symbols Compared [@]

PY	IPA	YALE	GR	W-G	ZYFH		PY	IPA	YALE	GR	W-G	ZYFH
b	$\underset{\circ}{b}$	b	b	p	ㄅ		zh	tʂ	j	j	ch	ㄓ
p	p^h	p	p	p'	ㄆ		ch	$tʂ^h$	ch	ch	ch'	ㄔ
m	m	m	m	m	ㄇ		sh	ʂ	sh	sh	sh	ㄕ
f	f	f	f	f	ㄈ		r	ɹ	r	r	j	ㄖ
d	$\underset{\circ}{d}$	d	d	t	ㄉ		j	tɕ	j	j	ch	ㄐ
t	t^h	t	t	t'	ㄊ		q	$tɕ^h$	ch	ch	ch'	ㄑ
n	n	n	n	n	ㄋ		x	ɕ	sy	sh	hs	ㄒ
l	l	l	l	l	ㄌ		g	ǧ	g	g	k	ㄍ
z	ts	dz	tz	ts,tz	ㄗ		k	k^h	k	k	k'	ㄎ
c	ts^h	ts	ts	ts',tz'	ㄘ		h	x	h	h	h	ㄏ
s	s	s	s	s	ㄙ							

[*] The tables for the initials and finals are adapted from Professor Chao's A *Grammar of Spoken Chinese*, p. 22 and p. 24.

[@] The abbreviations for the different phonetic symbols are for pinyin (PY), International Phonetic Alphabet (IPA), Yale System (Yale), Gwoyeu Romatzyh (GR), Wade-Gilees (W-G), and Zhuyin Fuhao (ZYFH).

B. Finals in Pinyin

Medial \ Ending	Open	-i	-u	-n	-ng	-r
Row-a	i a e	ai ei	ao ou	an en	ang eng ong	r
Row-i	i ia ie	iai	iao iu	ian in	iang ing iong	
Row-u	u ua uo	uai ui		uan un	uang weng	
Row-ü	ü üe			üan ün		

Pinyin and Other Symbols Compared

PY	IPA	YALE	GR	W-G	ZYFH
i	z̩,ʐ̩	z,r	y	ih,u	
a	ᴀ	a	a	a	ㄚ
e	ɤ	e	e	e,o	ㄜ,ㄛ
ai	ai	ai	ai	ai	ㄞ
ei	ei	ei	ei	ei	ㄟ
ao	au	au	au	ao	ㄠ
ou	ou	ou	ou	ou	ㄡ
an	an	an	an	a(e)n	ㄢ
en	ən	en	en	en	ㄣ
ang	aŋ	ang	ang	ang	ㄤ
eng	ʌŋ	eng	eng	eng	ㄥ
ong	ᴜŋ	ung	ong	ung	ㄨㄥ
er	ɚ	er	el	erh	ㄦ
i	i	i(y)	i	i	ㄧ
ia	iᴀ	ya	ia	ia	ㄧㄚ
ie	iɛ	ye	ie	ieh	ㄧㄝ
iai	iai	yai	iai	iai	ㄧㄞ
iao	iau	yau	iau	iao	ㄧㄠ
iu	iou	you	iou	iu	ㄧㄡ
ian	iɛn	yan	ian	ien	ㄧㄢ
in	in	in	in	in	ㄧㄣ
iang	iaŋ	yang	iang	iang	ㄧㄤ
ing	iŋ	ing	ing	ing	ㄧㄥ
iong	iᴜŋ	yung	iong	iung	ㄩㄥ
u	u	(w)u	u	u	ㄨ
ua	uᴀ	wa	ua	ua	ㄨㄚ
uo	uɤ	wo	uo	uo	ㄨㄛ
uai	uai	wai	uai	uai	ㄨㄞ
ui	uei	wei	uei	u(e)i	ㄨㄟ
uan	uan	wan	uan	uan	ㄨㄢ
un	uən	wu(e)n	uen	un	ㄨㄣ
uang	uaŋ	wang	uang	uang	ㄨㄤ
weng	uʌŋ	weng	ueng	weng	ㄨㄥ
ü(u)	y	yu	iu	ü	ㄩ
üe	yɛ	ywe	iue	üeh	ㄩㄝ
üan	yan	ywan	iuan	üan	ㄩㄢ
ün	yn	yun	iun	ün	ㄩㄣ

Comparative Table
of
Pinyin, YALE, Wade-Giles, Yhuyin Fuhao
and
Gwoyeu Romatzyh (Tonal Spelling) Systems

PY	YALE	WG	ZYFH	ROMATZYH 1	2	3	4
a	a	a	ㄚ	a	ar	aa	ah
ai	ai	ai	ㄞ	ai	air	ae	ay
an	an	an	ㄢ	an	arn	aan	ann
ang	ang	ang	ㄤ	ang	arng	aang	ang
ao	au	ao	ㄠ	au	aur	ao	aw
ba	ba	pa	ㄅㄚ	ba	bar	baa	bah
bai	bai	pai	ㄅㄞ	bai	bair	bae	bay
ban	ban	pan	ㄅㄢ	ban	barn	baan	bann
bang	bang	pang	ㄅㄤ	bang	barng	baang	banq
bao	bau	pao	ㄅㄠ	bau	baur	bao	baw
bei	bei	pei	ㄅㄟ	bei	beir	beei	bey
ben	ben	pen	ㄅㄣ	ben	bern	been	benn
beng	beng	peng	ㄅㄥ	beng	berng	beeng	benq
bi	bi	pi	ㄅㄧ	bi	byi	bii	bih
bian	byan	pien	ㄅㄧㄢ	bian	byan	bean	biann
biao	byau	piao	ㄅㄧㄠ	biau	byau	beau	biaw
bie	bye	pieh	ㄅㄧㄝ	bie	bye	biee	bieh
bin	bin	pin	ㄅㄧㄣ	bin	byn	biin	binn
bing	bing	ping	ㄅㄧㄥ	bing	byng	biing	binq
bo	bwo	po	ㄅㄛ	bo	bor	boo	boh
bu	bu	pu	ㄅㄨ	bu	bwu	buu	buh
ca	tsa	ts'a	ㄘㄚ	tsa	tsar	tsaa	tsah
cai	tsai	ts'ai	ㄘㄞ	tsai	tsair	tsae	tsay
can	tsan	ts'an	ㄘㄢ	tsan	tsarn	tsaan	tsann

PY	YALE	WG	ZYFH	1	2	3	4
cang	tsang	ts'ang	ㄘㄤ	tsang	tsarng	tsaang	tsanq
cao	tsau	ts'ao	ㄘㄠ	tsau	tsaur	tsao	tsaw
ce	tse	ts'e	ㄘㄜ	tse	tser	tsee	tseh
cen	tsen	ts'en	ㄘㄣ	tsen	tsern	tseen	tsenn
ceng	tseng	ts'eng	ㄘㄥ	tseng	tserng	tseeng	tsenq
cha	cha	ch'a	ㄔㄚ	cha	char	chaa	chah
chai	chai	ch'ai	ㄔㄞ	chai	chair	chae	chay
chan	chan	ch'an	ㄔㄢ	chan	charn	chaan	chann
chang	chang	ch'ang	ㄔㄤ	chang	charng	chaang	chanq
chao	chau	ch'ao	ㄔㄠ	chau	chaur	chao	chaw
che	che	ch'e	ㄔㄜ	che	cher	chee	cheh
chen	chen	ch'en	ㄔㄣ	chen	chern	cheen	chenn
cheng	cheng	ch'eng	ㄔㄥ	cheng	cherng	cheeng	chenq
chi	chr	ch'ih	ㄔ	chy	chyr	chyy	chyh
chong	chung	ch'ung	ㄔㄨㄥ	chong	chorng	choong	chonq
chou	chou	ch'ou	ㄔㄡ	chou	chour	choou	chow
chu	chu	ch'u	ㄔㄨ	chu	chwu	chuu	chuh
chua	chua	ch'ua	ㄔㄨㄚ	chua	chwa	choa	chuah
chuai	chwai	ch'uai	ㄔㄨㄞ	chuai	chwai	choai	chuay
chuan	chwan	ch'uan	ㄔㄨㄢ	chuan	chwan	choan	chuann
chuang	chwang	ch'uang	ㄔㄨㄤ	chuang	chwang	choang	chuanq
chui	chwei	ch'ui	ㄔㄨㄟ	chuei	chwei	choei	chuey
chun	chwun	ch'un	ㄔㄨㄣ	chuen	chwen	choen	chuenn
chuo	chwo	ch'o	ㄔㄨㄛ	chuo	chwo	chuoo	chuoh
ci	tsz	tz'u	ㄘ	tsy	tsyr	tsyy	tsyh

PY	YALE	WG	ZYFH	ROMATZYH 1	2	3	4
cong	tsung	ts'ung	ㄘㄨㄥ	tsong	tsorng	tsoong	tsonq
cou	tsou	ts'ou	ㄘㄨ	tsou	tsour	tsoou	tsow
cu	tsu	ts'u	ㄘㄨ	tsu	tswu	tsuu	tsuh
cuan	tswan	ts'uan	ㄘㄨㄢ	tsuan	tswan	tsoan	tsuann
cui	tswei	ts'ui	ㄘㄨㄟ	tsuei	tswei	tsoei	tsuey
cun	tswun	ts'un	ㄘㄨㄣ	tsuen	tswen	tsoen	tsuenn
cuo	tswo	ts'o	ㄘㄨㄛ	tsuo	tswo	tsuoo	tsuoh
da	da	ta	ㄉㄚ	da	dar	daa	dah
dai	dai	tai	ㄉㄞ	dai	dair	dae	day
dan	dan	tan	ㄉㄢ	dan	darn	daan	dann
dang	dang	tang	ㄉㄤ	dang	darng	daang	danq
dao	dau	tao	ㄉㄠ	dau	daur	dao	daw
de	de	te	ㄉㄜ	de	der	dee	deh
dei	dei	tei	ㄉㄟ	dei	deir	deei	dey
deng	deng	teng	ㄉㄥ	deng	derng	deeng	denq
di	di	ti	ㄉㄧ	di	dyi	dii	dih
dian	dyan	tien	ㄉㄧㄢ	dian	dyan	dean	diann
diao	dyau	tiao	ㄉㄧㄠ	diau	dyau	deau	diaw
die	dye	tieh	ㄉㄧㄝ	die	dye	diee	dieh
ding	ding	ting	ㄉㄧㄥ	ding	dyng	diing	dinq
diu	dyou	tiu	ㄉㄧㄡ	diou	dyou	deou	diow
dong	dung	tung	ㄉㄨㄥ	dong	dorng	doong	donq
dou	dou	tou	ㄉㄡ	dou	dour	doou	dow
du	du	tu	ㄉㄨ	du	dwu	duu	duh
duan	dwan	tuan	ㄉㄨㄢ	duan	dwan	doan	duann

PY	YALE	WG	ZYFH	1	2	3	4
dui	dwei	tui	ㄉㄨㄟ	duei	dwei	doei	duey
dun	dwun	tun	ㄉㄨㄣ	duen	dwen	doen	duenn
duo	dwo	to	ㄉㄨㄛ	duo	dwo	duoo	duoh
e	e	e,o	ㄜ,ㄛ	e	er	ee	eh
ei	ei	ei	ㄟ	ei	eir	eei	ey
en	en	en	ㄣ	en	ern	een	enn
eng	eng	eng	ㄥ	eng	erng	eeng	enq
er	er	erh	ㄦ	el	erl	eel	ell
fa	fa	fa	ㄈㄚ	fa	far	faa	fah
fan	fan	fan	ㄈㄢ	fan	farn	faan	fann
fang	fang	fang	ㄈㄤ	fang	farng	faang	fanq
fei	fei	fei	ㄈㄟ	fei	feir	feei	fey
fen	fen	fen	ㄈㄣ	fen	fern	feen	fenn
feng	feng	feng	ㄈㄥ	feng	ferng	feeng	fenq
fo	fwo	fo	ㄈㄛ	fo	for	foo	foh
fou	fou	fou	ㄈㄡ	fou	four	foou	fow
fu	fu	fu	ㄈㄨ	fu	fwu	fuu	fuh
ga	ga	ka	ㄍㄚ	ga	gar	gaa	gah
gai	gai	kai	ㄍㄞ	gai	gair	gae	gay
gan	gan	kan	ㄍㄢ	gan	garn	gaan	gann
gang	gang	kang	ㄍㄤ	gang	garng	gaang	ganq
gao	gau	kao	ㄍㄠ	gau	gaur	gao	gaw
ge	ge	ke,ko	ㄍㄜ	ge	ger	gee	geh

				ROMATZYH			
PY	YALE	WG	ZYFH	1	2	3	4
gei	gei	kei	ㄍㄟ	gei	geir	geei	gey
gen	gen	ken	ㄍㄣ	gen	gern	geen	genn
geng	geng	keng	ㄍㄥ	geng	gerng	geeng	genq
gong	gung	kung	ㄍㄨㄥ	gong	gorng	goong	gonq
gou	gou	kou	ㄍㄡ	gou	gour	goou	gow
gu	gu	ku	ㄍㄨ	gu	gwu	guu	guh
gua	gwa	kua	ㄍㄨㄚ	gua	gwa	goa	guah
guai	gwai	kuai	ㄍㄨㄞ	guai	gwai	goai	guay
guan	gwan	kuan	ㄍㄨㄢ	guan	gwan	goan	guann
guang	gwang	kuang	ㄍㄨㄤ	guang	gwang	goang	guanq
gui	gwei	kuei	ㄍㄨㄟ	guei	gwei	goei	guey
gun	gwun	kun	ㄍㄨㄣ	guen	gwen	goen	guenn
guo	gwo	kuo	ㄍㄨㄛ	guo	gwo	guoo	guoh
ha	ha	ha	ㄏㄚ	ha	har	haa	hah
hai	hai	hai	ㄏㄞ	hai	hair	hae	hay
han	han	han	ㄏㄢ	han	harn	haan	hann
hang	hang	hang	ㄏㄤ	hang	harng	haang	hanq
hao	hau	hao	ㄏㄠ	hau	haur	hao	haw
he	he	he	ㄏㄜ	he	her	hee	heh
hei	hei	hei	ㄏㄟ	hei	heir	heei	hey
hen	hen	hen	ㄏㄣ	hen	hern	heen	henn
heng	heng	heng	ㄏㄥ	heng	herng	heeng	henq
hong	hung	hung	ㄏㄨㄥ	hong	horng	hoong	honq
hou	hou	hou	ㄏㄡ	hou	hour	hoou	how

PY	YALE	WG	ZYFH	1	2	3	4
hu	hu	hu	ㄏㄨ	hu	hwu	huu	huh
hua	hwa	hua	ㄏㄨㄚ	hua	hwa	hoa	huah
huai	hwai	huai	ㄏㄨㄞ	huai	hwai	hoai	huay
huan	hwan	huan	ㄏㄨㄢ	huan	hwan	hoan	huann
huang	hwang	huang	ㄏㄨㄤ	huang	hwang	hoang	huanq
hui	hwei	hui	ㄏㄨㄟ	huei	hwei	hoei	huey
hun	hwun	hun	ㄏㄨㄣ	huen	hwen	hoen	huenn
huo	hwo	huo	ㄏㄨㄛ	huo	hwo	huoo	huoh
ji	ji	chi	ㄐㄧ	ji	jyi	jii	jih
jia	jya	chia	ㄐㄧㄚ	jia	jya	jea	jiah
jian	jyan	chien	ㄐㄧㄢ	jian	jyan	jean	jiann
jiang	jyang	chiang	ㄐㄧㄤ	jiang	jyang	jeang	jianq
jiao	jyau	chiao	ㄐㄧㄠ	jiau	jyau	jeau	jiaw
jie	jye	chieh	ㄐㄧㄝ	jie	jye	jiee	jieh
jin	jin	chin	ㄐㄧㄣ	jin	jyn	jiin	jinn
jing	jing	ching	ㄐㄧㄥ	jing	jyng	jiing	jinq
jiong	jyung	chiung	ㄐㄨㄥ	jiong	jyong	jeong	jionq
jiu	jyou	chiu	ㄐㄧㄡ	jiou	jyou	jeou	jiow
ju	jyu	chü	ㄐㄩ	jiu	jyu	jeu	jiuh
juan	jywan	chüan	ㄐㄩㄢ	jiuan	jyuan	jeuan	jiuann
jue	jywe	chüeh	ㄐㄩㄝ	jiue	jyue	jeue	jiueh
jun	jyun	chun	ㄐㄩㄣ	jiun	jyun	jeun	jiunn
ka	ka	k'a	ㄎㄚ	ka	kar	kaa	kah
kai	kai	k'ai	ㄎㄞ	kai	kair	kae	kay

PY	YALE	WG	ZYFH	1	2	3	4
kan	kan	k'an	ㄎㄢ	kan	karn	kaan	kann
kang	kang	k'ang	ㄎㄤ	kang	kerng	kaang	kanq
kao	kau	k'ao	ㄎㄠ	kau	kaur	kao	kaw
ke	ke	k'e,k'o	ㄎㄜ	ke	ker	kee	keh
ken	ken	k'en	ㄎㄣ	ken	kern	keen	kenn
keng	keng	k'eng	ㄎㄥ	keng	kerng	keeng	kenq
kong	kung	k'ung	ㄎㄨㄥ	kong	korng	koong	kong
kou	kou	k'ou	ㄎㄡ	kou	kour	koou	kow
ku	ku	k'u	ㄎㄨ	ku	kwu	kuu	kuh
kua	kwa	k'ua	ㄎㄨㄚ	kua	kwa	koa	kuah
kuai	kwai	k'uai	ㄎㄨㄞ	kuai	kwai	koai	kuay
kuan	kwan	k'uan	ㄎㄨㄢ	kuan	kwan	koan	kuann
kuang	kwang	k'uang	ㄎㄨㄤ	kuang	kwang	koang	kuanq
kui	kwei	k'uei	ㄎㄨㄟ	kuei	kwei	koei	kuey
kun	kwun	k'un	ㄎㄨㄣ	kuen	kwen	koen	kuenn
kuo	kwo	k'uo	ㄎㄨㄛ	kuo	kwo	kuoo	kuoh
la	la	la	ㄌㄚ	lha	la	laa	lah
lai	lai	lai	ㄌㄞ	lhai	lai	lae	lay
lan	lan	lan	ㄌㄢ	lhan	lan	laan	lann
lang	lang	lang	ㄌㄤ	lhang	lang	laang	lanq
lao	lau	lao	ㄌㄠ	lhau	lau	lao	law
le	le	le	ㄌㄜ	lhe	le	lee	leh
lei	lei	lei	ㄌㄟ	lhei	lei	leei	ley
leng	leng	leng	ㄌㄥ	lheng	leng	leeng	lenq

PY	YALE	WG	ZYFH	1	2	3	4
li	li	li	ㄌㄧ	lhi	li	lii	lih
lia	lya	lia	ㄌㄧㄚ	lhia	lia	lea	liah
lian	lyan	lien	ㄌㄧㄢ	lhian	lian	lean	liann
liang	lyang	liang	ㄌㄧㄤ	lhiang	liang	leang	lianq
liao	lyau	liao	ㄌㄧㄠ	lhiau	liau	leau	liaw
lie	lye	lieh	ㄌㄧㄝ	lhie	lie	liee	lieh
lin	lin	lin	ㄌㄧㄣ	lhin	lin	liin	linn
ling	ling	ling	ㄌㄧㄥ	lhing	ling	liing	linq
liu	lyou	liu	ㄌㄧㄡ	lhiou	liou	leou	liow
long	lung	lung	ㄌㄨㄥ	lhong	long	loong	lonq
lou	lou	lou	ㄌㄡ	lhou	lou	loou	low
lu	lu	lu	ㄌㄨ	lhu	lu	luu	luh
luan	lwan	luan	ㄌㄨㄢ	lhuan	luan	loan	luann
lun	lwun	lun, lun	ㄌㄨㄣ	lhuen	luen	loen	luenn
luo	lwo	lo	ㄌㄨㄛ	lhou	luo	luoo	luoh
lü	lyu	lü	ㄌㄩ	lhiu	liu	leu	liuh
lüan	lywan	lüan	ㄌㄩㄢ	lhiuan	liuan	leuan	liuann
lüe	lywe	lüeh	ㄌㄩㄝ	lhue	liue	leue	liueh
lün	lyun	lün	ㄌㄩㄣ	lhiun	liun	leun	liunn
ma	ma	ma	ㄇㄚ	mha	ma	maa	mah
mai	mai	mai	ㄇㄞ	mhai	mai	mae	may
man	man	man	ㄇㄢ	mhan	man	maan	mann
mang	mang	mang	ㄇㄤ	mhang	mang	maang	manq
mao	mau	mao	ㄇㄠ	mhau	mau	mao	maw

| | | | | ROMATZYH | | | |
PY	YALE	WG	ZYFH	1	2	3	4
mei	mei	mei	ㄇㄟ	mhei	mei	meei	mey
men	men	men	ㄇㄣ	mhen	men	meen	menn
meng	meng	meng	ㄇㄥ	mheng	men	meeng	menq
mi	mi	mi	ㄇㄧ	mhi	mi	mii	mih
mian	myan	mien	ㄇㄧㄢ	mhian	mian	mean	miann
miao	myau	miao	ㄇㄧㄠ	mhiau	miau	meau	miaw
mie	mye	mieh	ㄇㄧㄝ	mhie	mie	miee	mieh
min	min	min	ㄇㄧㄣ	mhin	min	miin	minn
ming	ming	ming	ㄇㄧㄥ	mhing	ming	miing	minq
miu	myou	miu	ㄇㄧㄡ	mhiou	miou	meou	miow
mo	mwo	mo	ㄇㄛ	mho	mo	moo	moh
mou	mou	mou	ㄇㄡ	mhou	mou	moou	mow
mu	mu	mu	ㄇㄨ	mhu	mu	muu	muh
na	na	na	ㄋㄚ	nha	na	naa	nah
nai	nai	nai	ㄋㄞ	nhai	nai	nae	nay
nan	nan	nan	ㄋㄢ	nhan	nan	naan	nann
nang	nang	nang	ㄋㄤ	nhang	nang	naang	nanq
nao	nau	nao	ㄋㄠ	nhau	nau	nao	naw
ne	ne	ne	ㄋㄜ	nhe	ne	nee	neh
nei	nei	nei	ㄋㄟ	nhei	nei	neei	ney
nen	nen	nen	ㄋㄣ	nhen	nen	neen	nenn
neng	neng	neng	ㄋㄥ	nheng	neng	neeng	nenq
ni	ni	ni	ㄋㄧ	nhi	ni	nii	nih
nian	nyan	nien	ㄋㄧㄢ	nhian	nian	nean	niann

PY	YALE	WG	ZYFH	ROMATZYH 1	2	3	4
niang	nyang	niang	ㄋㄧㄤ	nhiang	niang	neang	nianq
niao	nyau	niao	ㄋㄧㄠ	nhiau	niau	neau	niaw
nie	nye	nieh	ㄋㄧㄝ	nhie	nie	niee	nieh
nin	nin	nin	ㄋㄧㄣ	nhin	nin	niin	ninn
ning	ning	ning	ㄋㄧㄥ	nhing	ning	niing	ninq
niu	nyou	niu	ㄋㄧㄡ	nhiu	niou	neou	niow
nong	nung	nung	ㄋㄨㄥ	nhong	nong	noong	nonq
nou	nou	nou	ㄋㄡ	nhou	nou	noou	now
nu	nu	nu	ㄋㄨ	nhu	nu	nuu	nuh
nuan	nwan	nuan	ㄋㄨㄢ	nhuan	nuan	noan	nuann
nun	nwun	nun	ㄋㄨㄣ	nhuen	nuen	noen	nuenn
nuo	nwo	no	ㄋㄨㄛ	nhuo	nuo	nuoo	nuoh
nü	nyu	nü	ㄋㄩ	nhiu	niu	neu	niuh
nüe	nywe	nüeh	ㄋㄩㄝ	nhiue	niue	neue	niueh
ou	ou	ou	ㄡ	ou	our	oou	ow
pa	pa	p'a	ㄆㄚ	pa	par	paa	pah
pai	pai	p'ai	ㄆㄞ	pai	pair	pae	pay
pan	pan	p'an	ㄆㄢ	pan	parn	paan	pann
pang	pang	p'ang	ㄆㄤ	pang	parng	paang	panq
pao	pau	p'ao	ㄆㄠ	pau	paur	pao	paw
pei	pei	p'ei	ㄆㄟ	pei	peir	peei	pey
pen	pen	p'en	ㄆㄣ	pen	pern	peen	penn
peng	peng	p'eng	ㄆㄥ	peng	perng	peeng	penq
pi	pi	p'i	ㄆㄧ	pi	pyi	pii	pih

| | | | | ROMATZYH | | | |
PY	YALE	WG	ZYFH	1	2	3	4
pian	pyan	p'ien	ㄆㄧㄢ	pian	pyan	pean	piann
piao	pyau	p'iao	ㄆㄧㄠ	piau	pyau	peau	piaw
pie	pye	p'ieh	ㄆㄧㄝ	pie	pye	piee	pieh
pin	pin	p'in	ㄆㄧㄣ	pin	pyn	piin	pinn
ping	ping	p'ing	ㄆㄧㄥ	ping	pyng	piing	pinq
po	pwo	p'o	ㄆㄛ	po	por	poo	poh
pou	pou	p'ou	ㄆㄡ	pou	pour	poou	pow
pu	pu	p'u	ㄆㄨ	pu	pwu	puu	puh
qi	chi	ch'i	ㄑㄧ	chi	chyi	chii	chih
qia	chya	ch'ia	ㄑㄧㄚ	chia	chya	chea	chiah
qian	chyan	ch'ien	ㄑㄧㄢ	chian	chyan	chean	chiann
qiang	chyang	ch'iang	ㄑㄧㄤ	chiang	chyang	cheang	chianq
qiao	chyau	ch'iao	ㄑㄧㄠ	chiau	chyau	cheau	chiaw
qie	chye	ch'ieh	ㄑㄧㄝ	chie	chye	chiee	chieh
qin	chin	ch'in	ㄑㄧㄣ	chin	chyn	chiin	chinn
qing	ching	ch'inh	ㄑㄧㄥ	ching	chyng	chiing	chinq
qiong	chyung	ch'iung	ㄑㄩㄥ	chiong	chyong	cheong	chionq
qiu	chyou	ch'iu	ㄑㄧㄡ	chiou	chyou	cheou	chiow
qu	chyu	ch'u	ㄑㄩ	chiu	chyu	cheu	chiuh
quan	chywan	ch'uan	ㄑㄩㄢ	chiuan	chyuan	cheuan	chiuann
que	chywe	ch'ueh	ㄑㄩㄝ	chiue	chyue	cheue	chiueh
qun	chyun	ch'un	ㄑㄩㄣ	chiun	chyun	cheun	chiunn
ran	ran	jan	ㄖㄢ	rhan	ran	raan	rann
rang	rang	jang	ㄖㄤ	rhang	rang	raang	ranq

				ROMATZYH			
PY	YALE	WG	ZYFH	1	2	3	4
rao	rau	jao	ㄖㄠ	rhau	rau	rao	raw
re	re	je	ㄖㄜ	rhe	re	ree	reh
ren	ren	jen	ㄖㄣ	rhen	ren	reen	renn
reng	reng	jeng	ㄖㄥ	rheng	reng	reeng	renq
ri	r	jih	ㄖ	rhy	ry	ryy	ryh
rong	rung	jung	ㄖㄨㄥ	rhong	rong	roong	ronq
rou	rou	jou	ㄖㄡ	rhou	rou	roou	row
ru	ru	ju	ㄖㄨ	rhu	ru	ruu	ruh
ruan	rwan	juan	ㄖㄨㄢ	rhuan	ruan	roan	ruann
rui	rwei	jui	ㄖㄨㄟ	rhuei	ruei	roei	ruey
run	rwun	jun	ㄖㄨㄣ	rhuen	ruen	roen	ruenn
ruo	rwo	jo	ㄖㄨㄛ	rhuo	ruo	ruoo	ruoh
sa	sa	sa	ㄙㄚ	sa	sar	saa	sah
sai	sai	sai	ㄙㄞ	sia	sair	sae	say
san	san	san	ㄙㄢ	san	sarn	saan	sann
sang	sang	sang	ㄙㄤ	sang	sarng	saang	sanq
sao	sau	sao	ㄙㄠ	sau	saur	sao	saw
se	se	se	ㄙㄜ	se	ser	see	seh
sen	sen	sen	ㄙㄣ	sen	sern	seen	senn
seng	seng	seng	ㄙㄥ	seng	serng	seeng	senq
sha	sha	sha	ㄕㄚ	sha	shar	shaa	shah
shai	shai	shai	ㄕㄞ	shai	shair	shae	shay
shan	shan	shan	ㄕㄢ	shan	sharn	shaan	shann
shang	shang	shang	ㄕㄤ	shang	sharng	shaang	shanq

259

PY	YALE	WG	ZYFH	ROMATZYH 1	2	3	4
shao	shau	shao	ㄕㄠ	shau	shuar	shao	shaw
she	she	she	ㄕㄜ	she	sher	shee	sheh
shei	shei	shei	ㄕㄟ	shei	sheir	sheei	shey
shen	shen	shen	ㄕㄣ	shen	shern	sheen	shenn
sheng	sheng	sheng	ㄕㄥ	sheng	sherng	sheeng	shenq
shi	shr	shih	ㄕ	shy	shyr	shyh	shyy
shou	shou	shou	ㄕㄡ	shou	shour	shoou	show
shu	shu	shu	ㄕㄨ	shu	shwu	shuu	shuh
shua	shwa	shua	ㄕㄨㄚ	shua	shwa	shoa	shuah
shuai	shwau	shuai	ㄕㄨㄞ	shuai	shwai	shoai	shuay
shuan	shwan	shuan	ㄕㄨㄢ	shuan	shwan	shoan	shuann
shuang	shwang	shuang	ㄕㄨㄤ	shuang	shwang	shoang	shuanq
shui	shwei	shui	ㄕㄨㄟ	shuei	shwei	shoei	shuey
shun	shwun	shun	ㄕㄨㄣ	shuen	shwen	shoen	shuenn
shuo	shwo	shuo	ㄕㄨㄛ	shuo	shwo	shuoo	shuoh
si	sz	szu, ssu	ㄙ	sy	syr	syy	syh
song	sung	sung	ㄙㄨㄥ	song	sorng	soong	sonq
sou	sou	sou	ㄙㄡ	sou	sour	soou	sow
su	su	su	ㄙㄨ	su	swu	suu	suh
suan	swan	suan	ㄙㄨㄢ	suan	swan	soan	suann
sui	swei	sui	ㄙㄨㄟ	suei	swei	soei	suey
sun	swun	sun	ㄙㄨㄣ	suen	swen	soen	suenn
suo	swo	so	ㄙㄨㄛ	suo	swo	suoo	suoh
ta	ta	t'a	ㄊㄚ	ta	tar	taa	tah

| | | | | | ROMATZYH | | |
PY	YALE	WG	ZYFH	1	2	3	4
tai	tai	t'ai	去ㄞ	tai	tair	tae	tay
tan	tan	t'an	去ㄢ	tan	tarn	taan	tann
tang	tang	t'ang	去ㄤ	tang	tarng	taang	tanq
tao	tau	t'ao	去ㄠ	tau	taur	tao	taw
te	te	t'e	去ㄜ	te	ter	tee	teh
teng	teng	t'eng	去ㄥ	teng	terng	teeng	tenq
ti	ti	t'i	去ㄧ	ti	tyi	tii	tih
tian	tyan	t'ien	去ㄧㄢ	tian	tyan	tean	tiann
tiao	tyau	t'iao	去ㄧㄠ	tiau	tyau	teau	tiaw
tie	tye	t'ieh	去ㄧㄝ	tie	tye	tiee	tieh
ting	ting	t'ing	去ㄧㄥ	ting	tyng	tiing	tinq
tong	tung	t'ung	去ㄨㄥ	tong	torng	toong	tonq
tou	tou	t'ou	去ㄡ	tou	tour	toou	tow
tu	tu	t'u	去ㄨ	tu	twu	tuu	tuh
tuan	twan	t'uan	去ㄨㄢ	tuan	twan	toan	tuann
tui	twei	t'ui	去ㄨㄟ	tuei	twei	toei	tuey
tun	twun	t'un	去ㄨㄣ	tuen	twen	toen	tuenn
tuo	two	t'o	去ㄨㄛ	tuo	two	tuoo	tuoh
wa	wa	wa	ㄨㄚ	ua	wa	woa	wah
wai	wai	wai	ㄨㄞ	uai	wai	woai	way
wan	wan	wan	ㄨㄢ	uan	wan	woan	wann
wang	wang	wang	ㄨㄤ	uang	wang	woang	wanq
wei	wei	wei	ㄨㄟ	uei	wei	woei	wey
wen	wen	wen	ㄨㄣ	uen	wen	woen	wenn

PY	YALE	WG	ZYFH	ROMATZYH 1	2	3	4
weng	weng	weng	ㄨㄥ	ueng	weng	woeng	wenq
wo	wo	wo	ㄨㄛ	uo	wo	woo	woh
wu	wu	wu	ㄨ	u	wu	wuu	wuh
xi	syi	hsi	ㄒㄧ	shi	shyi	shii	shih
xia	sya	hsia	ㄒㄧㄚ	shia	shya	shea	shiah
xian	syan	hsien	ㄒㄧㄢ	shian	shyan	shean	shiann
xiang	syang	hsiang	ㄒㄧㄤ	shiang	shyang	sheang	shianq
xiao	syau	hsiao	ㄒㄧㄠ	shiau	shyau	sheau	shiaw
xie	sye	hsieh	ㄒㄧㄝ	shie	shye	shiee	shieh
xin	syin	hsin	ㄒㄧㄣ	shin	shyn	shiin	shinn
xing	sying	hsing	ㄒㄧㄥ	shing	shyng	shiing	shinq
xiong	syung	hsiung	ㄒㄩㄥ	shiong	shyong	sheong	shionq
xiu	syou	hsiu	ㄒㄧㄡ	shiou	shyou	sheou	shiow
xu	syu	hsü	ㄒㄩ	shiu	shyu	sheu	shiuh
xuan	sywan	hsüan	ㄒㄩㄢ	shiuan	shyuan	sheuan	shiuann
xue	sywe	hsüeh	ㄒㄩㄝ	shiue	shyue	sheue	shiueh
xun	syun	hsün	ㄒㄩㄣ	shiun	shyun	sheun	shiunn
ya	ya	ya	ㄧㄚ	ia	ya	yaa	yah
yai	yai	yai	ㄧㄞ	iai	yai	yae	yay
yan	yan	yen	ㄧㄢ	ian	yan	yean	yann
yang	yang	yang	ㄧㄤ	iang	yang	yeang	yanq
yao	yau	yao	ㄧㄠ	iau	yau	yeau	yaw
ye	ye	yeh	ㄧㄝ	ie	ye	yee	yeh
yi	yi	i	ㄧ	i	yi	ii	ih

				ROMATZYH			
PY	YALE	WG	ZYFH	1	2	3	4
yin	yin	yin	ㄧㄣ	in	yn	yiin	yinn
ying	ying	ying	ㄧㄥ	ing	yng	yiing	yinq
yong	yung	yung	ㄩㄥ	iong	yong	yeong	yonq
you	you	yu	ㄧㄡ	iou	you	yeou	yow
yu	yu	yu	ㄩ	iu	yu	yeu	yuh
yuan	ywan	yüan	ㄩㄢ	iuan	yuan	yeuan	yuann
yue	ywe	yüeh	ㄩㄝ	iue	yue	yeue	yueh
yun	yun	yün	ㄩㄣ	iun	yun	yeun	yunn
za	dza	tsa	ㄗㄚ	tza	tzar	tzaa	tzah
zai	dzai	tsai	ㄗㄞ	tzai	tzair	tzae	tzay
zan	dzan	tsan	ㄗㄢ	tzan	tzarn	tzaan	tzann
zang	dzang	tsang	ㄗㄤ	tzang	tzarng	tzaang	tzanq
zao	dzau	tsao	ㄗㄠ	tzau	tzaur	tzao	tzaw
ze	dze	tse	ㄗㄜ	tze	tzer	tzee	tzeh
zei	dzei	tsei	ㄗㄟ	tzei	tzeir	tzeei	tzey
zen	dzen	tsen	ㄗㄣ	tzen	tzern	tzeen	tzenn
zeng	dzeng	tseng	ㄗㄥ	tzeng	tzerng	tzeeng	tzenq
zha	ja	cha	ㄓㄚ	ja	jar	jaa	jah
zhai	jai	chai	ㄓㄞ	jai	jair	jae	jay
zhan	jan	chan	ㄓㄢ	jan	jarn	jaan	jann
zhang	jang	chang	ㄓㄤ	jang	jarng	jaang	janq
zhao	jau	chao	ㄓㄠ	jau	jaur	jao	jaw
zhe	je	che	ㄓㄜ	je	jer	jee	jeh
zhei	jei	chei	ㄓㄟ	jei	jeir	jeei	jey

PY	YALE	WG	ZYFH	ROMATZYH			
				1	2	3	4
zhen	jen	chen	ㄓㄣ	jen	jern	jeen	jenn
zheng	jeng	cheng	ㄓㄥ	jeng	jerng	jeeng	jenq
zhi	jr	chih	ㄓ	jy	jyr	jyy	jyh
zhong	jung	chung	ㄓㄨㄥ	jong	jorng	joong	jonq
zhou	jou	chou	ㄓㄡ	jou	jour	joou	jow
zhu	ju	chu	ㄓㄨ	ju	jwu	juu	juh
zhua	jwa	chua	ㄓㄨㄚ	jua	jwa	joa	juah
zhuai	jwai	chuai	ㄓㄨㄞ	juai	jwai	joai	juay
zhuan	jwan	chuan	ㄓㄨㄢ	juan	jwan	joan	juann
zhuang	jwang	chuang	ㄓㄨㄤ	juang	jwang	joang	juanq
zhui	jwei	chui	ㄓㄨㄟ	juei	jwei	joei	juey
zhun	jwun	chun	ㄓㄨㄣ	juen	jwen	joen	juenn
zhuo	jwo	cho	ㄓㄨㄛ	juo	jwo	juoo	juoh
zi	dz	tzu	ㄗ	tzy	tzyr	tzyy	tzyh
zong	dzung	tsung	ㄗㄨㄥ	tzong	tzorng	tzoong	tzonq
zou	dzou	tsou	ㄗㄡ	tzou	tzour	tzoou	tzow
zu	dzu	t.su	ㄗㄨ	tzu	tzwu	tzuu	tzuh
zuan	dzwan	tsuan	ㄗㄨㄢ	tzuan	tzwan	tzoan	tzuann
zui	dzwei	tsui	ㄗㄨㄟ	tzuei	tzwei	tzoei	tzuey
zun	dzwun	tsun	ㄗㄨㄣ	tzuen	tzwen	tzoen	tzuenn
zuo	dzwo	tso	ㄗㄨㄛ	tzuo	tzwo	tzuoo	tzuoh